Homework: The evidence

Homework: The evidence

Fully revised and expanded edition

Susan Hallam and Lynne Rogers

IOE Press

First published in 2018 by the UCL Institute of Education Press, University College London, 20 Bedford Way, London WC1H 0AL

www.ucl-ioe-press.com

British Library Cataloguing in Publication Data:
A catalogue record for this publication is available from the British Library

ISBNs
978-1-78277-247-7 (paperback)
978-1-78277-248-4 (PDF eBook)
978-1-78277-249-1 (ePub eBook)
978-1-78277-250-7 (Kindle eBook)

Typeset by Quadrant Infotech (India) Pvt Ltd
Printed by CPI Group (UK) Ltd, Croydon, CR0 4YY

Cover image © Bob Daemmrich/Alamy Stock Photo

Contents

List of figures and tables

Preface to the second edition

Since the first edition of *Homework: The evidence* was published in 2004, hundreds of studies relating to homework have been undertaken. This second edition aims to present this new evidence and link it with the existing research to present an up-to-date analysis of the field. While many of the underlying issues remain the same, since 2004 there has been a much greater emphasis on attempting to understand the complex relationship between homework and attainment, taking account of the amount of homework set by schools, the time spent by students completing homework and other student characteristics. Surprisingly, the amount of homework set by the school has emerged as a better predictor of attainment than the time students spend completing it. At the level of the individual pupil the evidence increasingly shows that there is little or no positive relationship between the amount of homework undertaken and attainment, and in some cases the relationship is negative.

Research has continued to focus on teachers, particularly the way that they link homework with classwork, while the introduction of flipped learning has created considerable interest. The role of parents has been clarified, suggesting that their strongest impact on attainment is in relation to aspirations for their children, and that controlling or interfering with homework has a negative effect. The greatest positive impact occurs where parents support the development of autonomous learning, though the tensions caused by homework in the family have continued to be evidenced. Since 2004 there has been an increase in the ways that technology has supported homework – its setting, management and assessment – while the number and types of after-school activities and programmes supporting learning have increased substantially. The second edition of the book provides a detailed account of these advances, providing up-to-date evidence that will be useful to a wide range of stakeholders.

About the authors

Susan Hallam is Emerita Professor of Education and Music Psychology at the UCL Institute of Education. She pursued careers as both a professional musician and a music educator before joining the Institute of Education in 1991. Her research interests include attendance and exclusion, behaviour improvement, school–home links, ability grouping in primary and secondary schools, formative feedback in learning, instrumental music services and policy evaluation. In addition to the first edition of *Homework* her many sole- and co-authored books include *Music Psychology in Education* (2005); *Preparing for Success: A practical guide for young musicians* (2012); and *Active Ageing with Music: Supporting well-being in the third and fourth ages* (2014), all published by UCL IOE Press. She was awarded an MBE in the 2015 New Year's Honours list.

Lynne Rogers is Reader in Education at the UCL Institute of Education, where she is Co-Director of the Centre for Post-14 Education and Work. She has long-standing interests in teacher/lecturer training and learning in further and higher education and other professional settings. With careers in teaching and management before entering academia, she has undertaken research on behaviour in school, disengagement from education (including the role of alternative curricula), learning, studying and homework in adolescents and issues relating to music education. She is the author of publications on behaviour and attendance in school, alternative curriculum, disengagement, prison education, music education, teacher education and studying, including *Disengagement from Education* (2015), published by UCL IOE Press.

Chapter 1

Introduction

This chapter sets out the historical context of homework and considers its definitions, purposes and types, and its advantages and disadvantages. It provides a brief overview of international perspectives and sets out the English policy context. The chapter concludes by presenting a model of homework that serves to outline its complexity.

Homework is controversial. Its pros and cons have been and continue to be debated by politicians, educators, parents and children. Such discussions are frequently characterized by polemic and based on personal experience that may have been more or less positive. Typically, there is disagreement about homework's benefits. Alongside the debates, there has been much research on homework. This is rarely referred to in consideration of its usefulness. In part, this may be because most people are unaware of it. The purpose of this book is to synthesize key findings from the research, providing an evidence base that can be used in future considerations of the role of homework in the lives of children and young people.

This chapter will provide a brief account of the history of homework in the United Kingdom (UK) and the United States of America (USA), where much of the early research was undertaken. It will outline the main definitions, purposes and types of homework and set out what are typically perceived as its main advantages and disadvantages. Recent English policy regarding homework will be presented. The chapter will conclude by considering the complexity of issues relating to homework and setting out a model that will provide the basis for the research evidence presented in the remainder of the book.

Historical origins

Homework is not new. It has a long and controversial history (Gordon, 1980; Cooper, 1989a, 1989b, 1994; Bonyun, 1992; Earle, 1992; Foyle, 1992). Since the mid-nineteenth century it has been used to supplement the curriculum and in the UK, as elsewhere, it has been more or less fashionable depending on political, economic, social and educational factors. For instance, when public examinations were introduced and the professions looked increasingly to academic qualifications rather than patronage as a basis for entry, schools were obliged to prepare their students accordingly. This encouraged the setting of greater amounts of homework. At elementary school level, payment of teachers by results, competition for scholarships and the introduction of the New Code in 1883 (intended to raise levels of achievement and standards of teaching) put considerable pressure on schools. As a result, levels of homework increased. This led some parents and social reformers to campaign for a reduction in homework. Although the Royal Commission on Elementary Education of 1886 examined the question of homework, it made no firm recommendations (UK Parliament, 1886: xxv Evidence. Q. 5930–6060, 7 April).

In 1928, the first research on homework was undertaken by the West Kent Branch of the Incorporated Association of Assistant Masters. The survey revealed wide divergence in practice, weekly homework set for boys aged 11 varying from 1 to 12 hours, while for those over 11 it ranged from 7.5 to 20 hours. In most schools, there was no policy for distributing homework fairly across different evenings and no attempt to balance written and other forms of homework. Respondents were divided as to whether homework caused mental fatigue but they were concerned about the unfavourable home conditions of some children, which were considered to be a barrier to good performance. In almost half of the schools, parents were not consulted about the time that should be spent on homework and in general were not invited to express any opinion on the effect of homework. There was wide agreement that public examinations were responsible for the long hours of homework and that homework interfered with the pursuit of hobbies and the development of natural abilities, particularly music (Incorporated Association of Assistant Masters in Secondary Schools, 1928). As a result of the survey, the *Times Educational Supplement* (19 January, 1929) had a special article across its front page asking the question 'Is homework necessary?'. Laying stress on the social aspects of the question, it concluded that, in a changing world where knowledge was available in homes and where transport meant that the world could be freely experienced at first hand, homework tasks must be of a very high educational value to justify the school extending its control into the home and encroaching on family life. A similar argument would be equally valid today.

In 1935, a major survey of homework was undertaken by His Majesty's Inspectors of Schools (HMI). This report concluded that homework was useful in allowing pupils to develop self-reliance and initiative, enabling them to learn to settle down to work and resist distractions, accustoming them to the idea that they could work profitably out of school, and providing opportunities for individual work, e.g. revision and memorizing of facts. Problems identified in relation to homework included insufficient control of the setting of homework so that unsuitable tasks were sometimes assigned, underestimation of the length of tasks, and pupils being required to do too much. The report recommended the adoption of four types of homework: giving pupils practice in particular operations or processes, verbal memorizing, revision of previous work and preparation for a coming lesson. Overall, the report recommended a reduction in the amount of homework and no homework for children under 12 (Board of Education, 1937). However, as the cause of excessive homework (the examination system) remained, little difference was made in practice, although some schools and Boards of Education did carry out experiments in reducing homework (London County Council, 1937) and the early equivalents of homework clubs were set up.

With the establishment of secondary modern schools after 1944, practices in setting homework between and within different types of school continued to vary. A survey in 1947 (Ward, 1948), showed that 24 per cent of secondary modern boys were set up to one hour of homework each evening and 5 per cent did more than an hour, but 71 per cent had none. The corresponding percentages for grammar school boys were 43, 55 and 2. Calls for this to change were made in 1963 when the Central Advisory Council (Newsom, 1963) reported on the education of pupils of average and less than average abilities (aged 13–16). The report called for a programme of liberal education, as pupils were bored with school, with life outside school and, later, with their jobs. More able pupils, it argued, had a longer school day because of homework, and it suggested that the less able would also benefit from homework, albeit of a more varied form. Extra facilities would be needed for this, for example quiet rooms in schools and public libraries to enable all pupils to do their homework properly. Additional staff resources would also be required. This brief historical review of research on homework in the UK indicates that many of the concerns frequently raised about homework are not new, and neither are the solutions that are often proposed.

In the USA, homework has experienced similar cyclical changes in popularity depending on social, economic and educational factors. In the early part of the twentieth century homework was seen as an important means of disciplining children's minds (Brink, 1937). Memorization was the key task, being seen as mental exercise, and homework provided an appropriate means for such exercise to be undertaken. By the 1940s, the development of problem-solving skills and of student initiative and interest in learning had become fashionable, and the use of homework began to be questioned (LaConte, 1981). In the late 1950s, after the Russians developed Sputnik, the question of rigour in the educational system was raised, and knowledge of subject matter was perceived to be important. Homework came into vogue again. By the 1960s, the trend had reversed and homework was seen as placing excessive pressure on students. In 1983, the tide turned yet again (Cooper, 1989a, 1989b, 1994; Foyle, 1992) with the publication of *A Nation at Risk: The imperative for education reform* (National Commission on Excellence in Education, 1983). With renewed pressure to raise standards, homework came back into fashion. At the end of the twentieth century homework was set for pupils in the earliest school grades, sometimes even in kindergarten (Gill and Schlossman, 2000).

This brief outline of the history of homework demonstrates how attitudes towards homework reflect current political and economic concerns and the dominant philosophical approach to the aims of education. Research on homework can only be understood by taking account of the cultural and historical framework within which it is undertaken.

Definitions of homework

While there has been controversy about the setting of homework, there is little controversy about its definition. Homework is usually taken to mean any work set by the school and undertaken out of school hours for which the learner takes the primary responsibility. Of course, it may actually be undertaken on school premises and where very young children are involved the primary responsibility for making sure that it is undertaken usually lies with the parent(s) or carer(s). Cooper (1989a, 1989b) argues that homework explicitly excludes in-school guided study, home-study courses delivered through the post, television, audio- or videocassettes or the internet that are not determined by the school, and extra-curricular activities such as sports and participation in clubs. Homework can vary in its amount, its purpose, the skill area utilized, the degree of individualization, the degree of choice the student has, the completion deadline, and the social context (that is, whether it is undertaken in groups or individually). In addition to its relation to academic work, it may have other purposes related to the teacher, the school or the wider educational administration (Epstein and Van Voorhis, 2001).

Purposes of homework

Over the years many purposes have been suggested for homework. Some of these may appear contradictory in nature, but this is in part because they are defined by different kinds of tasks set for pupils of different ages and abilities. Drawing on a number of sources (Lee and Pruitt, 1979; LaConte, 1981; Epstein, 1983, 1988, 1998; Cooper, 1989a, 1989b; MacBeath and Turner, 1990; DfEE, 1998b; North and Pillay, 2002), we can group the purposes of homework into a number of categories: promoting academic learning, the development of generic skills, school purposes, promoting home–school links, and promoting communication between parents and children.

Homework for promoting academic learning can:

- allow practice and consolidation of work done in class;
- allow preparation for future classwork;
- extend school learning;
- encourage creativity.

Homework for the development of generic skills can:

- provide opportunities for individualized work;
- foster initiative and independence;
- develop skills in using libraries and other learning resources;

- train pupils in planning and organizing time;
- develop good habits and self-discipline;
- encourage ownership of and responsibility for learning.

Homework for the school can:

- ease time constraints on the curriculum;
- enable particular examination demands to be managed;
- allow assessment of pupils' progress and their mastery of the work covered;
- exploit resources not available in school for learning of all kinds at home;
- enable the punishment of students;
- provide evidence for the evaluation of teaching;
- fulfil the expectations of parents, pupils, teachers, politicians and the public;
- enable accountability to external inspection agencies.

Homework that promotes home–school links can:

- bring the school and home closer together;
- inform parents about what is going on in the school;
- create channels for home–school dialogue;
- develop an effective partnership between the school and parents.

Homework for promoting family communication can:

- provide opportunities for establishing communication between parent and child;
- provide opportunities for parental co-operation and support.

The perceived importance of each of these purposes will vary over time, depending on circumstances. No single piece of homework will satisfy them all.

The emphasis on particular purposes varies between primary and secondary schools. At primary level, the role of parents tends to be seen as more important, while at secondary school the emphasis tends to be on the development of independent study skills.

Types of homework

The type of homework set by schools varies according to the age and ability of the pupil and the demands of the curriculum. In the early years, it usually consists of working on basic skills with the help of parents. As pupils progress through the primary school they may be asked to learn spellings, undertake a range of reading tasks, practise simple mathematical skills or learn tables. As they approach the end of their time at primary school, they are likely to be required to undertake more written work, and less parental support is expected. At secondary level pupils are expected to do much more homework covering the whole curriculum. Issues relating to types of homework are discussed in depth in Chapter 3.

The advantages and disadvantages of homework

The perceived advantages of homework reflect many of the purposes of homework outlined above. While there is evidence that homework can support learning and academic achievement, and have non-academic, parental and family benefits (e.g. Cooper, Robinson and Patall, 2006; Eren and Henderson, 2008), there can also be negative effects. These can include boredom on the part of pupils, lack of time for leisure and community activities, parental interference, and increased differences between high achievers on the one hand and low achievers and those of low socio-economic status and minority groups on the other. These issues have been raised consistently over the years (e.g. Cooper, 1989b; Earle, 1992). Table 1.1 sets out the perceived advantages of homework in terms of promoting academic attainment, the development of generic skills, the advantages for the school, promoting home–school liaison and supporting family communication. The disadvantages of homework are categorized under school, personal, family and societal factors. Within the historical homework cycle, change seems to occur when the amount of homework required of pupils is so great that the disadvantages of homework come to be perceived as outweighing the advantages.

Table 1.1: Perceived purposes, advantages and disadvantages of homework

Perceived purposes and advantages of homework	Perceived disadvantages of homework
Homework can promote academic learning by	**Homework can act to the disadvantage of schools when**
* increasing the amount of time students spend studying	* it increases negative attitudes
* providing opportunities for practice, preparation and extension work	* it reduces the opportunities for pupils to develop academic skills from involvement in everyday life
* assisting in the development of a range of intellectual skills	* parents pressure children too much
Homework can assist in the development of generic skills by	* parents create confusion in explaining material
* providing opportunities for individualized work	* parents have different approaches to teaching from those adopted by the school
* fostering initiative and independence	* parents do homework for their children or contribute excessively

Perceived purposes and advantages of homework	Perceived disadvantages of homework
* developing skills in using libraries and other learning resources	* pupils cheat or copy
* training pupils in planning and organizing time	* the differences between high and low achievers are increased
* developing good habits and self-discipline	**Homework can have a negative impact on the family when it**
* encouraging ownership and responsibility for learning	* disrupts family life
Homework can be beneficial to schools through	* causes friction within the family
* easing time constraints on the curriculum and allowing examination demands to be met	**Homework can be detrimental to the individual when it**
* allowing assessment of pupils' progress and mastery of work	* causes anxiety
* exploiting resources not available in school	* reduces motivation to learn
* fulfilling the expectations of parents, pupils, politicians and the public	* creates boredom, fatigue and emotional exhaustion
* enabling accountability to external inspection agencies	* reduces time for leisure activities
Homework can promote home–school liaison by	**Homework can have a negative impact on society when it**
* encouraging the involvement of parents	* reduces time for involvement in community activities
* developing links and opportunities for dialogue between parents and the school	* polarizes the opportunities for children from different economic circumstances because some have better facilities and resources than others
Homework can promote family communication by	
* encouraging parents and children to work together	

Derived from Cowan and Hallam (1999)

International perspectives on homework

Homework practices and attitudes towards them vary across cultures. An early survey prepared by the Eurydice National Unit for England, Wales and Northern Ireland (Le Métais, 1985) examined the role of homework in the curriculum of each of the then European Community Member States. The survey revealed that policies on the place of homework in the curriculum were usually left to the discretion of individual institutions. Ministerial recommendations tended to deal with maximum duration, co-ordination of work in different subjects to ensure an even spread of tasks throughout the week, and the need for children to be allowed sufficient free time to relax and engage in non-school leisure pursuits. At the time of the survey, Denmark, Luxembourg and several of the Länder in West Germany forbade the setting of homework tasks at weekends. The Spanish regulations specifically forbade teachers to ask pupils to do work of a general, regular or periodic nature outside of schools, and in Greece, in response to parents' wishes, guidelines about methods of teaching and the structure of lessons meant that homework was generally perceived as unnecessary. While the length of time stipulated for homework, where it was set, varied from none for primary school pupils to half an hour for 11–12-year-olds and to about two hours for senior secondary pupils, it was generally perceived that the quality of the tasks set within an overall programme determined their value. Repetitive exercises or those which did not build on work already covered in class were felt to lead to a reaction against education as a whole. Where parents were forced to put pressure on children or attempt to provide explanations that should have been given in class the relationship between parents and pupils was seen to be put under pressure, undermining the spirit of co-operation between the school and the home.

A further comparison, based on evidence from the Third International Mathematics and Science Study (TIMSS) (Keys, Harris and Fernandes, 1997a), showed that mathematics homework was set less frequently for Year 5 pupils in England than in every comparison country except the Netherlands. In Hungary, France, Singapore and the USA, in over 80 per cent of schools mathematics homework was set for pupils more than three times a week. In Germany and Canada the rate was over 70 per cent, and in Switzerland 67 per cent. This compared with 5 per cent in England. In contrast, in science, in Year 9 88 per cent of teachers in England set homework at least once or twice a week, more frequently than in most other countries. However, in mathematics in Year 9, England was in the minority in generally setting less than three pieces of homework a week. In seven countries over two-thirds of mathematics teachers set homework at least three times a week. These comparisons undoubtedly contributed to the decision in England to provide schools with guidelines about homework. These are set out later in the chapter.

Doing ever increasing amounts of homework may not be productive. Evidence from Programme for International Student Assessment (PISA) 2009 data suggested that after around four hours of homework per week the additional time invested had a negligible impact on performance. A reduction in homework between 2003 and 2012 in 31 of the 38 countries meant that most OECD countries were closer to this four-hour threshold (OECD, 2014). Details of more recent research focusing on the amount of homework that teachers set and the time spent by children completing it are set out in Chapters 4 and 5.

The policy context in England

With the introduction in 1988 of the National Curriculum in England, homework became a focus of interest as a means of raising attainment. In 1998, the then DfEE introduced national guidance on homework, as the research evidence had suggested that schools varied considerably in their approach towards setting homework at both primary and secondary levels (Ofsted, 1994). An Ofsted survey in 1995 concluded that homework was not an integral part of the school curriculum in primary schools, and that while homework policies were in place in most secondary schools they were rarely monitored to ensure that they were being implemented effectively.

Another source of pressure to increase the amount of homework set was examinations. At primary level the need for schools to perform well in Standard Attainment Tasks (SATs) may have had an impact on the amount of homework given, while at secondary level the course work requirements of many GCSE and GCE AS and A-level syllabuses required students to undertake a considerable amount of independent work (Ofsted, 1995). While a small-scale study of parents' perceptions of GCSE requirements (Kibble, 1991) indicated that students were coping well with homework, parents reported that students often found it difficult to deal with distractions. They were also concerned that teachers were not always aware of how long some homework tasks actually took, which led to overloading of their children.

The guidelines set out in 1998 (DfEE, 1998b) recommended time allocations for homework at primary and secondary level and gave indicative tasks that might be set (see Tables 1.2 and 1.3). At primary level the main aim was perceived to be engaging parents in children's learning, while for older students it was suggested that homework should provide opportunities for independent study.

Table 1.2: DfEE recommendations for Homework in Primary Schools (1998)

Year group	Time allocation	Subjects
Years 1 and 2	1 hour/week	Reading, spellings, other literacy work and number work
Years 3 and 4	1.5 hours/week	Literacy and numeracy as for Years 1 and 2 with occasional assignments in other subjects
Years 5 and 6	30 minutes/day	Regular weekly schedule with continued emphasis on literacy and numeracy but also ranging widely over the curriculum

Table 1.3: DfEE recommendations for Homework in Secondary Schools (1998)

Year group	Time allocation
Years 7 and 8	45–90 minutes per day
Year 9	1–2 hours per day
Years 10 and 11	1.5–2.5 hours per day

In addition to recommendations for the amount of time to be spent on homework, schools were offered guidance on other aspects of homework policy. Secondary schools were encouraged to have a homework timetable so that the balance of work required of students was equitable across the week, and also to provide a balanced programme of different kinds of assignments so that students had opportunities to develop a range of different types of skills. Schools were encouraged to establish a homework strategy, ensure clear communication with pupils and parents, and plan homework to complement classwork and not merely be a means of completing it. Teachers were exhorted to take account of their pupils' learning needs, devise strategies to involve parents, and provide formative feedback to students. Schools were advised to put money into homework, produce a list of tasks and ensure that staff and students complied with the policy. In addition, they were advised to monitor, review and evaluate homework policy.

These guidelines seemed to have an impact. In 1997, Osgood and Keys (1998) reported that over half of primary schools had a homework policy. In 1998 the figure was similar (Birmingham, Keys and Lee, 1999), but by the end of 1999 90 per cent had homework policies. This included 100 per cent of junior and middle schools and 75 per cent of infant and first schools. There was also much greater guidance in schools regarding time allocation for homework, marking and feedback (Felgate and Kendall, 2000). Ninety-one per cent of primary schools provided guidance on the type of homework activities to be set, 79 per cent on the amount of homework to be given each week, 73 per cent on the consolidation of classwork, 63 per cent on marking and feedback, 45 per cent on the time allocation of homework in different subjects and 31 per cent on follow-up strategies. In all cases, these percentages represented an increase on what had been reported in 1997.

Despite the positive impact of the guidelines on the way that schools managed homework, in March 2012 Michael Gove, then Secretary of State for Education, indicated that schools no longer needed to follow them. This placed the responsibility for decisions about homework on the leadership team in each individual school. Following this change, in a document offering guidance on how to emerge as an 'outstanding' school following inspection, Ofsted (2012) indicated that homework should only be set if it was appropriate to the needs of the children. It should have clear and relevant objectives and should develop children's learning. The document also suggested that homework chat rooms could maximize the potential for learning from homework and personalize children's learning in a safe environment. Particular reference was made to the US-based Northwest Educational Technology Consortium as an example of how teachers could improve the effectiveness of homework. The use of chat rooms to support homework is considered in greater detail in Chapters 3 and 7. The role of the school and teachers in homework is considered in Chapter 4.

Models of homework

The effectiveness of homework in increasing pupil attainment depends on a wide range of factors. Historically, this complexity led a number of authors to propose explanatory models of homework. Coulter (1979) suggested that the homework process could be divided into three phases, the initial classroom phase, the home-community phase and the classroom follow-up phase. Cooper (1989a) extended this to include six sets of factors: exogenous factors such as student characteristics, subject matter and grade level; assignment characteristics; initial classroom factors; home-community factors; classroom follow-up; and outcomes or effects. Keith (1982) explored the relative influences of some of these factors in a path analysis that included the amount of time spent on homework as a predictor of high school grades. The model suggested that students' race, and family background, affected their abilities and whether they were working in vocational or academic fields. Time spent on homework was seen as a function of all of these. De Jong, Westerhof and Creemers (2000) found in a multilevel analysis that the only homework variable predictive of achievement was the amount of homework given. The most powerful factors predicting attainment were prior knowledge and ability, time on task, absence from school, motivation and self-confidence. Other variables included class prior achievement, the number of homework tasks in the year and the quality of instruction, specified as clear, task-directed and positive teaching. While such analyses and the models derived from them incorporate many factors important for predicting the relationships between attainment and homework, they have not attempted to consider the dynamic relationships between them.

Model of homework

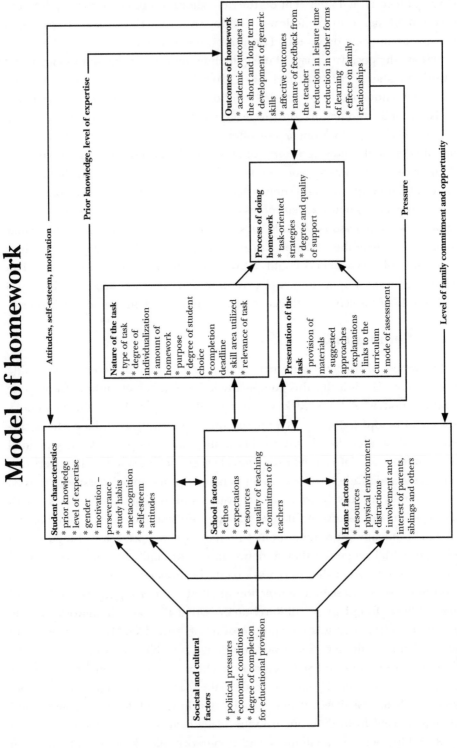

Figure 1.1: Model of homework

Cowan and Hallam (1999) proposed a model that sets out the factors involved and also attempts to outline some of the interactions between them. The model, illustrated in Figure 1.1, suggests that societal and cultural factors influence the behaviour of students, schools and families. In turn, there are complex interactions between aspects of each of these. The nature of the homework task and its presentation are largely determined by the school, although teachers may take account of student characteristics and home factors. The nature and presentation of the task will to some extent determine the processes involved in doing homework. The processes include the strategies available to the student for undertaking the task itself and for supporting their learning, such as maintaining concentration and organizing time. The process will also be influenced by the degree and quality of support that pupils receive at home from parents/carers, siblings, friends or other family members. The outcomes of homework can be both academic and affective and may be related to school, family, personal or social factors. Student characteristics may directly influence learning outcomes through prior knowledge and level of expertise factors, while the outcomes of homework will influence student characteristics, changing not only academic and metacognitive characteristics but also those relating to self-esteem, attitudes and motivation. The outcomes of homework are affected directly by time factors, in particular opportunities to do homework, while the home environment can be influenced by the degree of family commitment to school and their child's progress. School factors can be affected by the outcomes of homework. Teachers respond more favourably to pupils if they are working hard and doing well, and the school's reputation may improve and its ethos become more positive. The reverse can also apply: negative outcomes of homework can contribute to a downward spiral in which teacher morale is low, which can lead to cycles of blame and the emergence of a more negative ethos.

While this model does not take account of all the complexities of interactions between factors affecting homework, it does provide a broad framework in which to consider them. To understand homework and its potential role in enhancing learning, those making and implementing policy and those undertaking research need to acknowledge the complexity of the homework process and its relationship to a range of different outcomes.

The remaining chapters explore current evidence relating to the elements of the model. Chapter 2 considers homework and attainment, taking account of a range of possible mediating factors. Chapter 3 looks at different types of homework, and a range of ways in which support for homework has been offered. The role of schools and teachers is considered in Chapter 4 and factors relating to children and young people in Chapter 5. In Chapter 6, the ways in which parents engage with their children and their homework are discussed, along with how parents can best support the homework process. The final chapter considers new developments and ways in which the effectiveness of homework can be improved.

Susan Hallam and Lynne Rogers

CHAPTER 1: KEY POINTS

There is a long history of research on homework.

Homework is controversial.

Much discussion about homework is polemic and based on opinion rather than evidence.

The way homework is viewed tends to be cyclical, and is based on the political, social, economic and educational factors of the time.

Homework can serve a range of purposes. No individual piece of homework can satisfy them all.

There are advantages and disadvantages to homework that operate at national, school, home and pupil levels.

There are international differences in policies and practice relating to homework.

There have been changes in England in policy relating to homework in the recent past. Responsibility for all issues relating to homework now resides in individual schools.

Models of homework are needed to take account of the many interacting factors that contribute to its effectiveness.

14

The role of homework in attainment

This chapter addresses, first, issues of methodology in the research on homework and attainment, and then research reviews and meta-analyses. The roles of the school, the learner and the home are explored, comparisons are made between findings in different countries, including England, and the longer-term implications of doing homework are considered.

Logically, homework should enhance attainment. It gives schools the opportunity to cover the curriculum more fully and provides learners with opportunities to spend more time in learning guided by teachers. Research on the development of expertise suggests that the longer an individual engages with any particular activity, the higher the level of expertise they will attain in that field. However, a range of factors mediate the relationship between time spent and expertise developed, including the prior knowledge of the learner, their commitment and focus as they are working on tasks, their metacognitive skills, the strategies available to them, and the study environment (for reviews see Ericsson, Charness, Feltovich and Hoffman, 2006; Hallam, 2010). Research on the extent to which homework has an impact on achievement needs to take account of these and other mediating factors including those related to the school and the home. Recently, researchers have begun to address the complexity of studying homework and have adopted approaches that make it possible to take account of a range of confounding or mediating factors. Despite this, much of the research has been criticized as being of poor quality (Cooper, Robinson and Patall, 2006). This chapter will consider the research to date and whether any meaningful conclusions can be drawn from it about the relationship between homework and attainment.

There are many methodological challenges in relation to research on the impact of homework on achievement. For instance, where comparison groups have been used there have often been problems in controlling for confounding variables, e.g. teaching quality, school ethos and the prior attainment of pupils. The amount of homework has been measured by assessing how often it is set, how much is completed and how long it took. The last-named has variously been based on teachers' estimates and on those of pupils and parents. Teachers cannot estimate accurately how long it will take each child to undertake a particular piece of homework and parents and pupils may distort their accounts for a range of reasons, for instance wishing to appear conscientious, forgetfulness, or inaccuracy in keeping records.

The quality or type of homework is rarely taken into account in studies that assess its effectiveness, although a few studies have considered its nature. There are also differences in the way that the impact is assessed, for example teacher tests, examination results, standardized tests and teacher grades. The nature of the assessment can affect the findings. For instance, Maltese, Tai and Fan (2012) found that time spent on homework had a stronger relationship with standardized examination scores than with grades. Research has also been undertaken over different time scales, from a few days to several months, or years. Most of the research has concentrated on mathematics, perhaps because the outcomes are relatively easy to measure. This, however, limits the extent to which the findings can be generalized to other subject domains. In comparison with secondary education, little work has focused on homework in primary schools. Research has also tended to ignore the impact of homework on motivation in the long term and the effect this may have on future decisions about education and on career choice.

Interpreting the findings from research on homework is difficult, because of the many different approaches adopted, the variable quality of the research, and the many factors that contribute to academic learning outcomes in school. Many of these are irrevocably intertwined, which makes it extremely difficult to isolate the effects of homework from other factors, particularly the quality of teaching and teacher expectations. It is perhaps not surprising, therefore, that the research findings are often inconclusive or contradictory in nature. The remainder of this chapter will provide an overview of the key findings from the research and attempt to draw some conclusions about the relationship between homework and achievement.

Reviews of research on homework

Historically, there have been many reviews of research on homework, particularly in the USA. The purpose of most has been to inform policy. Overall, the reviews are inconsistent in their conclusions. Some have concluded that homework does not raise standards and, particularly at primary level, has many disadvantages (Wiener, 1912; Otto, 1941, 1950; Barber, 1986). Some have concluded that the evidence is inconclusive (Harding, 1979; LaConte, 1981; Strang, 1960; Epps, 1966; Friesen, 1979; Knorr, 1981; Rickards, 1982; Otto, 1985). Other reviews have indicated that homework has positive effects in relation to attainment for some pupils, often those who are older and more able, but not for all (Marshall, 1983; Austin, 1979; Coulter, 1980; Goldstein, 1960; Strang, 1968; Cooper, 1989a, 1989b). Some reviews have stressed the many mediating factors that influence the impact of homework on attainment (Holtzman, 1969; LaConte, 1981), while others have concluded that homework does have a positive impact (Cartledge and Sasser, 1981; Coulter, 1979; Austin,

1979; Faulkner and Blyth, 1995; Keith, 1982, 1986, 1987; Foyle, 1984; Pendergrass, 1985; North Carolina Department of Public Instruction, 1983; Walberg, Paschal and Weinstein, 1985, 1986; Paschal, Weinstein and Walberg, 1984; Foyle and Bailey, 1988; Fan, Xu, Cai, He and Fan, 2017; Baş, Şentürk and Ciğerci, 2017). The more recent reviews have tended to stress the positive relationship between homework and attainment, particularly at secondary level.

In England, political interest in homework and the introduction of homework guidance by the DfEE in 1998 led to a number of reviews being undertaken in the late 1990s and the early twenty-first century. Weston (1999) concluded that it was very difficult to identify a clear 'homework effect' on attainment separate from the influence of all the other associated factors, such as home and family background, which are commonly associated with achievement. Sharp, Keys, Benefield *et al.* (2001) drew similar conclusions, which indicated that while there was a case for homework at secondary level, the case at primary level was less clear. Time spent on homework was reported to explain only a small amount of the variance in pupils' achievement scores even at secondary level.

Meta-analyses

One strand of research has attempted to identify the size of the impact of homework on attainment by carrying out meta-analyses that combine the outcomes of several studies. Such research identifies effect sizes. Typically, effect sizes between 0.20 and 0.50 are considered small, those between 0.50 and 0.80 moderate, and those above 0.80 large (Cohen, 1992).

Cooper and colleagues (Cooper 1989a, 1989b; Cooper, Lindsay and Nye, 2000; Cooper, Robinson and Patall, 2006) carried out a series of meta-analyses in the USA. Studies before 1962 that compared homework with no homework generally found that homework had a positive effect on achievement in mathematics but findings were inconsistent in other subject areas. Studies between 1962 and 1986 showed that the average high school student in a class doing homework outperformed 69 per cent of the students in a no-homework class as measured by standardized tests or grades. In junior high school the average homework effect was half of this magnitude, and in elementary school homework had no association with achievement gains. Effects were found over short time periods and where several homework assignments were given each week. Class tests and grades revealed larger homework effects than standardized tests. There were differences between subjects, homework being more effective for science and social studies than for mathematics. Analysis of longitudinal studies showed that for students at elementary school the average correlation between amount of homework and achievement was almost nil, for students in the middle grades it was 0.07 and for high school students it was 0.25. All of the correlations were low. The higher level for the more advanced grades perhaps reflects the fact that teachers set more homework for students who are more advanced and who have more positive attitudes towards school. Overall, Cooper concluded that the relationship between time spent on homework and related academic outcomes was positive and significant except at elementary level, where the findings were predominantly negative (Fetler, 1984; Harding, 1979). Only one study (Singh, 1969) showed a positive relationship for elementary students. There may be a number of explanations for this, perhaps the most obvious being that parents spend longer supporting their children in their acquisition of basic skills at primary level when they are experiencing problems with literacy or numeracy.

On the basis of these findings, Cooper (1989a, 1989b) suggested that homework was ineffective for young children but that there were close relationships at high school level. A later study focusing on elementary school children found that classroom grades were predicted by how much homework the student completed, student ability and the amount of parent facilitation of homework. Parents' support for autonomous student behaviour showed a positive relationship with achievement, whereas direct parental involvement in homework showed a negative relationship (Cooper, Jackson, Nye and Lindsay, 2001; see also Chapter 6).

A later meta-analysis (Cooper, Robinson and Patall, 2006) included 30 studies based on longitudinal data. Most of the included studies found positive relationships between the amount of homework and achievement when various potentially confounding variables were controlled for. Nine studies contained multivariate analysis, although a wide variety of outcome measures and predictor variables were used. Every regression coefficient associated with homework was positive and all but one were statistically different from zero. Six studies compared homework with no homework. All revealed a positive effect of homework on unit tests. Overall, however, Cooper and colleagues were critical of the quality of much of the research and indicated that no firm conclusions could be drawn.

Fan and colleagues (Fan, Xu, Cai *et al.*, 2017) analysed research on homework and achievement in mathematics and science over the thirty years from 1986 to 2015. They concluded that there was an overall small and positive relationship between homework and academic achievement. In contrast to the earlier syntheses, their findings indicated that the effect was stronger for elementary and high school students than for middle school students. The relationship was strongest in studies undertaken in the USA, weakest in studies involving Asian students. They found small differences in outcomes for mathematics and science. Most important was the difference in effect size depending on measures of homework activity. Homework completion, homework grade and effort had larger effect sizes (0.59, 0.52, 0.31) than those for the frequency of homework and time spent doing homework (0.12, 0.15).

Another meta-analytic review (Baş, Şentürk and Ciğerci, 2017) identified 11 studies suitable for inclusion, dating from 2006 to 2015. The review included research from elementary school, secondary school and higher education. Seven of the 11 studies had positive effect sizes, four negative effect sizes. Three main subjects were involved in the analysis, namely science, mathematics and chemistry. The science courses had positive effect sizes, the mathematics outcomes, overall, were negative. In a comparison of the three types of institution, the mean effect size for studies at elementary level was 0.15, at high schools 0.48 and in higher education 0.45, although these were not significantly different from each other. The overall effect size was 0.23. When grade levels were considered the mean effect size for grades 1–4 was 0.21, for grades 5–8 0.41 and for grades 9 and above 0.48. Although these differences were not statistically significant, across most of the research the relationship between homework and attainment increased as students progressed through school and on to higher education. This may be in part because older students tend to be given more homework but also because more ability grouping occurs in the later school years. It is also possible that as students progress through school they become more responsible, acquire higher levels of self-awareness, and have a wider range of learning strategies that support their completion of homework.

Hattie (2009), drawing together several of the meta-analyses of homework (Cooper, 1989a, 1994; Cooper, Robinson and Patall, 2006; DeBaz, 1994; Paschal, Weinstein and Walberg, 1984), included 161 studies involving more than 100,000 students and showed an average effect size of homework on attainment of 0.29. He argued that homework enhanced children's progress by about one year, improving the rate of learning by 15 per cent. Across the studies about 65 per cent of the outcomes were positive in relation to homework, 35 per cent were zero or negative and the average achievement level of students in classes that prescribed homework exceeded 62 per cent of the achievement levels of the students not given homework. Overall, the research suggested that primary school pupils gained the least from homework (d = 0.15) with secondary students having greater gains (d = 0.64). Hattie reiterated earlier comments about the poor quality of the research.

Overall, these meta-analyses suggest that homework can have a small positive effect on homework that increases as children progress through school. However, the inconsistency in the findings indicates that other factors play a mediating role. The next sections will examine research that has attempted to take account of at least some of these factors. These will be considered in relation to the school, the individual learner and parents.

The school, homework and attainment

The amount of homework set by the school

The amount of time spent doing homework varies depending on the type of school that students attend. International comparisons have shown that those who attend schools in which the students are predominantly advantaged and which are in urban areas report doing more homework than those who attend schools in rural areas and in which the student body is more disadvantaged. Students who attend private schools, and upper secondary school (typically pupils aged 15 and over), spend more time doing homework than students who attend public schools and those who attend lower secondary schools (OECD, 2013).

In schools where teachers give a lot of homework attainment tends to be higher (Rutter, Maughan, Mortimore, Ouston and Smith, 1979). McMullen and Busscher (2010), using data for 1st- to 5th-grade students from the US Early Childhood Longitudinal Study, found that the amount of time teachers expected students to spend on homework had positive effects on mathematics and reading achievement. Analysis of PISA data showed that students who attended a school where more mathematics homework was given experienced a particularly large effect, 17 score points or more for each extra hour of homework.

There is a tendency for pupils considered to be of lower academic ability to do less homework, perhaps because their teachers do not set it (Hargreaves, 1967). The giving of homework may depend on tracking, setting or streaming systems. Homework is assigned more frequently in the higher-ability groups (Hallam and Ireson, 2003; Trautwein, 2007). Keith and Cool (1992) found that students who attended an advanced course in mathematics or an elite school spent more time on homework than those enrolled on a basic course or in a less academic school type. Brandsma and van der Werf (1997), in a national longitudinal study with 19,000 participating students, found that the higher-ability classes reported doing more homework. While homework time and mathematics achievement were positively correlated, it was at a very low level (0.12).

Further support for the positive relationship between the amount of homework set and attainment comes from research by Trautwein (2007). He reanalysed data from the Trends in International Mathematics and Science Study (TIMMS) German sample, using multilevel modelling and distinguishing between homework set at the school or class level, homework frequency (number of days) and the amount of time spent doing homework. The findings showed that homework frequency was a significant but moderate predictor of achievement at the class and school levels, while time spent on homework was negatively related to achievement and achievement gains at the student level. Several other large-scale studies support this. For instance, Trautwein, Schnyder, Niggli, Neumann and Lüdtke (2009) studied 1,275 students from 70 classes in Switzerland in relation to the impact of homework on learning French as a second language. At the class level, achievement was higher in classes set frequent homework assignments. Track level (a relatively permanent type of ability grouping) and homework frequency were also positively associated. In a study of 26,543 Spanish students in the 8th grade, Fernández-Alonso, Álvarez-Díaz, Suárez-Álvarez and Muñiz (2017) found that the relationship between academic results and homework time was negative at the individual level, but positive at the school level for Spanish, mathematics, science and citizenship. An increase in the amount of homework a school assigned was also associated with an increase in the differences in student time spent on homework.

In summary, where schools set a lot of homework it has a positive impact on attainment. Typically, children in high-achieving schools or high-ability groups are given more homework. The more homework is given, the greater the variability in the time it takes individuals to complete it. There is a negative association between the time taken to complete homework at the individual level and attainment. The most likely explanation for this is that it takes students with less prior knowledge and lower current attainment in a subject longer to complete homework assignments.

Grade level

Taken together, most of the evidence suggests that homework has a greater impact on attainment in secondary than in primary schools (e.g. Cooper and Valentine, 2001). But not all of the evidence supports this. There may be many reasons for the inconsistencies in findings. There has been less research at primary level, which means that issues relating to whether homework time is based on frequency of homework set or time taken to complete homework have not been fully investigated. Homework at primary level may be more focused on basic skills in literacy and numeracy, so prior knowledge may play a more important role than at secondary level. Some have suggested that younger students have less effective study habits and are easily distracted, which may affect the impact on attainment (Núñez, Suárez, Rosário, Vallejo, Valle and Epstein, 2015). Parents tend to be more involved in the homework of children at elementary school (Skaliotis, 2010). Their support may mediate individual differences, for instance in ability, and so ensure that homework is completed even if it takes a long time. Xu (2005) suggests that older students may be more intrinsically motivated to do homework, whereas younger students may rely on extrinsic motivators, although Hong, Peng and Rowell (2009) analysed Chinese students' (7th- and 11th-graders) approaches to homework and concluded that the older students were less engaged, persisted less, and expressed less enjoyment of doing homework. Other research supports this, showing that some older students do not value school and display less effort with homework (Epstein and Van Voorhis, 2012).

To summarize, the effects of homework on attainment at the elementary school level tend to show little or no effect, although there are exceptions. There may be a range of reasons for this. The tasks set as homework at primary level tend to be related to the development of literacy (particularly reading) and numeracy, where the effects of prior knowledge may be particularly important. Parents may play a different role when their children are at primary school from when they are at secondary school. Some children may be less able to work independently. The research undertaken to date does not enable clear conclusions to be drawn.

The role of teachers in the effectiveness of homework

In many education systems, teachers are responsible for giving students overall attainment grades. These may depend on a combination of attainment and effort. Where effort is included, the grades given are likely to be influenced directly by the extent to which students complete homework. For instance, in a study in Israel, Chen and Ehrenberg (1993) found that the strongest influence on the grades that teachers gave was homework. Students who, according to their teachers, invested more time in homework received higher grades. This influence was greater than the influence of pupils' achievements in tests. The role of teachers in grading students presents a particular challenge for research assessing the impact of homework on attainment.

The way teachers manage homework is crucial for the extent to which homework has a positive impact on attainment. This is clearly illustrated by an early study by Paschal, Weinstein and Walberg (1984), who showed that when doing homework was compared with doing no homework there was an overall effect size of 0.28. However, if homework was given frequently the effect size rose to 0.49 and if teachers checked and graded homework the effect size was 0.80. Similarly, Murillo and Martínez-Garrido (2013), studying the impact of homework on the academic performance in mathematics and language of 5,603 Iberoamerican 3rd-grade students in 98 elementary schools, found that school performance improved if teachers monitored homework, homework was reviewed and corrected in the classroom, and students with lower performance had homework adapted to their needs.

Teachers make decisions about the extent to which homework is used as a substitute for work in class (Rønning, 2011). Falch and Rønning (2012) showed that there were relationships between the effect of homework, instruction time and teaching time. They suggested that homework was more effective when it was used as a complement to classroom learning. In similar vein, Murillo and Martínez-Garrido (2014), focusing on 200,000 children in the 3rd and 6th grades in 16 Latin American countries, concluded that there was a strong dependence between the improvement of academic achievement and the way the teacher used homework in the classroom. This applied for mathematics across all grades. Only homework that was supported by its efficient use in the classroom had an important role in the improvement of students' academic achievement.

De Jong, Westerhof and Creemers (2000) explored a number of issues relating to the teachers' role in the effectiveness of homework. Time devoted in the class to giving homework was related to achievement ($r = 0.13$), although the average amount of time spent giving homework was low. The frequency of setting homework was not related to achievement, perhaps because there was little variance as homework was given frequently by most teachers. However, the total number of tasks given by the teacher was related to attainment ($r = 0.25$). Checking whether homework was completed was negatively related to achievement (–0.21), while classes in which students evaluated homework themselves had higher achievement (r = 0.13). Overall, three class variables explained 8 per cent of the variance, class prior achievement in mathematics, the number of homework tasks set during the year, and the quality of instruction.

Overall, teachers play a critical role in the effectiveness of homework. The way they explain homework in the classroom and ensure that feedback is given on it, either to the whole class, individually or by arranging for students to evaluate homework themselves, contributes to its effectiveness. They can also contribute to making homework tasks interesting, which leads to an enhancement of student motivation. Generally, homework is most successful when it complements classroom activities. Where teachers assign class grades they may also take homework effort and completion into account. This makes it impossible to determine the independent effect of homework on attainment.

Homework in different subjects

Types of homework vary between and within subject domains. Research on the relationship between the type and amount of homework set in different subject areas in schools is limited. Typically, the research has focused on the differences in subjects rather than the differences in specific tasks. This subsection gives examples of the findings related to subject differences. Chapter 3 focuses on types of homework and systems that can support homework.

In an early study, Farrow, Tymms and Henderson (1999) found that there was a moderate correlation in primary schools between the amount of homework that teachers set in mathematics and the amount they set in science. The highest test scores were achieved by those pupils who reported doing homework once a month in each of the core subjects. Homework reported more frequently than once a month was generally associated with lower attainment. However, there was little connection between the amount of homework reported by schools in reading and the other two subjects studied. Similar variation was reported by Eren and Henderson (2011), who showed that while homework had a significant and positive impact on all subjects, adding an additional hour of mathematics or English homework significantly increased attainment, while this was not the case for history, and in science scores decreased. In a meta-analysis, Baş, Şentürk and Ciğerci (2017) compared the effect sizes for homework in general science, mathematics and chemistry. For science, the effect size was 0.66, for mathematics the effect was negative (–0.08) and for chemistry 0.81. In contrast, Fan and colleagues (2017) in their meta-analysis compared homework in mathematics and science and found relatively small effect differences.

Given the inconsistency in the findings of research on the impact of homework in different subjects it is not possible to draw any clear conclusions. A more systematic analysis of the different amounts of homework set for different subject domains and their effects on learning outcomes would clearly be useful, as would a comparison of time spent on homework and its effects within subject domains in different classes and schools. Such research would also need to take account of the kinds of tasks set in each subject.

The learner and homework

Homework attainment and individual time spent on homework

At the level of the individual student, there is frequently a negative relationship between time spent on homework and attainment. For instance, research in the Netherlands by Kuyper and Swint (1996) followed 900 students during their first years in secondary education (grades 7–9). The average correlation between reported time spent on homework and achievement in the first school year was –0.19. Similarly, De Jong, Westerhof and Creemers (2000) studied 1,394 students in their first year of junior high school (average age 12.3 years) in 28 schools in the Netherlands. They found a small negative correlation between time spent on homework and mathematics achievement (r = –0.15). The time students reported spending on mathematics homework was strongly influenced by their prior knowledge. Students scoring high on prior knowledge spent less time on homework. There was also a relationship between the amount of homework time reported by a class and the amount of time devoted to work undertaken independently in class. The relationship was negative (r= –0.55). De Jong and colleagues suggested that when students start their homework in class, they spend less time working at home. Those who already have high levels of competence, who work quickly, may spend very little time on 'homework', completing most of it in class.

These findings are supported by a study in Germany. Trautwein, Köller, Schmitz and Baumert (2002) collected data from 1,976 German 7th-graders (aged 12–13) in 125 classes. The researchers controlled for prior knowledge, intelligence, socio-economic background, motivation and type of secondary school. Homework frequency, frequency of teachers monitoring homework completion and time spent on homework on a typical day were included in the analysis. At the class level, the frequency of homework assignments correlated positively with mathematics achievement, although lengthy homework assignments had a negative, but non-significant, effect. At the individual level, time spent on homework correlated negatively with achievement. Later research (Trautwein, 2007; Trautwein, Schnyder, Niggli, Neumann and Lüdtke, 2009) supported these findings, showing that the relationship between homework and achievement was moderate and positive at the school level but negative at the individual level. Weaker students took longer to do assigned homework and had negative emotions related to homework, which were related to lower achievement. Similarly, Núñez and colleagues (Núñez, Suárez, Cerezo *et al.*, 2015) studied 454 students aged 10 to 16 and found a small negative association between the amount of time spent to complete homework and students' academic achievement. They concluded that the negative association may have been due to problems with assessing the actual time spent or problems in students' ability to self-regulate learning, which resulted in the inefficient use of time and unmotivated homework completion (Rosário, Mourão, Baldaque *et al.*, 2009).

Overall, the research that has adopted a multilevel approach has found that at the individual level the time spent doing homework has little or no positive effect on academic attainment (e.g. Farrow, Tymms and Henderson, 1999; De Jong, Westerhof and Creemers, 2000; Dettmers, Trautwein, Lüdtke, Kunter and Baumert, 2010; Murillo and Martínez-Garrido, 2013; Núñez, Suárez, Rosário, Vallejo, Cerezo and Valle, 2015). Where the findings are statistically significant the significance tends to be in a negative direction (Trautwein, 2007; Trautwein, Schnyder, Niggli, Neumann and Lüdtke, 2009; Lubbers, van der Werf, Kuyper and Hendriks, 2010; Chang, Wall, Tare, Golonka and Vatz, 2014). Spending a long time on homework may indicate that this time was needed because of a lack of prior knowledge or inefficient study habits (Trautwein and Lüdtke, 2007; Núñez, Suárez, Rosário, Vallejo, Valle and Epstein, 2015; Rosário, González-Pienda, Cerezo *et al.*, 2010; Rosário, Núñez, Valle, González-Pienda and Lourenço, 2013; Rosário, Núñez, Valle, Paiva and Polydoro, 2013).

Student characteristics, attainment and homework

Some research has investigated the association between different student homework behaviours and academic achievement, including:

- procrastination and the adoption of specific learning strategies (Lubbers, van der Werf, Kuyper *et al.*, 2010);
- the frequency of homework assignments, the time spent on homework and homework emotions (Núñez, Rosário, Vallejo *et al.*, 2013; Núñez, Suárez, Rosário, Vallejo, Cerezo and Valle, 2015; Núñez, Vallejo, Rosário, Tuero, E. and Valle, 2014; Trautwein, Schnyder, Niggli, Neumann, M. and Lüdtke, 2009);
- homework management (Oubrayrie-Roussel and Safont-Mottay, 2011; Xu, 2010b, 2011);
- attitudes towards homework and reasons for doing homework (Xu and Wu, 2013);
- homework effort (Trautwein, Lüdtke, Kastens and Köller, 2006; Trautwein, Lüdtke, Schnyder and Niggli, 2006; Trautwein, Niggli, Schnyder *et al.*, 2009); and
- help-seeking strategies (Bembenutty and White, 2013; Puustinen, Lyyra, Metsäpelto and Pulkkinen, 2008).

The student factors that contribute the most towards explaining attainment relate to prior knowledge and existing intellectual skills. De Jong, Westerhof and Creemers (2000) found that prior knowledge and intelligence explained 53 per cent of the variance in mathematics achievement. Adding time on task, absence, motivation and self-confidence increased the variance explained to 55 per cent. All ability measures had a negative correlation with homework time. Prior knowledge (mathematical and information-processing) correlated negatively with homework time ($r = -0.23$). The same applied to intelligence ($r = -0.12$), number speed ($r = -0.06$) and average mathematics mark ($r = -0.17$). Similarly, Keith and Cool (1992) found that the strongest effect on achievement was ability, followed by the academic courses previously taken by the student. Eren and Henderson (2011), using NELS:88 data from 8th-grade students, also found a strong positive relationship between homework and test outcomes, but when ability measures were added to the model the co-efficient was zero.

Some students benefit more than others from doing homework. Flunger, Trautwein, Nagengast *et al.* (2015) undertook a latent profile analysis in relation to a longitudinal data set of information on 1,915 8th-grade students from Switzerland (average age 13.6 years) who had been surveyed on their homework behaviour in French as a second language. They identified five learner types that were stable over time: fast, high-effort, average, struggling and minimalist. Time spent on homework and the association with attainment depended on learner type. The fast and high-effort learners displayed favourable achievement outcomes, struggling learners the lowest. For high-effort learners, large amounts of homework could have a positive impact on attainment. Adopting a different approach, Bhandarkar, Leddo and Banerjee (2016) compared the impact of mathematics homework on high- and low-aptitude middle school students and found that it was the average-attainment students who gained the most from being set homework.

Attitudes towards homework have been shown to be related to measured achievement. For instance, Cooper, Lindsay, Nye and Greathouse (1998) studied 709 students in grades 2–12 who completed a homework process inventory. Correlational analyses showed that, although the homework attitudes of lower-grade students (grade 4 and below) were not associated with achievement, those of students of grade 6 and above were. Upper-grade students' attitudes were positively correlated with their reports of the proportion of homework completed and the time spent, as well as with their grades, but not with test scores. However, the size of the correlation between attitudes and grades was quite small ($r = -0.11$).

Effort on homework is also associated positively with achievement. Trautwein and Lüdtke (2007) showed a substantial negative association between homework effort and negative homework emotions ($r = -0.48$). Time spent doing homework was not highly correlated with homework effort ($r = 0.20$). High homework effort and low levels of negative emotions predicted favourable achievement in French whereas high negative emotions and low homework effort predicted lower achievement.

The approach to learning adopted and homework management also have an impact on the effectiveness of homework. In a study focused on 535 children in elementary school (i.e., aged 5–13), Valle, Regueiro, Núñez *et al.* (2016) compared academic goals, student homework engagement and academic achievement. The findings showed that students in the last years of elementary education reported a high level of motivation to learn and master, tended to use a deep approach to homework, did the homework assigned by their teachers most of the time, usually spent an hour a day on homework and reported managing their study time effectively. In the last years of elementary education, academic achievement was related to the amount of homework completed. In turn, homework completed was related to homework time management, which in turn was related to approach to homework, which in turn was related to academic goals and motivation. The study showed the importance of students' effort and commitment to doing homework in relation to its impact on attainment.

Homework time management can also explain a significant proportion of the variance in homework completion (Xu, 2010b, 2011; Xu and Wu, 2013). Núñez and colleagues (Núñez, Rosário, Vallejo and González-Pienda, 2013; Núñez, Suárez, Cerezo *et al.*, 2015) reported that students' perceptions of the quality of their homework time management (concentration on the assignment) were significantly and positively associated with student achievement. Perhaps doing homework on a daily basis helps students to develop good study habits, as some research has suggested (Cooper, Robinson and Patall, 2006; Rosário, Mourão, Baldaque *et al.*, 2009; Xu and Corno, 2006; Xu and Yuan, 2003).

The evidence presented here indicates that prior knowledge and children's current level of attainment has the greatest impact on future achievement. For students who have a positive approach to homework and good homework-management skills there is a positive relationship between homework effort and achievement. Conversely, there are also relationships between low achievement and high levels of negative homework emotions. These issues and those relating to the impact of homework on stress are discussed more fully in Chapter 5.

The effects of homework on the achievement of minority groups

Some research has explored the effects of homework on the achievement of a range of minority groups. Keith and Benson (1992) found that Asian-American students tended to spend more time on homework and that that time was spent more productively in relation to academic achievement. In the UK, in a study taking account of a wide range of family and individual variables, Strand (2011) demonstrated that Indian students were more likely than others to do homework on five evenings a week. Between the ages of 11 and 14 they made greater progress than their White British peers. This cannot be attributed to homework alone as they were also most likely to have a computer and to have private lessons. In contrast, the Black Caribbean students did the least homework and fell further behind the performance of other groups. Strand discusses a range of reasons for this. In Australia, Dandy and

Nettelbeck (2002) compared the relationship between IQ, homework, aspirations and academic achievement for Chinese, Vietnamese and Anglo-Celtic Australian children. The Chinese and Vietnamese children had higher mathematics scores and higher aspirations and spent more time studying, but the regression analysis did not indicate that these students gained higher academic grades directly because of more study time or higher aspirations.

In the USA, Eren and Henderson (2011) found that the impact of mathematics homework for black students compared with white students was much lower and statistically insignificant, although there was a beneficial effect of science homework for Hispanic students. Kitsantas, Cheema and Ware (2011), working with US high school students, explored the effect of time spent completing homework, homework support resources and students' mathematics self-efficacy across race and gender by using data from the 2003 PISA study. Racial achievement gaps were reduced when homework resources and self-efficacy were taken into consideration. Overall, the proportion of time spent on mathematics homework was negatively associated with mathematics achievement scores. Featherstone (1985) found no relationship between race, homework and achievement but suggested that girls did more homework than boys despite the fact that parental expectations were lower for girls. Of course, parental expectations for girls may have changed since the time of this research.

Recently, some research has focused on homework and immigrant children. Suárez, Regueiro, Epstein *et al.* (2016) compared students from immigrant and native families aged 10–16. The results showed higher involvement in homework from native than from immigrant students. Immigrant students who were engaged with homework had better academic achievement in mathematics at secondary grades than less involved immigrant students. Overall, the students tended to be less involved in homework at secondary school than at elementary school. A key issue was the disadvantage of having poor language skills. Homework completion and English language proficiency have a significant impact on class grades (Bang, Suárez-Orozco, Parkes *et al.*, 2009). A further study found that strong academic skills, classroom engagement and a safe school environment were significant predictors of homework completion (Bang, Suárez-Orozco and O'Connor, 2011).

Socio-economic differences

There are concerns that homework can perpetuate differences in performance related to socio-economic status (SES). Dettmers, Trautwein and Lüdtke (2009) found that SES was a significant predictor of mathematics achievement in 9–10-year-olds, although it was confounded with homework time as teachers in schools with economically privileged students tended to assign more homework. Their multilevel analysis found a positive association between school-average homework time and attainment in mathematics in almost all the countries studied, but the size of the association decreased considerably once socio-economic background and data on ability grouping were included. Similarly, Falch and Rønning (2012) found that in some countries the effect of assigning homework was most positive for the students with most books at home. The effect was on average twice as large for girls than boys. Rønning (2011) and Eren and Henderson (2011) found that only students with college-educated parents benefited from homework, while Farrow, Tymms and Henderson (1999), working at primary level, also found that homework time was related to pupils' assessed cultural capital. In every country and economy that participated in PISA 2012, socio-economically advantaged students spent more time doing homework or other study required by their teachers than disadvantaged students (OECD, 2013).

In contrast, in a study of 1,776 Turkish students in grades 5 to 8, students with low-SES backgrounds reported more positive attitudes towards homework than did those with high-SES backgrounds. More students with low-SES backgrounds reported that they were self-motivated to do well on homework, organized assignments in a certain order before starting homework, had a set place for homework, and preferred less background sound and more authority figures present than students with high-SES background (İflazoğlu and Hong, 2012). Baş, Şentürk and Ciğerci (2017), in a meta-analytic review, concluded that there was no indication that SES played a role in homework's effects on academic success.

Of course, some pupils from disadvantaged groups may have greater pressures on their time and be unable to complete homework. They may need to take paid employment (Cooper, 1989b) or look after younger children (DfEE, 1998a). Some children are young carers, which limits the time that can be spent on homework. There is also evidence that employment and many hours working while still at school negatively affect academic outcomes and the probability of completing high school (e.g. Dustmann and van Soest, 2007). Not completing homework may contribute to this effect.

Low-income pupils are likely to have a home life that is less conducive to progress at secondary school than that enjoyed by more affluent pupils. It may be that the role of parents differs in relation to SES. For instance, in the Netherlands, elementary school children from the lowest SES received less help from their parents with homework than other children (Rønning, 2011). Advantaged students are also more likely than disadvantaged students to have an appropriate place to study at home and parents who can convey positive messages about schooling and the importance of doing what teachers ask (OECD, 2013). Low-SES children are less likely to experience a high-quality home learning environment with effective homework routines, material resources for home learning such as books and computers, and academically enriching cultural and sporting activities (Sammons, Sylva, Melhuish *et al.*, 2014).

Overall, the evidence suggests that homework tends to maintain existing inequities in attainment between those of different SES and ethnic minority groups, although there are some exceptions. In countries where there is considerable poverty some children and parents, with high aspirations, may view education and the completion of homework as a means of ensuring greater economic success in the future. In developed countries, those of low SES, in low-attaining schools or ability groups, may find the education system unsupportive and see little hope of gaining high-level qualifications regardless of any homework that they complete.

The home

Parents play an important role in their children's education but parental activity in relation to homework is not a strong predictor of attainment. It is parental aspirations that have the most important influence on children's achievement, while supervision in the forms of monitoring homework, students' time watching TV and time going out with friends tends to have a negative effect (S. Hong and Ho, 2005; see also Chapter 6). Jeynes (2005) showed that while, overall, parental involvement was related to school achievement grades, the best predictor was expectations (d = 0.58). At secondary level, there were greater effects from parental expectations (d = 0.88) than from any other parent factors, including checking homework (Jeynes, 2007).

Despite this, parental support for doing homework can have a positive effect in some contexts. Research in the USA has shown that the effects are greatest in high-SES families, in elementary compared to high schools and in Asian and Latino compared to white and African American families. The family variables that are negatively related to achievement are external rewards, homework surveillance, negative control and restrictions for unsatisfactory grades (Rosenzweig, 2000). Similarly, De Jong, Westerhof and Creemers (2000) found three things were negatively related to achievement, namely parents telling students to start homework, students experiencing problems doing homework and students doing homework with the TV playing.

Children's perceptions of their parents' role in homework are also linked to attainment. Núñez, Suárez, Rosário, Vallejo, Valle and Epstein (2015) explored the relationship between perceived parental involvement in homework (control and support) and student behaviours and academic achievement in 1,683 Spanish students at different stages of schooling. Academic achievement was significantly explained by students' homework behaviours and children's perceptions of parental control and support for homework. These explained 26 per cent of the variance in elementary school, 32 per cent in junior high school and 29 per cent in high school. Núñez, Suárez, Rosário, Vallejo, Valle and Epstein (2015) argued that for the time spent on homework to affect or be affected by time-management skills parents must be involved in ways that support the development of student autonomy. In addition, if students are to improve their knowledge and skills they must be motivated when they do their homework, and the tasks set must facilitate the development of self-regulation skills, including those related to cognition, motivation, behaviour and goal setting.

In summary, the greatest positive impact on attainment that parents' involvement can have is through their aspirations for their children (see also Chapter 6). With regard to homework, negative effects occur when parents attempt to control or interfere with homework. The most positive impact is when parents support the development of autonomous self-regulation in their children (see also Chapter 5).

The impact of homework on attainment in different countries

Exploration of differences between countries in relation to homework is valuable, as it enables homework to be put in context, taking into account national differences in attitudes towards education in general and homework more specifically, towards the role of the family in children's education, and towards the nature of childhood. In an early study, C. Chen and Stevenson (1989) interviewed 3,500 elementary school children, with their mothers and teachers, from China, Japan and the USA. The findings revealed that the Chinese children were assigned more homework and spent more time doing it than the Japanese, who in turn did more than the US children. The amount of homework set varied between schools. The study found no consistent relationship between time spent doing homework and the child's academic achievement. However, the comparison may be misleading. Although Japanese children reported doing less homework, they tend to go to study classes after school. This may have distorted the findings. Overall, the relationships between achievement and time spent on homework varied across the cities involved and at different grade levels.

Other international studies have explored the relationship between attainment and time spent doing homework. At primary level the research has suggested within-country relationships between time spent on homework and achievement in mathematics or science, but the relationships have been inconsistent and weak (C. Chen and Stevenson, 1989; Keys, Harris and Fernandes, 1997b; Mullis, Martin, Beaton *et al.*, 1997). Similar studies undertaken at secondary level (Beaton, Martin, Mullis *et al.*, 1996; Beaton, Mullis, Martin *et al.*, 1996; Keeves, 1995; Keys, Harris and Fernandes, 1997a; Lapointe, Mead and Askew, 1992) have not shown consistent positive correlations between homework and attainment in all countries. Where positive relationships did occur they accounted for only a small proportion of the variation in attainment scores. It was more common for the relationship between time on homework and achievement to be curvilinear (Beaton, Martin, Mullis *et al.*, 1996; Beaton, Mullis, Martin *et al.*, 1996; Keys, Harris and Fernandes, 1997b; Mullis, Martin, Beaton *et al.*, 1997). Moderate amounts of homework time were linked with higher subject scores. Spending a lot of time or very little time was less productive. While the definition of moderate amounts of homework varied between countries,

Beaton and colleagues (Beaton, Martin, Mullis *et al.*, 1996; Beaton, Mullis, Martin *et al.*, 1996) reported a trend in several countries for 13-year-olds spending between one and three hours a day on homework in all subjects to score highest in both mathematics and science. In England, the research showed that being set homework or doing more homework in a subject was slightly positively associated with subject outcomes in mathematics at Year 5 and Year 9, but in the international comparisons the link between how often homework was set and attainment did not hold up in mathematics (Beaton, Martin, Mullis *et al.*, 1996; Beaton, Mullis, Martin *et al.*, 1996; Keys, Harris and Fernandes, 1997a, 1997b). Support for the curvilinear relationship between time spent on homework and attainment comes from work by Cooper (1989a, 1989b) and Lam (1996). Lam found that students who dedicated between 7 and 12 hours to homework each week had a noticeable improvement in attainment over those spending between 13 and 20 hours each week.

In more recent research, Dettmers, Trautwein and Lüdtke (2009) drew on data from 213,759 students in 9,791 schools and 40 countries who participated in PISA 2003. Multilevel analyses revealed a positive association between school-average homework time and mathematics achievement in almost all countries. Students attending schools with lengthy and frequent homework assignments outperformed students attending schools with fewer or shorter assignments. However, the size of the association decreased considerably once socio-economic background and ability group were controlled. At the student level, no clear-cut relationship was established between homework time and achievement. In some countries, there was a negative association between homework time and achievement, in others the association was positive, and in others still it was not significantly different from zero. Overall, homework time explained 4 per cent of the variance at the student level and up to 46 per cent at the school level, with wide variation between countries. Similarly, Falch and Rønning (2012) drew on data on 9-year-olds from 16 OECD countries participating in TIMSS 2007. They found that all students in all countries were given at least some homework in mathematics. Those given homework in all lessons scored on average five to six test points higher than students never given homework. Student achievement was highest in classes where homework was given in half, not all, of the lessons, and lowest where there was no homework.

Overall, the findings from international comparisons regarding the impact of homework on attainment are inconclusive. There may be cultural differences that distort the impact of homework, for instance the extent to which private tutoring or additional educational support is provided. There may also be a curvilinear relationship between the amount of homework given or completed and attainment. Ever increasing amounts of homework may not contribute to enhanced attainment and may lead to student stress. The impact may also differ in relation to primary and secondary education and the extent to which the homework set has direct links with the attainment being measured (see also Chapter 3).

Research on homework in England

There has been very little systematic research on the effects of homework on individual academic achievement in England. Most research has been focused on the school level. One strand of research considered the homework practices of 'effective' schools. Overall, successful schools were characterized as setting more homework (M. Barber, Myers, Denning, Graham and Johnson, 1997). Farrow, Tymms and Henderson (1999) found that schools that set a lot of homework got better results in mathematics and science at primary level but that there was no support for this with regard to reading. Ofsted (1995) reported that most schools set homework and that where it was treated seriously by staff and pupils it had the potential to raise standards, extend coverage of the curriculum, allow more effective use to be made of lesson time, and improve pupils' study skills and attitudes to learning. In general, many pupils and their parents saw work done at home as valuable and as helping to create a partnership between home and school.

In relation to the level of homework assigned, Tymms and Fitz-Gibbon (1992), in their study of homework and A-level performance, which took account of individual pupil differences, found that classes where more homework was given did not do better than classes which reported doing less homework. Broadly similar amounts of homework were set for different curriculum areas, except for general studies, where more homework was given. In contrast, Dudley and Shawver (1991) found that grades were higher in classes where daily homework was set. These apparently contradictory findings may be explained by a range of mediating factors, for instance the quality of the teaching or the nature and quality of the homework.

In a study exploring the relationships between attainment and perceptions of studying among students taking public examinations at age 16, Rogers (2013a) used cluster analysis to classify 826 students in terms of their use of metacognitive, effort-management and study strategies. Six groups were identified. These differed in relation to attainment and the amount of homework that students reported completing. Students in the highest-achieving clusters were hard-working, but differed in their use of strategies. Students in Cluster 2 displayed high anxiety and were ranked second in attainment level. Students in Cluster 4 were the highest achievers. They adopted many self-checking strategies and gained the highest results. Those in Cluster 5 demonstrated effective strategy use and were ranked third. Overall, students in Clusters 1, 3 and 6 achieved less highly. These students demonstrated poor perceptions of studying, which could be conceptualized as the adoption of a surface approach to learning, i.e., a lack of concern for developing a deep understanding of what they were learning. Cluster 3 represented students who directed little effort into their work. They had the poorest results. Students in Cluster 1 had poor time management and little conception of what they were required to do and how to do it. Unsurprisingly, they had the poorest results, followed by cluster

6, who demonstrated a lack of interest and effort. Overall, students who recognized the effort required for study and sought to utilize effective strategies to achieve it did better than those who did not, although there were complex relationships between time spent on homework, students' approaches to studying, student anxiety, prior knowledge and achievement.

The most recent study undertaken in England (at the time of writing) showed that more time spent on homework at secondary school predicted better progress for children aged between 11 and 16 even when other factors – prior attainment, background and neighbourhood – were taken into account (Sammons, Sylva, Melhuish *et al.*, 2014). The greatest progress was made by those completing two to three hours of homework per night. Students who spent more time on homework during Year 9 were almost ten times more likely to achieve five A*–C grades than those who did less homework. A similar result was found for the time spent on homework in Year 11, with positive effects for total GCSE score, specific GCSE grades and benchmark indicators as well as for overall academic progress in specific subjects. In Year 11, the effect sizes did not decrease for those doing more than three hours' homework. Spending more than three hours on homework in Year 11 was significantly associated with obtaining higher total GCSE scores, better grades in GCSE English and in GCSE mathematics, being entered for more GCSE exams, and being more likely to have achieved five A*–C including English and mathematics and the English Baccalaureate. While these findings strongly support the importance of homework in relation to attainment, they must be interpreted with some caution as, at the time of this research, GCSE examinations included a considerable element of course work. This requires students to complete projects independently, and involves much time being spent doing work at home. A further confounding factor is that those in high-ability groups, who would be expected to have high levels of attainment, are set more homework (Hallam and Ireson, 2003).

A further issue to be taken into account in assessing the impact of homework on attainment in England is the extent to which some children are engaged in home tutoring. In a large-scale study of over 3,000 children and 1,100 parents, Ireson and Rushforth (2011) found that, of Year 6 pupils, almost 8 per cent were in receipt of tutoring in mathematics, 8 per cent in English and 3 per cent in science. In Year 11, as students were preparing for GCSE examinations, 8 per cent were receiving tutoring in mathematics and 3 per cent in English and science. Overall, 27 per cent of responding students reported that they had received tutoring at some stage during their school career (see also Chapters 3 and 6). This is likely to have had a positive impact on attainment regardless of the amount of homework completed.

Long-term effects of homework

Kalenkoski and Pabilonia (2017) studied the impact of homework while at school on 20-year-olds. They used the combined Child Development Supplement (CDS) and the Transition to Adulthood Survey (TA) of the Panel Study of Income Dynamics. Homework was assessed in four ways: homework time (as a primary activity or as a secondary activity while listening to music or watching TV), time spent on homework as a primary activity, time spent as a sole activity (the only activity being undertaken), and whether homework was undertaken over the two diary days of the research. The outcomes assessed were long-term academic outcomes, high school Grade Point Average (GPA), and college attendance by age 20. A wide range of student characteristics, family background factors, school characteristics and other external factors were taken into account. All positive associations of homework time with the academic achievement of girls had disappeared by age 20, but total homework time, time spent in homework as a primary activity and sole-tasked homework time all increased the probability of college attendance for boys, although on average they did less homework than girls. Homework time without distractions had a small positive effect on high school boys' GPAs. However, when variables relating to ability and motivation were included the positive relationships were reduced.

Conclusions

The relationships between homework and attainment are complex, and there are many confounding factors, which much of the research does not take into account. Depending on the approach adopted, homework and achievement may be associated negatively, positively or not at all. Attainment has been assessed in many different ways, which may explain some of the inconclusive findings, particularly when school grades given by teachers take into account effort, which might include homework completion. When prior knowledge and other potential confounding variables are included in the models the strength of the association between homework and achievement decreases considerably. While homework can contribute to increased attainment, it accounts for only a very small amount of the variance. Most of the variance is explained by pupils' prior knowledge.

School-level variables, such as the amount of homework assigned, have more explanatory power in terms of attainment than the amount of time the individual spends doing homework. The amount of homework set tends to reflect the academic standing of the school and the level of ability grouping, higher groups being given more homework. Schools that assign more homework tend to exhibit more variation in the time that students spend completing homework. The amount of time individual students spend is usually negatively related to attainment, which suggests that those who have less prior knowledge, poor time management skills or fewer homework strategies take longer to do their homework. Where homework involves finishing off work started in class, those with already higher attainment levels are likely to complete much of it in class, which leads them to spend less time on 'homework'.

Some of the research suggests that there is a curvilinear relationship between homework and attainment. In other words, after a certain point doing additional homework has no benefit. This fits well with what we know about skill development. Extensive practice of a skill produces large benefits in the early stages of learning, but once the skill is acquired longer-term improvement is much slower and the gains are much smaller.

The effects of homework on attainment seem to be much stronger at secondary level than at primary level. In primary schools, the effects tend to be negligible. This may be because younger children have less effective independent learning strategies, because parents support their children in completing homework (in part because they feel able to do so), or because the nature of homework tasks at primary level differs in important ways from what is set at secondary level. In addition, at primary level, where the concern is with the development of basic skills, teachers and parents are likely to encourage children to spend longer doing homework related to those skills so that they do not fall behind. While the principles underlying these relationships do not change at secondary level, the attitudes of educators do. There is an acceptance of differences in attainment and an expectation that children will not all achieve at the same levels beyond primary school.

Teachers have a crucial role to play in pupil attainment in terms of the quality of their teaching, irrespective of their role in relation to homework. In addition, where homework is explained clearly and students are given feedback on it, the impact on attainment is greater. In contrast, the greatest parental impact on attainment is in terms of their aspirations for their children. Where parents attempt to control and interfere in homework activities there tends to be a negative impact. Support for the development of autonomous learning has the most positive effect.

Despite the body of research on homework, there is still much that is not known. The research to date suggests that the effect of homework on attainment varies as a function of the way attainment is assessed, cultural factors, the school system, the age of the students, student characteristics (prior knowledge, skill set, motivation, ethnicity, SES), the way in which homework is assigned and followed up, and how parents support homework completion. Future research needs to take these factors into account. There has been very little recent research on homework in England at a time at which there have been major changes in the education system. This clearly needs to be addressed.

CHAPTER 2: KEY POINTS

The relationships between homework and attainment are complex.

There are many challenges in undertaking and interpreting research on homework. Much early research was of poor quality.

Most of the research suggests that homework makes a small positive contribution to attainment. The effect tends to be larger in secondary education. At primary level the effects tend to be small or negligible.

The amount of homework set by the school is a better predictor of attainment than the time that students spend completing homework. High-attaining schools and teachers of higher-ability groups tend to set more homework.

Students with less prior knowledge and skills take longer to complete homework.

Homework has less of an impact on the attainment of those of low SES and those from some ethnic minority groups.

Prior knowledge and skills explain most of the variance in attainment.

Being able to manage homework and adopt a deep approach to learning, and having positive attitudes towards homework, affect attainment.

Teacher explanations of homework and feedback on outcomes have a considerable impact on its effect on attainment.

The strongest impact of parents on attainment is in relation to aspirations. Controlling or interfering with homework has a negative effect. Support for the development of autonomous learning has the most positive impact.

There is limited recent UK research on homework. Given the major changes in the educational system in the twenty-first century and in guidance for schools concerning homework, this needs to be addressed.

Chapter 3

Homework types and support

In this chapter issues relating to the design of homework and its relationship with the curriculum and assessment are considered. There are sections focusing on different types of homework, computer based assisted learning, differences in homework in primary and secondary schools, differentiation, and a variety of initiatives to support homework including telephone helplines, homework clubs and study centres, supplementary education and support for parents.

This chapter considers how homework relates to the curriculum and assessment; the nature of different types of homework and how they might impact on motivation; the contribution that technology can make to homework; and whether homework should be differentiated and how this might be achieved particularly for children with special educational needs. The role of homework clubs and study centres is discussed and ways in which parents can be supported to play a positive role in relation to their children's homework.

The design of homework and its relationship with the curriculum and assessment

While considerable effort has been made to attempt to establish whether homework is effective in enhancing achievement, there has been little concern in much of this research with the nature or quality of the homework set and its relationship to the particular learning outcome that is being assessed. Clearly, the closer the relationship between the nature of the homework and what is being tested, the more likely it is that there will be positive effects. The amount of time spent on homework alone can be, at best, only a very crude predictor of learning outcomes. The nature of the homework, its value in contributing to the curriculum and the motivation and concentration of the individual undertaking it will be equally, if not more, important. Several authors have argued that for homework to impact positively on attainment its design and purpose have to be clear. Marzano and Pickering (2007) suggest that it needs to have legitimate purpose and be at an appropriate level of difficulty, while Danielson, Strom and Kramer (2011) argue that to have value it should be reasonable, relevant and reinforcing. Baker, LeTendre and Akiba (2005) showed that in countries where teachers set poorly designed homework, the average academic performance decreased even if students completed a lot of homework.

Earle (1992) suggested that homework should be framed within instructional design theory to maximize its effects. He cited the Gagné, Briggs and Wager (1988) model as an appropriate framework, suggesting that homework should be a valid component of instruction and that a lack of understanding of its instructional significance would lead to it being inappropriately used by teachers. This is supported by the findings of MacBeath and Turner (1990), who showed that pupils perceive that homework is useful when it is an integral part of schoolwork. Earle suggested that homework can meet six of the nine 'events' outlined by Gagné as functions of instruction: stimulating recall of prerequisite material, presenting the stimulus material, eliciting performance, providing feedback about performance correctness, assessing performance, and enhancing retention and transfer. He further suggested that if materials were prepared as a self-instructional module the remaining three events – gaining attention, informing learners of objectives, and providing learning guidance – could also be included. He proposed that consideration of these would elevate homework to a position of value in the learning process. Whether one agrees that the model suggested by Earle would provide the best framework within which to consider homework, it is clear that homework is likely to be more effective if it is planned to satisfy designated aims and objectives within the curriculum (DES, 1987; Ofsted, 1995).

While there has been no UK research on the effectiveness of different kinds of homework, the DES (1987) reported, on the basis of their observations, that successful homework was interpreted and implemented within flexible guidelines which avoided adherence to a rigid time allocation and made allowance for widely differing circumstances, age, ability and home conditions. Quality was more important than quantity and, although homework might include some routine work, other, more creative activities were seen as beneficial.

The link between class and homework has been found to be particularly important in terms of homework's effectiveness. Murillo and Martínez-Garrido (2014) worked with Latin American teachers, teaching mathematics and language to 3rd- and 6th-grade children. They asked them how homework was linked to classwork. Thirty-three per cent indicated that they built on homework in all of their classes, while a further 33 per cent indicated that they used homework in more than 70 per cent of their teaching sessions. Only 4.5 per cent did not build on work done at home in class. Reported differences seemed to reflect the cultural background and tradition of the countries where the research was undertaken. The extent to which homework was integrated into classroom work had a statistically significant impact on attainment in most cases. Similarly, a study of 3,483 German students showed that it was possible to increase the efficiency of learning if the teacher adjusted homework to the topics taught in the classroom and supervised its execution (Dettmers, Trautwein, Lüdtke, Kunter and Baumert, 2010).

To be effective in supporting attainment, homework must be an integral part of the curriculum, with strong links to activities in the classroom. Only where homework is aligned with the educational aims and the system of assessment is it likely that there will be a positive impact on students' academic achievement.

Types of homework

Homework can include finishing off work started in class, self-contained or parallel homework (distinct from classwork), spontaneous work arising out of a project or activity, and preparation reading or research done in advance of the lesson. Suggestions for providing variety in homework have included investigations, research, reading, interviews, public library visits, designing, word processing, simple experiments, drafting, revision, desktop publishing, essay writing, report writing, making a model, and projects.

Cooper (1989a, 1989b), in a meta-analysis, found that the instructional purpose of homework, whether it was practice or preparation, had little effect on students' attitudes, but that on immediate and delayed achievement measures homework that included preparation, practice or both was more effective than homework concerned only with current curriculum content. On tests of achievement given immediately after the topic lessons were completed, the average student who did preparation, practice or both types of homework in addition to current-content homework outperformed 54 per cent of the students who did current-content homework only. Where learning outcomes were measured over the longer term, preparation homework seemed more effective than practice homework. In general, Cooper concluded that preparation homework and practice homework were more beneficial than working on current topics. The effects seemed to occur regardless of ability (Laing, 1970; Camp, 1973; Butcher, 1975; Dadas, 1976), gender (Foyle, 1984) and whether students had independent or dependent learning styles (Peterson, 1969). Studies that consider extension homework suggest that it is no more effective than other types of homework (Baughman and Pruitt, 1963; Peterson, 1969). However, caution is needed in generalizing these findings, as the studies considered were all related to secondary schools and mainly focused on mathematics homework.

In the USA, research in the 1990s showed that more than 70 per cent of homework assignments at all levels of schooling were designed to enable students to finish classwork or practise skills (Roderique, Polloway, Cumblad, Epstein and Bursuck, 1994). In Malaysia, a study of the homework set by teachers of English revealed an extensive list of 26 types of homework. The most frequent were grammar exercises, guided writing, corrections, reading comprehension and writing compositions (North and Pillay, 2002).

There has been interest in what have been called 'flipped classrooms'. Here students are asked to prepare material in advance of lessons so that lesson time can be spent in practical activities or practice. They may watch online videos about the topic, made by their teacher or from other sources, or engage before lessons with other materials, for instance worksheets or textbook excerpts. They are responsible for learning the basic content of the topic on their own before class time (Sparks, 2011; Lage, Platt and Treglia, 2000; Bergmann and Sams, 2012). The model has been used most frequently in higher education, although there are examples at school level. One advantage of flipped learning is that it makes students more aware of their own learning processes.

Flipped learning mirrors an approach called flexible learning, which was developed in the UK in the 1990s (Hughes, 1993). The approach was developed for use in geography at secondary level to increase student motivation and improve attainment. Students learned through independent study supervised through tutorials, regular planned meetings between the teacher and a small group of four to six students. The tutorials were used for planning, clarifying, explaining, monitoring general progress and assessment. The key principles were that pupils should take increasing responsibility for their learning, that teaching and learning should take place at an individual level, and that pupils should be made aware of how they learned and how specific learning activities contributed to or detracted from their progress. The students were gradually shaped into this way of learning, beginning with small steps in Year 7 and progressing to much greater independence in Year 11. Data were collected over a four-year period for four cohorts of students. Where students had been taught in this way, there was an improvement in GCSE grades A*–C from 41 per cent to 85 per cent compared with students taught by traditional methods, whose performance increased from 16 per cent to 59 per cent. Pupils and parents reported increased motivation, effort and level of work. The students indicated that this was because they were given greater responsibility, independence and choice, were able to work at their own pace, did not have to go over things they already knew and had access to individual help when they needed it. For flexible learning to be successful, students need to have close support and guidance on a regular basis and teachers need to have appropriate resources. Models in which students learn more independently offer the possibility of transforming the way homework is conceptualized (Bishop and Verleger, 2013).

In the USA, one study focused on the value of different types of homework. Danielson, Strom and Kramer (2011) categorized homework into practice, preparation and integration assignments (applying new knowledge to new tasks, longer-term projects). Data were collected from 48 teachers. In both phases of education, elementary and secondary, most homework was categorized as practice, a lesser proportion as preparation and the least as integration. At all levels the central focus seemed to be practice. Further analysis drew on Kramer's 2008 consideration (cited by Danielson, Strom and Kramer, 2011) of the value of homework as being reasonable, relevant and reinforcing. In the elementary grades, 33 per cent of tasks could be assessed in terms of value, judged by these criteria. Of those, 25 per cent were categorized as having appropriate educational value for the subject and the grade level. At secondary level 55 per cent of tasks were able to be assessed for value and 96 per cent were found to have value. All of the tasks required time, an appropriate work place and basic materials. Of the 750 tasks that were assigned, 22 per cent required some explicit level of adult support at elementary level. In the secondary grades, no adult support was expected. Technological items were required for 6 per cent of tasks and reference material for 14 per cent. Overall, the findings suggest that more consideration needs to be given to the kinds of homework set at elementary level for the homework to have value.

In the Netherlands, Buijs and Admiraal (2013) undertook an intervention designed explicitly to devise homework assignments to challenge student disengagement. Four different assignments were adopted: preparing analytical skills (which promoted knowledge acquisition at home to prepare the practice of analytic skills in class); fragmented assessment (preparation for a test spread over six lessons); jigsaw assignment; and student choice. In jigsaw assignment, students prepared different materials at home related to a complex concept. In class, they discussed each element in order to get an overview of the whole concept. They were then required to apply their knowledge in another assignment in class. In student choice, assignments were grouped by topic and difficulty and students chose their own assignment. Work started at home but was completed in class. The jigsaw assignment and the preparation of analytical tasks increased time on task and class participation. In the longer term, students were most motivated by the fragmented test, which was perceived as meaningful and challenging. This was also perceived as achieving the best learning outcomes. As this work was completed entirely at home, no information about students' time on task or class participation was available.

Other research has also explored whether giving students a choice of homework tasks increases completion rates. Patall, Cooper and Wynn (2010) randomly assigned 207 students to a homework choice or no-choice condition. Students who were able to select the particular homework exercises that they undertook completed more homework, scored better on unit tests, felt more competent in relation to the homework and reported more interest and enjoyment in doing it. Providing students with more control over their homework in this way seems to enhance motivation and engagement.

Few studies explore the particular skills utilized in homework. Nadis (1965) conducted a study relating to history homework for pupils in grade 9. The effectiveness of reading only, reading plus answering related questions and reading plus outlining the material read was compared. No significant differences were found, although the students reported that written homework assignments were more effective because they assisted with memorization and ensured that homework was actually undertaken.

In an interesting study, Zohar, Schwartzer and Tamir (1998) examined the level of thinking skills required for completing homework while studying biology in schools in Israel. They found that higher-order thinking and enquiry skills were likely to be required in homework for which pupils were set a medium number of questions to answer. Such questions were posed more often in homework and tests than in the classroom. This suggests that homework may have an important role to play in the development of high-level cognitive skills.

Overall, the most commonly assigned types of homework are those relating to practice, preparation and the completion of work started in class. The benefits for attainment tend to be greater when skills are practised or work is prepared before lessons. The latter tends to increase motivation and enables the classroom to be used for discussion, follow-up and practical work. The difficulty here is ensuring that all students undertake the preparation work. Giving students choice, creating opportunities for independent learning and devising interesting approaches to homework enhance motivation. Teachers need to consider whether homework has value, i.e., is reasonable, relevant and reinforcing. While most homework meets these criteria at secondary level, that is not always the case at primary level.

Computer-assisted learning

An emerging means of supporting student learning is the use of interactive computer programs. Students work through these at their own pace and are given immediate feedback on their performance. This is important as formative assessment plays a major role in enhancing learning (Black and Wiliam, 1998a, 1998b). Timely, supportive and specific feedback and guidance are very beneficial to students (e.g. Shute, 2008; Butler, Karpicke and Roediger, 2007).

The findings from research on computer-assisted learning are mixed. Lee and Heyworth (2000) found no significant effect on retention from using electronic homework, although the particular system being used was reported by students to be slow. Penn, Nedeff and Gozdzik (2000) evaluated the use of a web-based approach to homework and testing called the WE_LEARN System. A multiple-choice database of questions was created that were similar in style to those which had previously been assigned from a textbook. Students using the system obtained higher test scores and were more confident when taking exams. They used the system as a learning tool as it gave them greater knowledge of the extent of their understanding of the materials. As a result of the implementation of the system, the questions that students raised with their academic advisers changed from ones concerned with basic concepts to ones concerned with high levels of understanding. Hall, Butler, McGuire *et al.* (2001) also used a web-based homework system to enable university students to complete problem-solving tasks in chemistry and gain feedback on their performance independently of their tutors. Correlations with end-of-semester grades showed that students who participated earned better grades than those who did not. The increased time on task, the dispelling of misconceptions and the emphasis on correcting mistakes proved very helpful. Student feedback was overwhelmingly positive. An unexpected outcome was that the students reported more collaborative working. The project also enabled instructors to set a greater quantity and variety of homework questions because they were not limited to marking them by hand. Other projects have explored the development of materials for use on home computers in mathematics (Wain and Flower, 1992), physics (Thoennessen and Harrison, 1996) and general science (Ronen and Eliahu, 1999). In all cases the students rated the use of the systems positively. In physics students spent more time on assignments. Fewer teaching assistants were needed and their time was diverted from grading to more interactive contact with the students.

ASSISTments is another interactive program designed to give immediate feedback to students. In one study, it was used with 28 7th-grade mathematics students. Comparison of pre- and post-tests showed a positive effect (d = 0.6) (Mendicino, Razzaq and Heffernan, 2009). Another study with 63 students compared immediate feedback from the computer with next-day feedback from a teacher. The computer-based group had higher post-test scores (Kelly, Heffernan, Heffernan *et al.*, 2013). Singh, Saleem, Pradhan *et al.* (2011) worked with 172 students divided into control and intervention groups. Both groups answered homework questions on a computer. The computer-based-feedback group received both correctness feedback and tutorial guidance if they got a question wrong. The control group did not receive such feedback. The feedback group had higher post-test scores. Roschelle, Feng, Murphy and Mason (2016) studied two elements of ASSISTments content. One element linked to existing textbook homework problems or problems that teachers had written themselves, the second was designed for mastery-oriented skill practice. Forty-three schools participated with a total sample size of 2,850 6th-grade students. For those students with scores at or below the median the scores for the treatment group were 13.35 points higher than controls. For the students above the median the mean score was 5.84 points higher. Overall, the ASSISTments program had a greater impact for lower-performing students.

The US-based Northwest Educational Technology Consortium has provided examples of how teachers can use a range of new technology to support student learning. They highlighted an example of a teacher who posted relevant reading material online and encouraged students to debate issues in chat forums. The class website also had a space for teachers to communicate directly with parents and one where students could ask specific questions regarding reading and homework. The times when the chat room would be open were specified (for 90 minutes after school and for an hour on one evening a week), and the teacher controlled access to the forum. The students who engaged with activities in the chat room were more engaged and asked more questions (Ofsted, 2012).

In summary, computer-based interactive systems have the potential to assist with homework, particularly where there are correct answers to problems, as they can provide immediate feedback and support. In some subject domains, student chat rooms where issues can be discussed with their peers and teachers are likely to be more effective in engaging students and enhancing their learning.

Differences in homework in primary and secondary schools

Typically, the homework set by schools varies according to the age and ability of the pupils and the demands of the curriculum. In the early years, it usually consists of working on basic skills with the help of parents. As pupils progress through the primary school they may be asked to learn spellings, undertake a range of reading tasks, practise simple mathematical skills or learn tables. As they approach the end of their time at primary school, they are likely to be required to undertake more written work, and less parental support is expected. At secondary level pupils are expected to do much more homework, covering the whole curriculum. MacBeath and Turner (1990), in their study of homework in Scottish schools, found that at secondary level English, mathematics and French homework dominated, particularly in the early years; the amount of English and mathematics homework increased while the amount of French homework declined. Homework for other subjects increased as pupils progressed through school, although there was considerable variation from school to school, class to class, and teacher to teacher.

Differentiation of homework

In the UK, in 1987, the then Department for Education and Science suggested that it was not possible to be definite about the kind or amount of homework desirable for all pupils as students differ greatly (DES, 1987). This has been reflected in school practice in the UK, particularly at secondary level. It has been assumed that lower-achieving children should get less homework, and in practice they do (Gordon, 1980; Hallam and Ireson, 2003; Mirza, 1992; MacBeath, 1996; Ofsted, 1994). Those in lower-ability groups may resent this (MacBeath, 1996). As teachers often set the same homework tasks for all pupils in a class regardless of their different needs, there can be issues when classes are mixed-ability (Costa, Cardoso, Lacerda, Lopes and Gomes, 2016). Teachers may set less homework for those of lower attainment because they tend not to complete it (DES, 1987). In part, it may be this that has led to demands that homework be differentiated for pupils of different abilities (MacBeath, 1996; DfEE, 1998b). Where lower-ability students do complete regular homework, they can achieve higher average grades than more able pupils who do no homework at all (Keith, 1982).

At primary level the position is not so clear. Studies in the USA have found that low achievers spend more time on homework (Epstein, 1988), while in the UK Farrow, Tymms and Henderson (1999) found no difference in the amount of homework set and pupils' measured ability. At secondary level, in addition to being set more homework high-ability pupils are likely to receive the most support from teachers.

Teachers tend to reinforce and exaggerate differences between high and low achievers through their differential expectations (Natriello and McDill, 1986), although it is possible for these to be overcome (Walberg, Paschal and Weinstein, 1986). The way in which more homework has tended to be set for more able pupils raises issues relating to the purpose of homework. If there is indeed a trade-off between ability and time spent learning, as suggested by Carroll (1963) and as operationalized through mastery learning programmes (Bloom, 1976), then homework could operate as a means of increasing learning time for the less able, increasing the possibility of them keeping up with their more able peers. In practice this does not seem to happen.

Does individualizing homework lead to higher achievement? The evidence is mixed. Schunert (1951) found that differentiated homework led to increases in performance in mathematics (algebra and geometry). In contrast, Bradley (1967), also studying mathematics performance, found no clear advantage for individualization. He compared homework set for the whole group with individualized assignments. In the individual condition students played a role in deciding on the nature of the assignment, whether it would be remedial or for enrichment, and how long it would take. In the group condition homework was taken from the textbook and was identical for all students. This procedure was adopted for eight weeks. The outcomes were assessed by achievement gains, interest levels, and time spent on homework. The individualistic homework group achieved more but the effect was not found in all schools. Overall, individualized homework was more effective for girls and for students in the top third of ability. There was no overall effect on interest levels, although there were gender differences. Boys receiving individualized homework chose mathematics activities more than others, while the opposite was true for girls. Achievement did not relate to activity choices. In relation to time, boys spent more time when they had group homework (that is, they were all set the same homework). Almost half of the bottom third of achievers spent more than the desired time on group homework compared with only one in six when it was individualized. The time teachers spent preparing and correcting homework was much greater in the individualized condition. Grant (1971) allowed students to choose between two types of mathematics assignment, which differed in level of difficulty but were similar in format and covered the same material, and found no overall significant differences in performance; however, girls, in contrast to Bradley's study, did better in the group homework. In Scotland teachers reported that, particularly at secondary level, homework should vary in amount and type for different pupils (MacBeath and Turner, 1990). However, they were concerned about the increased amount of teacher time this would take. Where work was already individualized through graded schemes of learning this was not perceived as a problem.

These studies indicate mixed benefits from individualizing homework. The issue to be addressed is what the purpose of homework is. Should schools be attempting to ensure that every child spends the same amount of time doing homework? If so, individualization is clearly essential. If the aim is to ensure that every child has covered the same curriculum, individualization is inappropriate and some students will need to spend a greater amount of time on homework to keep up with their peers. If the aim is to ensure that every child is given work that will be of maximum benefit to their overall intellectual development then individualization will be necessary. While this implies that schools need to establish the overall aims and purpose of homework, it is likely that there will be variation dependent on the nature of the subject domain, the particular topic being studied, and other characteristics of the pupils. The necessity for individualization of homework is also related to the ability-grouping procedures adopted in the school. Where pupils are grouped by ability there should be less need for individualization. Where classes are mixed-ability it may be more important, particularly as teachers in the UK tend to give the same homework to the whole class regardless of the type of ability-grouping procedures adopted (Hallam and Ireson, 2003).

What can research tell us about the role of homework for children who have identified learning difficulties? The evidence suggests that they have problems completing homework, particularly in mainstream school settings (McNary, Glasgow and Hicks, 2005). The challenges include short attention span, memory deficits, poor receptive language, and lack of organizational skills (Polloway, Foley and Epstein, 1992). They need specific support in undertaking homework (Jayanthi, Bursuck, Epstein and Polloway, 1997). A major challenge is getting teachers to develop assignments that are developmentally appropriate in terms of their difficulty and the length of time required to complete them. Bryan and Burstein (2004) found a discrepancy between the time teachers thought homework would take and the actual time it took, as some students had not understood the assignments, had attention problems or experienced distractions at home. Despite this, children with special educational needs can benefit from doing homework (Strukoff, McLaughlin and Bialozor, 1987; Salend and Schliff, 1989; Mims, Harper, Armstrong and Savage, 1991). The extra attention and closer home–school liaison resulting from homework being set can lead to marked progress, particularly if the work is presented as an integral part of the overall learning aims (Rosenberg, 1989). However, it is important to recognize the challenges. Polloway, Foley and Epstein (1992) found that students aged 8–17 with learning difficulties experienced two and a half times the level of difficulty with specific homework problems as their peers.

Children with learning difficulties require particular support in undertaking homework (Jayanthi, Bursuck, Epstein and Polloway, 1997). Quite simple strategies can be effective in helping them. Bryan and Sullivan-Burstein (1997, 1998) engaged a team of elementary school teachers in participatory action research for two years to study the effects of teacher-selected homework strategies on students with and without learning difficulties. Following a baseline period teachers introduced rewards for homework completion, such as extra break time or special treats when students had completed all assignments. A further strategy was graphing homework completion and enabling students to show the graphs to their parents during parent–teacher meetings. Real-life assignments were used to help students connect classwork to daily home routines, events and activities, and students were also given homework planners. The intervention strategies significantly increased homework completion and performance on weekly mathematics and spelling tests, the effects being strongest for mathematics. Students with learning difficulties and average-achieving students benefited more from the interventions than higher-achieving students with no homework problems. The effects were sufficiently strong that homework planners and graphing progress strategies were still being used two years later. The effectiveness of graphing and self-monitoring in increasing the number of daily homework assignments completed by students with learning difficulties in grades 7–10 was also tested by Trammel, Schloss and Alper (1994). Self-monitoring resulted in an increase in assignment completion, and even when these visual aids were no longer used the increase in completion rates continued.

Similarly, Hughes, Ruhl, Schumaker and Deshler (2002) developed a strategy involving nine middle school students who had learning difficulties and problems with homework. They were taught skills for doing homework independently, listening for and correctly recording an assignment, planning how much time to allow for identifying what materials were needed, recruiting help when needed, monitoring progress and self-rewarding for task completion.

The findings showed that direct instruction of this nature resulted in independent completion of more homework. However, instruction in organizational skills alone was insufficient to produce a 100 per cent submission rate. The researchers suggested that the students needed to be motivated to master the required skills and complete assignments. This meant that the appropriateness of the assignments needed to be considered.

A contrasting approach focused on students monitoring each other's homework in groups. O'Melia and Rosenberg (1994) developed a co-operative homework model for students with learning difficulties and behaviour issues in 6th- to 8th-grade special education classrooms. Homework was assigned to three of four member teams. During a daily 10-minute meeting teams submitted completed work to one team member, who checked assignments and reported the grades to the teacher. Papers were then returned for review and corrections. Team members were encouraged to help each other with corrections. Students who worked in these co-operative groups showed significantly higher rates of homework completion and correct responses than controls, although there were no statistically significant differences on a global measure of mathematics achievement. Although there are only a small number of studies that investigate training in self-management strategies for students with special education needs, such as there are tend to show positive outcomes in relation to homework completion (Cancio, West and Young, 2004).

There has been little research into the views of teachers on setting homework for pupils with special educational needs. This is surprising given that homework performance in students with special educational needs is influenced by the perceptions and attitudes of teachers, including their ability to communicate effectively with each other and with parents (Epstein, Munk, Bursuck *et al.*, 1999; Polloway, Foley and Epstein, 1992; Soderlund, Bursuck, Polloway and Foley, 1995). Epstein and colleagues reported that special education teachers had similar homework priorities to mainstream teachers (Epstein, Munk, Bursuck *et al.*, 1999). When asked to put a list of recommendations for homework communication in order, Bursuck and colleagues (Bursuck, Harniss, Epstein *et al.*, 1999) found that special education teachers in the USA ranked requiring students to keep a daily homework assignment book the highest. They also wanted parents to ask their children about homework each day, and indicated that the school should promote better communication with parents through telephone hotlines and releasing teachers to talk to parents. In some schools learning support staff help teachers to devise differentiated homework and work with parents to help them support their children while they do their homework (MacBeath and Turner, 1990).

Where classes are grouped by ability, or through tracking, streaming or setting, homework is already differentiated. Where classes are mixed-ability, teachers need to judge whether homework should be differentiated for different groups. In some cases, where tasks are assessed by outcome, all students can be given the same task; in others, this may not be possible, and teachers may have to consider differentiating homework, although there is a danger that this can perpetuate existing attainment differences. Where students have special educational needs, teachers need to consider how homework is structured and organized to be most effective. Keeping records of homework completion seems to be beneficial to all students, and some may benefit from learning self-management strategies.

Interventions to support pupils in doing homework

In recent years, in acknowledgement of the difficulties some children and young people experience in completing homework, a range of initiatives have been developed that offer support. These include general support in developing strategies on how to do homework, telephone helplines, homework clubs and study centres, and support for parents.

Early initiatives provided booklets for pupils that contained advice on how to do homework (e.g. Lash, 1971). Loitz and Kratochwill (1995) evaluated a self-help manual on children's homework problems. Two families experiencing problems with their child's homework participated. One child demonstrated improved homework accuracy and completion rates, while the parent of another reported a perceived improvement in daily homework behaviour. Both sets of parents reported overall improvement in homework behaviour during the concurrent evaluation and three months later.

Other interventions have offered indirect support to students, for instance by identifying homework problems through the use of checklists (e.g. Anesko, Schoiock, Ramirez and Levine, 1987; Foley and Epstein, 1993; Polloway, Foley and Epstein, 1992), providing study skills courses or support in managing homework (e.g. Olympia, Sheridan, Jenson and Andrews, 1994), introducing a homework calendar (Chavous, 1990), and encouraging the adoption of self-monitoring procedures (e.g. Trammel, Schloss and Alper, 1994).

Another approach to supporting learning at home has been to provide 'summer home learning packets'. Evaluations of these indicated that students did use them over the summer and many worked with parents in completing the activities. For some students, there was better-than-expected performance on a post-test (Epstein, Herrick and Coates, 1996).

Telephone helplines

One approach to supporting homework has been the introduction of telephone helplines (e.g. Blackwell, 1979; Barrett and Neal, 1992). Cooper (2001) defines them as 'telephone services in which teachers or other knowledgeable people are available to answer questions related to homework problems' (p. 48). Some hotlines enable parents or students to get a recorded message from the teacher about the homework to be completed. The automated message may include other information and be directed towards a whole school, a class or an individual. If the recording is student-specific it might include information on whether the previous assignment has been completed, the nature of the current assignment and additional telephone numbers for help (Garner, 1991). The advantage of these automated systems is that they are available 24/7. Other mechanisms include answering-machine systems that allow students to call, leave a number and have their call returned when convenient, and educational TV that incorporates on-air calls.

Hotlines have had variable success. In some cases they have rarely been used, although when well established they are used regularly. Reach and Cooper (2010) argue that before such lines are set up it is necessary to establish that there is a need. Following this, goals should be established, and agreement reached on the frequency and length of calls, the times and duration of the hotline, the level of staffing, the population to be targeted, the academic material to be covered, the location, the funding resources, and how to make people aware of the hotline's existence. Barrett and Neal (1992) conducted a randomized experiment evaluating the effectiveness of hotlines with 5th-grade students. Forty-six students in an experimental group were encouraged to call the hotline, while the control group were not informed about it. Only 12 students called the hotline, making a total of 79 calls. Most of the calls concerned either mathematics or spelling. Students who called the hotline did not exceed the controls on class grades or standardized test scores. Overall, hotlines have not lived up to expectations; they may well have been overtaken by the massive increase in apps and social networking sites for young people to use in support of homework (see Chapters 5 and 7).

Homework clubs and study centres

A range of initiatives have provided direct support for students through the provision of homework clubs or study centre support (see e.g. Gordon, 1980; Faulkner and Blyth, 1995). For many years, out-of-school-time study programmes have been provided in US schools, targeted on disadvantaged children. Activities in such centres might include curriculum extension, revision schemes, study skill development, curriculum support, technological resources, access to qualified staff or volunteers and an appropriate environment for completing homework. The number and types of after-school activities and programmes supporting learning have increased substantially since 2000 (Huang and Cho, 2009; Kremer, Maynard, Polanin, Vaughn and Sarteschi, 2015). Not all study programmes take place on school sites; many are hosted in community settings and libraries. In Victoria, Australia, homework clubs draw extensively on the local community, with assistance generally provided by volunteers (Kronberg, 2014). Increasingly universities are supporting homework clubs within their local communities. These are run by volunteer university students. In many countries, including for example Australia, the USA and Ireland, after-school programmes tend to be targeted at disadvantaged pupils or those at risk of disengagement from education.

A state-wide evaluation of after-school programmes in California (involving 542 elementary and 433 middle school pupils) indicated that 60 per cent of elementary and 51.3 per cent of middle school pupils attended in response to their parents' recommendation or parents' work commitments (Huang, Wang and the CRESST Team, 2012). Forty-six per cent of middle school pupils reported attending for homework help, compared with 37.8 per cent of elementary students. In the focus group interviews, many students identified homework as one of the ways in which the programme had helped them do better in school. Students commented that they had fewer distractions when doing homework at the programme compared with school, and that the staff helped them.

Organized academic activities after school typically have a positive impact on behaviour, relationship with peers, motivation, self-confidence and study habits. However, they do not necessarily impact on academic achievement (Posner and Vandell, 1994). When activities focus on school academic work the relationship with academic attainment is stronger (De Kanter, 2001; Huang, Gribbons, Kim, Lee and Baker, 2000; Miller, 2003). The programmes have benefit for elementary and secondary students in terms of reading. The benefits for mathematics are mainly in secondary school (Lauer, Akiba, Wilkerson *et al.*, 2006). Programmes find it more difficult to recruit older children (Grossman, Walker and Raley, 2001). The strongest effects occur when the programmes focus on small groups of students and provide individual and small group support (Cooper, Jackson, Nye and Lindsay, 2001; Elbaum, Vaughn, Tejero Hughes and Watson Moody, 2000; Fashola, 1998). There is some evidence that children from low-SES families are more likely to benefit than those from moderate-SES families (Cosden, Morrison, Albanese and Macias, 2001; Miller, 2003), and that students who were previously low achievers benefit more than high achievers (McComb and Scott-Little, 2003). Overall, out-of-school programmes in the USA improve academic performance, with low to moderate gains in mathematics and reading (Apsler, 2009; Durlak, Weissberg and Pachan, 2010; Lauer, Akiba, Wilkerson *et al.*, 2006). The extent to which this occurs depends on their focus and goals.

Huang and Cho (2009) studied seven high-functioning homework programmes. In addition to providing students with ample time and resources to complete their homework, the programmes focused on teaching students study skills and stressed the importance of homework completion for academic achievement. They all employed motivational strategies and provided positive and nurturing environments and mentoring and reward systems to encourage students to complete homework. Staffing included volunteers, hired instructors, and after-school staff. Where homework programmes were near universities, recruitment of volunteers tended to be easier. Some programmes used peer-to-peer tutoring, while others provided one-to-one tutoring. Building study skills was seen as a way of enhancing academic confidence as well as achievement; it included teaching time management and organizational skills, note taking, test preparation skills and the use of reference materials. Homework planners were the most commonly used organizational tool. Local mentors were involved and aimed to provide positive role models and the opportunity to develop relationships with community members. A range of reward systems motivated homework completion, including points, stars or tickets and engagement with other activities. Communication with teachers in schools was perceived as an element critical to success. Some instructors communicated regularly but there was huge variability. The means of communication was often informal and in passing, although written communication was sometimes used to inform the school about planners, agendas and homework assignment logs.

Case study visits to homework clubs established in libraries have indicated that pupils, teachers and parents felt that the centres provided a valuable resource (Train, Nankivell, Shoolbred and Denham, 2000). Duffett and Johnson (2004) found that it was low-income and minority parents who were most likely to want after-school academically based programmes. However, in some cases the quality of support was low (James-Burdumy, Dynarski and Deke, 2008). Where workers did not receive adequate training, students' academic performance was barely enhanced (Fashola, 2002). The best programmes are those that provide structure, a strong link to the curriculum, well-qualified staff, and small group settings (Apsler, 2009; Durlak, Mahoney, Bohnert and Parente, 2010; Lauer, Akiba, Wilkerson *et al.*, 2006; Miller, 2003).

In the UK, the implementation of some form of out-of-school programme became widespread in secondary schools around the beginning of the 2000s (MORI, 2004). MacBeath (1993) identified a range of benefits deriving from school-based homework centres that served a range of deprived populations and intended to provide students with a supportive learning environment that might not be possible at home. The centres provided access to learning resources, created an appropriate learning environment, and offered support from teachers. Overall, there were positive reports from parents, head teachers and teachers about the value of the centres in supporting pupils' learning. Pupils felt that the clubs had made homework more enjoyable and had given them a better chance of passing exams. Evaluation of 50 pilot study support schemes funded by the then DfEE involving primary, secondary and special schools showed that projects that supported children's transfer from primary to secondary school were particularly successful. Overall, there were positive effects on participants' behaviour, self-esteem, confidence and motivation. Attendance was generally good, but there were fluctuations related to imminent examinations, homework, dark evenings and religious festivals (Mason, Bhabra, Mawson *et al.*, 1999). These findings are supported by other, similar evaluations (MacBeath, Kirwan, Myers *et al.*, 2001).

Pocklington (1996) evaluated a two-year school improvement project involving eight secondary schools in London. The schools developed a range of study support activities, for example flexible learning centres, revision classes, coursework clinics and homework centres. Teachers reported that the students showed improved motivation, self-esteem and behaviour. In addition, the teachers themselves became more motivated. Students who attended the revision sessions achieved higher grades than students who did not. An evaluation of the Tower Hamlets project (Tower Hamlets Study Support Project, 1997) produced similar findings. Participating schools experienced larger gains in national GCSE results over a three-year period than did non-participating schools, while at the student level a positive association was found between GCSE performance and attendance at Easter revision classes. More recently, in Ireland, Mc Loughlin (2012) found in a small-scale study that students participating in the homework club had a stronger sense of school belonging and made more of an effort with schoolwork than non-participants, but there were no statistical differences between those attending and those not attending, in either aspirations for the future or academic performance.

In a major survey, Keys and colleagues (Keys, Mawson and Maychell, 1999) explored the kinds of out-of-lesson support activities provided by schools. While overall provision was not targeted at particular pupils, in some secondary schools study skills or homework clubs aimed to meet the needs of low achievers. Mathematics clubs tended to focus on high achievers in both primary and secondary schools. Virtually all mainstream schools and about three-quarters of special schools provided some study support activities. Half of all the pupils taking part in the research reported attending an out-of-school-hours club or activity during the survey week. Despite this, fewer than 10 per cent of responding Local Education Authorities (LEAs) had a written policy regarding study support activities (Keys and Wilkinson, 1999), although about three-quarters of LEAs had been involved in study support activities in some way since 1997. The most frequent areas of provision were homework study clubs and literacy support; the most frequently targeted pupils were low achievers, gifted pupils, and ethnic-minority pupils.

Pensiero and Green (2017) studied the effectiveness of out-of-school-time study programmes for secondary school students with a large sample of almost 16,000 students in Year 10 (aged 13–14). Forty-four per cent of the sample participated in teacher-led out-of-school groups, while 32 per cent took part in self-directed study groups. Participation was relatively low among the children of the long-term unemployed and those in routine occupations, and was lower outside London and other major cities. In London, children of those in routine occupations or who were unemployed participated significantly more than all other groups. Where programmes were teacher-led, they were moderately effective in improving the academic performance as measured by the GCSE total score. This was not the case for self-directed programmes, perhaps because students left unsupervised by trained teachers may tend to work less effectively. Teacher-led programmes were able to compensate for previous social disadvantage, the children of those who were unemployed or in a routine occupation benefiting the most. More advantaged children did not benefit significantly from participation. The findings suggest that it is possible to compensate to some extent for a disadvantageous home learning environment and previous low performance, but the quality of the programmes has to be high, and the leadership of teachers must be active.

Overall, well-run study support centres offer a valuable resource for supporting homework. It is clear that well-qualified staff who have the relevant expertise need to be involved, and that where students are unsupervised they are less effective. The drawback of the centres is that they may disenfranchise parents and break the link between parents and their child's life in schools. However, the evidence to date suggests that the centres offer pupils an avenue for achievement, raise self-esteem and feed back positively into the home, making children more disposed to talk about their learning and share their success.

Supplementary education

Internationally, there are numerous ways in which students and their parents can purchase additional out-of-school learning support, including one-to-one tutoring, distance learning packages and cramming school places. These have grown in popularity (Mori and Baker, 2010). In the mid-1990s, an international study using TIMMS data found that, across 41 nations, on average four out of every ten 8th-graders participated weekly in some form of additional education, as a means of enhancing performance and taking advantage of future opportunities (Baker, Akiba, LeTendre and Wiseman, 2001). There were high rates of participation in so-called shadow education in Colombia, Slovakia and the Philippines, but also appreciable rates of between 10 and 20 per cent in some European countries, such as Norway, Germany, Sweden, France and the Netherlands.

Support for parents

Some interventions to support homework have operated through providing guidance and support to parents (e.g. Anesko and O'Leary, 1982; Kahle and Kelley, 1994; Miller and Kelley, 1994; Gennaro and Lawrenz, 1992). Several programmes have had considerable success in involving parents in work in schools (see Merttens and Newland, 1996; Capper, 2000). Callahan, Rademacher and Hildreth (1998) worked with a group of 26 students in one US school who were at risk of school failure through drug or alcohol abuse, contravening school rules, or poor academic and social skills. The parents participated in a three-hour training programme to familiarize themselves with homework materials and to be introduced to techniques that would enable them to support their children in developing self-management. There was a significant improvement in homework completion and quality of homework following the training.

Also in the USA, Balli, Wedman and Demo (1997) and Balli, Demo and Wedman (1998) developed an intervention to increase family involvement with the mathematics homework of their middle-grade children. The Teachers Involve Parents in Schoolwork (TIPS) scheme required pupils to interact with a member of the family while doing homework (Epstein, 2001; Epstein and Associates, 2009). Parents reacted positively to this and indicated that they felt better informed about their child's work as a result. The assignments were successful in increasing family/parental involvement with homework but did not have a significant impact on pupils' achievement. There were positive results for families and students of different ages in a variety of subjects (Balli, 1995; Balli, Demo and Wedman, 1998; Epstein, Simon and Salinas, 1997; Van Voorhis 2001, 2003). For instance, Van Voorhis (2011) reported on three two-year TIPS interventions in elementary mathematics, middle school language arts and middle school science. Each weekly TIPS assignment included materials for students to involve a family partner in a discussion, interview, experiment or other interaction. Following the programme, TIPS students and families responded significantly more positively than controls to questions about their emotions and attitudes to homework and revealed more family involvement in TIPS subjects. Although no differences emerged in the time spent on homework, TIPS students gained significantly higher standardized test scores than did controls. However, not all of the research showed an improvement in academic attainment.

A number of interventions have attempted to help parents in supporting their children with homework based on reading. Sénéchal and Young (2008) reviewed 13 studies of training programmes that had been set up to help parents in this way. Training parents to teach their children to read was more effective than training them to listen to their children read, although both had an impact on achievement. Reading to their children did not seem to have an impact. The findings were consistent across grades, the reading level of the children, and SES.

Focusing on homework more generally, Patall, Cooper and Robinson (2008) reviewed 14 studies that provided training relating to homework. There was no statistically significant impact on student achievement, regardless of the measure of achievement, the subject matter type or the duration of training, although there was a stronger effect when children were in the earlier grades. However, parent training for homework involvement did have a significant positive impact on homework completion rate, and on the frequency of problems with homework assignments.

In a meta-analysis, Erion (2006) focused on the impact of learning activities at home on mathematics, reading and spelling. Thirty-seven studies were included. The findings showed that parent tutoring positively affected academic achievement and did not vary in relation to the length of the tutoring period or any written instructions or modelling the parents may have been provided with. It did depend on the duration of the training sessions that some parents were involved in before they provided tutoring for their children. There were no differences in impact in relation to the grade level of the children or the skill area in which the children received tutoring. A meta-analysis carried out by Jeynes (2012) investigated the types of programmes that were effective, including shared reading programmes, partnerships between teachers and school, checking homework, communication between teachers and parents, Head Start, and English as a second language programmes. Fifty-one studies were included. The findings showed a positive relationship between parental involvement programmes and the academic success of students across school grades. The impact was stronger when achievement was measured by standardized tests. Shared reading was most effective with regard to academic outcomes. Partnership programmes also had positive results, as did the checking homework programme. Similarly, Gorard and See (2013) reviewed 68 studies that evaluated interventions to increase parental involvement. Although critical of the quality of the research, they concluded that interventions were most likely to succeed when they were aimed at young children and involved parents and staff meeting regularly. There should be training, ongoing support and co-operative working with teachers.

There is considerable evidence that offering training to parents can support them in helping with homework. Depending on the kind of training, there may be an impact on attainment. Programmes tend to be more successful when they focus on supporting the parents of younger children. All of the projects served to raise the awareness of schools, teachers, children and their parents of the importance of homework. This in itself is likely to have had an impact on the monitoring of homework completion, the care with which it was undertaken, and the effort made, regardless of the specific intervention.

Conclusions

Compared with research exploring the extent to which homework can improve attainment, little work has considered the nature of homework tasks, their relative appropriateness for different groups of children and the extent to which they develop generic or specific skills. Different kinds of homework are likely to be more effective than others in attaining particular educational aims; teachers need to consider this carefully when setting homework and situate homework within broader curriculum planning. Frequently, homework needs to be tailored for specific groups of students. The nature of the subject may make this more or less important. Particular attention needs to be given to those with special educational needs, who need more support in undertaking homework, although all learners may benefit from help with time, motivational and studying management.

Policy makers and those in senior management positions in school need to give careful consideration to the reasons they require pupils to undertake homework. Once these are clearly established, teachers can ensure that the nature of homework tasks is aligned with those aims. If the aims are to raise attainment in examinations across the school then homework must be given to all pupils and be focused on improving the skills required in those examinations. If a broader range of skills are to be developed, homework needs to be planned to ensure that a balance is obtained across different subject areas. For instance, the acquisition of literacy skills in young children can be enhanced through reading and writing across a range of subjects. Allowing children and parents to choose materials and topics is likely to enhance motivation and commitment and ensure that homework is completed. If the aim is to develop independence in learning, tasks need to be set at an appropriate level so that the child can complete them unaided. The level of challenge needs to take account of the current level of attainment so that they can experience success. Over time, and as metacognitive skills develop, more challenging tasks can be set. The question teachers need to ask themselves constantly is 'What is the purpose of this particular piece of homework?'

Technological advances mean that computer programs can be of great benefit in providing immediate feedback and guidance as students do homework. Where homework requires higher-level cognitive skills, chat rooms can enable peer learning and provide online support from the teacher. Telephone helplines have had mixed success.

Homework clubs and other study support centres can be particularly beneficial in motivating students and supporting them in their learning. They serve to raise the awareness of the importance of homework and offer particular benefits to those from lower-SES homes and lower attainers. Staff and volunteers working in these centres need to have appropriate levels of expertise for students to benefit. Where students are unsupervised the outcomes in terms of homework completion tend to be less positive.

Support with homework for parents is most beneficial when children are young. It seems to be most productive when parents are taught how to tutor their children.

CHAPTER 3: KEY POINTS

A consideration of homework needs to take account of broad educational aims and systems of assessment, and homework needs to be planned alongside the curriculum.

The main types of homework are practice, preparation and completion of classwork.

The nature of homework is different at primary and secondary school.

Different homework designs can be more motivating for students, as can giving them some choice.

Flipped learning changes the relationship between homework and classwork and can be effective. The difficulty is ensuring that learners complete the preparation work.

Homework may be automatically differentiated when children are ability-grouped. Where children are taught in mixed-ability classes teachers need to decide whether homework should be differentiated. This may depend on the subject being taught.

Interactive computer systems can be effective in providing immediate feedback and guidance in some subject areas.

Internet chat rooms can support discussion about homework, providing peer and teacher support.

Homework clubs and study centres are very effective in supporting learning when teachers or those with the relevant expertise supervise study. Where students are unsupervised they are less effective. The effects are particularly strong for low-attaining students and those of low SES.

Initiatives to support parents in relation to homework are more effective for younger children and when parents are taught how to tutor their children.

Teachers and homework

This chapter considers the role that teachers play in homework. The role of the school in influencing teachers' approaches to homework and the place of homework policies provide the starting point for the chapter. Thereafter consideration is given to teachers' behaviours and attitudes towards homework, their views on the purposes of homework and how this may vary with different groups of students. Attention is given to how teachers design and assign homework, the different types of feedback that they provide to students and how teachers motivate students to complete homework.

The role of the school in influencing teachers' behaviour and attitudes

Changes to policy in 2012 in England mean that individual schools have the responsibility for all issues relating to homework, including whether homework is set or not (see Chapter 1). In practice, most schools continue to have a homework policy. Many schools make theirs available on their websites and have school-based virtual learning environments or apps that enable parents/carers and students to access information about their homework electronically. Most homework policies set out the school's perspective on the purpose of homework, the types of homework activities that will be set, the time that these will take according to year group, and the responsibilities of teachers, parents/carers and pupils in relation to homework. In more detailed policies information is provided about the frequency of teacher feedback and the different types of feedback that may be provided. In some there are examples of good homework and poor or inadequate homework. This would suggest that there is a level of teacher accountability in meeting the demands of the school policy.

In primary schools in England emphasis is placed on reading, writing and mathematics, and parents/carers are encouraged to support their child's learning alongside the teachers. Homework is seen as an opportunity for children to practise and consolidate skills, and, as they grow older, to enable them to become independent learners. In many primary schools homework completion is rewarded through systems of certificates, stickers or merits.

At secondary level, further to the above there is usually more information on the monitoring and tracking of homework in relation to the larger organizational structures that exist in secondary schools. For instance, in addition to requirements set out for the class teacher, parents/carers and pupils, it is common to see responsibilities listed for the head of department, the senior leadership team and form tutors/pastoral staff. Often these are linked to sanctions for non-completion of homework, or to the provision of additional support.

To what extent are teachers influenced by the homework policies and practices in the schools in which they teach? Research by Wiesenthal, Cooper, Greenblatt and Marcus (1997) found that teachers' beliefs about and attitudes towards homework were significantly different in schools that did or did not have clear policies and support for homework. The schools influenced the behaviour of the teachers in relation to the extent to which homework was set, to the collection of assignments from students, to grading and marking homework, and to returning homework to students. There were significant differences between schools in the extent to which homework was assigned as repetition of classwork, as the introduction of new skills or topics, or as the opportunity to pursue imaginative ideas or learning. Despite these school influences, teachers still saw homework as being primarily under their control. The research also found strongly significant relationships between teachers' attitudes towards homework and their behaviour.

International perspectives on homework policies

In some countries homework policies are set at the level of the district or state. This means that there can be variation within a country. In Australia, many states (e.g. Victoria and Queensland) have a government school homework policy that requires that schools have a documented approach to homework and that the homework policy is developed in consultation with the school community, including the principal, the teachers, the school council, parents/carers and students. Overarching guidelines on good practice are provided, but schools develop their policies within their communities. In New South Wales, while schools are similarly required to have a homework policy, the setting of homework and indicative time allocations across year groups are not compulsory. This approach is based on an understanding that community expectations about homework are variable, that research regarding the value of homework is inconclusive and that schools are best placed to make decisions about homework in consultation with their communities (New South Wales Department of Education and Communities, 2012).

So, should teachers be required to set homework? And who should take responsibility for this? Kohn (2006), for instance, has argued that homework policies can shift power away from teachers, thereby removing some of their autonomy in order to achieve greater consistency across classrooms. There is, though, much variation in the employment of homework policies internationally. Finland has a history of setting no homework or very low levels of homework for students, and yet is frequently placed high in the international league tables. Denmark has never had a specific policy about doing homework. Where homework has been given, this has been the decision of each individual teacher (Kryger and Ravn, 2009). In Norway, although decisions about whether or not to set homework rest with the teachers, legislation requires municipalities to provide eight hours of homework support per week (Holte, 2016). In Sweden homework is not regulated in the national curriculum; however, research carried out by Gu and Kristoffersson (2015) involving 201 lower secondary teachers found that 83 per cent reported setting homework in their subject. Most homework was designed to reinforce knowledge that had already been taught and to enable students to practise skills through repetition.

By contrast, in Nova Scotia, Canada, before September 2015 decisions about what homework to set and how much were made by individual teachers, schools or boards. There had also been a ban on setting homework for students in primary before grade 3. The province-wide homework policy established by the Department of Education in 2015 has changed this and introduced an expectation that teachers will assign developmentally appropriate homework at each grade level to enhance student learning (Nova Scotia Department of Education and Early Childhood Development, 2015a, 2015b).

International perspectives: Homework set in primary school

Research, using the TIMMS 2007 data from 16 OECD countries, focused on 9-year-olds (Falch and Rønning, 2012). This showed that in most OECD countries homework was set in mathematics and science. However, there were differences; for instance, across all countries, 43 per cent of students were given homework in every or almost every mathematics lesson, 19 per cent in about half of lessons and 30 per cent in some lessons. Seven per cent were not given homework. Germany, Hungary and Austria were the countries in which over 90 per cent of students were given mathematics homework in every or almost every lesson. In the Netherlands, the proportion was only 0.5 per cent, with 64 per cent getting no homework in mathematics. In England, 2 per cent were given homework in every or almost every lesson, 14 per cent in about half of the lessons and 81 per cent in some lessons. Only 3 per cent of teachers reported giving no mathematics homework. Interestingly, 8 per cent of teachers in Scotland reported giving mathematics homework in every or almost every lesson, 28 per cent in about half of the lessons and 62 per cent in some lessons. Homework was not given by only 1 per cent. It seems that at the time of the data collection children in Scotland were given more mathematics homework than those in England. For science across all countries 12 per cent of children were given homework in every or almost every lesson, 9 per cent in about half of lessons and 45 per cent in some lessons. Thirty-four per cent were not given homework. There were many more countries giving no homework or a very small amount of homework in science. Hungary reported the greatest percentage (62 per cent). In

England, the percentage of teachers who reported giving science homework in some lessons was 52 per cent, and 43 per cent reported not giving homework in science. The percentages for Scotland were similar. Overall, these data suggest that 9-year-old children are set more homework in mathematics than science but also that there are huge differences between countries in the extent to which homework is set.

International perspectives: Homework set in secondary school

A US survey involving 1,000 teachers across all grades found that on average high school teachers set 3.5 hours of homework each week (University of Phoenix College of Education, 2014). At the time most high school students generally had five classes with different teachers, amounting to as much as 17.5 hours homework each week. There were differences in the amount of homework set by teachers according to their length of experience in teaching. Teachers with more than 20 years' experience in the classroom on average allocated 2.8 hours of homework per week, compared with 3.1 hours where teachers had 10 to 19 years' experience and 3.6 hours of homework set from teachers with less than 10 years' experience in the classroom (Stainburn, 2014)

Also in the USA Snead and Burris (2016) identified that time spent on homework per week varied widely among the 118 participating middle school teachers. More than 80 per cent of the teachers stated homework was not mandatory. Across all classrooms, time reported for completing homework ranged from zero hours (where homework was not assigned) to seven hours per week. However, the average amount of time to complete homework for all grade levels ranged from 0.77 to 1.78 hours per week. Grade level was not a significant factor in the amount of time required to complete homework.

In Victoria, Australia, state guidance for Year 10 to 12 pupils is that homework will require from one to three hours per week night and up to six hours at weekends during peak Victorian Certificate of Education periods.

Teachers' views on the purpose of homework

Historically, the evidence suggests that teachers and schools have used homework as a means of ensuring that their pupils have covered and thoroughly learned the curriculum in preparation for tests or examinations that will be used to assess teacher or school performance (Gordon, 1980). When schools and teachers are under pressure, the amount of homework set for pupils appears to increase. Especially at secondary school, where the relationship between time spent on homework and outcomes in examinations is mediated by a range of other factors, simply increasing pupil workloads will not of itself improve standards, and in some cases, where pupils become overloaded, may have a negative impact on the performance of individual children (see Chapter 1).

Johnson and Pontius (1989) reported that teachers believe that homework develops student responsibility and benefits students in relation to their mastery of content. Savage (1966) found that teachers favoured homework assignments that involved a combination of regular nightly written assignments as well as regular nightly reading assignments and long-range projects. There may also be differences in subject domain, with mathematics, science and foreign language teachers being supportive of daily homework (Johnson and Pontius, 1989; Wallinger, 2000; Villas-Boas, 1998).

A review of effective primary teaching practice in England revealed three types of homework tasks, each with a different purpose: practice and recapitulation, extension, and new learning or pre-work (Keeble, 2016). Of these the weakest evidence was found for the effectiveness of new learning or pre-work. It was suggested that, unless schools were clear about the capacity of their pupils, the quality of resources and the levels of support and explanations that pupils received, this approach to homework was best avoided. Extension tasks were longer-term projects, often of a voluntary nature. These gave pupils and their families the flexibility to manage projects around their home lives. Practice of reading, mathematics and grammar, tasks of recapitulating learning undertaken in class through quizzes and no-stakes tests, and letting students test themselves, were seen as the most helpful approach if homework was set.

International perspectives on the purpose of homework

At primary level, research involving 297 Malaysian teachers identified the following reasons for assigning homework: to provide practice of what has been learnt, to obtain feedback on pupils' strengths and weaknesses, and to improve pupils' study habits (Sidhu and Fook, 2010). Teachers were less likely to set homework to encourage autonomous learning in relation to becoming more independent as learners, to encourage individual development and to provide a more individualized programme of learning. Important here is the notion that homework can have a role in providing feedback to the teacher, an aspect that is seldom addressed explicitly in research.

In the USA, Snead and Burris (2016), using data from 118 middle school teachers, revealed reinforcement (20 per cent) as the most frequent reason for setting homework, followed by practice (19 per cent). Somewhat remarkably, in this study 37 per cent of teachers gave no reason for setting homework, and neither was mention made of homework as a vehicle to support autonomous learning. This is similar to the study of 133 elementary US teachers by Brock, Lapp, Flood, Fisher and Han (2007), in which practising skills and teaching discipline, as well as meeting parental expectations and system requirements, were important aspects of homework.

At secondary level, reasons for assigning homework among 1,000 US teachers included: to help students practise skills or prepare for tests (86 per cent), to help students develop good working habits (80 per cent), to develop students' critical thinking skills (67 per cent), to motivate students to learn (65 per cent) and to assess students' skills and knowledge (63 per cent) (Markow, Kim and Liebman, 2007).

Findings from a survey of 168 Turkish middle school (grades 6–8) science teachers identified problem-solving and research as the most commonly assigned homework types (Tas, Vural and Öztekin, 2014). Poster preparation, the development of concept maps (diagrams that depict relationships), project work and setting up an experiment were assigned frequently. Making summaries and memorizing information and formulas were least preferred. Almost one-third of the teachers (31.3 per cent) reported that they never assigned homework that required the memorization of information or formulas and almost 41.1 per cent that they rarely assigned this type of homework. By contrast, Singaporean grade-8 teachers reported a preference for review, practice and drill types of assignments (Kaur, 2011).

Overall, it would seem that teachers perceive homework as an opportunity for pupils to practise skills and for reinforcement. There is little evidence on the setting of group work for homework. Most often teachers set individual homework tasks (e.g. Tas, Vural and Öztekin, 2014; Costa, Cardoso, Lacerda, Lopes and Gomes, 2016). Interestingly, one study of primary school children indicated that they would like teachers to set homework based on group work (mentioned by 69.5 per cent of pupils) as well as on research on the internet (51.6 per cent of pupils) (Costa, Cardoso, Lacerda, Lopes and Gomes, 2016). This may be worthy of further research given the wider contributions to student learning that are facilitated by group work.

Differences between primary and secondary schools in the purpose of homework

In primary schools in the UK, MacBeath and Turner (1990) found that the most important perceived purposes of homework as reported by teachers were: developing links between home and school; reinforcement of work; review and practice; involvement of parents; enrichment and extension work; and the development of good study habits. By contrast, secondary school teachers tended not to consider the role of parents. The most important functions of homework were regarded as the reinforcement, review and practice of work. Enrichment and extension of work were seen as important, but to a lesser extent (MacBeath and Turner, 1990). There were also differences about the perceived purposes of homework between teachers in the primary and secondary sectors and between and within schools. Sometimes teachers in a school agreed about purpose, in others they did not; the differences among secondary teachers were less marked than among primary.

In primary and elementary schools, teachers tend to use homework to enhance students' basic skills and to enforce good study habits. These teachers see homework as a tool for enhancing student self-regulation and time use. The involvement of parents is encouraged. By contrast, in secondary education emphasis tends to be placed on reinforcing academic content (Gu and Kristoffersson, 2015) rather than on developing independent study habits, presumably because their educational agenda is focused more closely on attempting to ensure that their pupils perform well in tests and examinations. This may be, in part, because they see their pupils' performance as a reflection of their own effectiveness as teachers. This is particularly likely given the current public interest in national examination performance.

Overall, for teachers the main function of homework seems to be in relation to mastery of the curriculum.

Teachers' attitudes towards homework

Although the effectiveness of homework has been challenged by many (see Chapters 1 and 2) homework continues to be used by most teachers to extend the learning experience of students. Overall, there is considerable agreement among teachers that homework is worthwhile (see for example MacBeath and Turner, 1990; Deslandes, 2009; Sidhu and Fook, 2010; Gu and Kristoffersson, 2015; Costa, Cardoso, Lacerda *et al.*, 2016). Teachers perceive homework as playing an important role that complements and consolidates the learning that has taken place in class. This is despite evidence that devising and setting homework significantly adds to teachers' workload, as does the assessment of homework (Cooper, Robinson and Patall, 2006; Cameron and Bartel, 2009). Research to date has explored teachers' views of the purpose and function of homework (Brock, Lapp, Flood, Fisher and Han, 2007; Bang, 2012), preferences in the types of assignments and tasks (Trautwein, Niggli, Schnyder and Lüdtke, 2009; Kaur, 2011) and problems with homework (Hong, Wan and Peng, 2011). The prominence given to homework may in part reflect current policies of publishing schools' examination results and comparisons made in international league tables.

Notwithstanding teachers' preferences concerning different functions and purposes of homework, if homework is to be of any value in supporting pupil learning, clear expectations and the commitment of teachers are essential (DES, 1987). Cross-cultural research indicates that where teachers feel that homework is unimportant they may communicate this feeling to parents and pupils (Chen and Stevenson, 1989). Pupils themselves have indicated that teacher expectations are one of the most decisive factors motivating them to do their homework (MacBeath and Turner, 1990). Where teachers set high standards for school and homework pupils tend to do better (Natriello and McDill, 1986). Keys, Harris and Fernandes (1995) showed in a large-scale survey that 62 per cent of primary and 57 per cent of secondary pupils said the teacher always ensured that their homework had been completed, and a further 23 per cent and 36 per cent indicated that this was nearly always the case. Approximately 4 per cent of pupils at primary level and 7 per cent at secondary level, however, indicated that homework was hardly ever or never checked by their teacher. While this suggests that in the UK most teachers do value homework, it also suggests that a small minority do not.

Teachers' attitudes and beliefs about the importance of homework tend to reflect current cultural, social and economic factors and so cannot be taken as absolutes, although there may be a core of beliefs that persist across time. Research undertaken in Hong Kong by Tam and Chan (2016) provides clear indications of how beliefs can change over time. They identified in teachers a move away from preferences for drill-type assignments towards those involving thinking, imagination, peer collaboration and reading. This was in response to changing cultural and societal demands and the educational reforms taking place in Hong Kong.

Homework styles

Other research has put forward distinctions between teachers who adopt controlling homework styles and those who favour student autonomy styles (Trautwein, Niggli, Schnyder and Lüdtke, 2009), and posed questions about how teachers' homework control practices relate to student homework effort and motivation. In self-determination theory (Deci and Ryan, 2002; Ryan and Connell, 1989) a distinction is made between informational feedback, which is associated with positive consequences, and controlling feedback and external rewards, which are perceived to undermine students' intrinsic motivation. If this theory is applied to homework completion, it suggests that grading and intensive control of homework are at odds with increasing student motivation and might also result in negative emotional states for students during homework. Trautwein, Niggli, Schnyder and Lüdtke (2009), for example, using a sample of 63 teachers of French and 1,299 grade-8 students from 71 classes, found a controlling homework style to be negatively associated with homework effort. By contrast, an emphasis on student responsibility positively predicted homework effort. In addition, a controlling homework style predicted an increase in negative homework emotions. It is also plausible that where teachers adopt an over-controlling homework style students may feel tempted to copy from high-achieving peers to avoid negative consequences.

Teacher assignment and preparation of homework

There is enormous variation in the amount of homework set by teachers (Weston, 1999; Snead and Burris, 2016). For pupils in the UK in Year 10, Weston (1999) reported a median of 10 hours' homework set each week, but the differences in the time allocated for homework for different pupils could amount to an extra 100 hours' homework in a school year. However, the accuracy of these figures is debatable. Weston (1999) indicated that at Key Stages 2 and 3 pupils reported completing less homework than their teachers set. Other studies have confirmed discrepancies between the amount of homework set by teachers and that reported by students. Analysis of the TIMMS data for mathematics homework among 4,972 Hong Kong students shows that 44 per cent of the students said they were set homework that took between 15 and 30 minutes, 34 per cent chose between 31 and 60 minutes, and nearly 10 per cent reported that they were given homework exceeding 60 minutes per day. In contrast, teachers anticipated that assigned homework would take up to 30 minutes for 65 per cent of students and more than 60 minutes for about 2 per cent (Zhu and Leung, 2012). In spite of this, the potential for inequitable homework loads is vast, given the differences between school policies, the amount of homework set by individual teachers and the amount of time actually required to complete homework by individual pupils.

Important decisions are made by teachers in the process of setting homework: (1) the design, planning and setting of homework (Epstein and Van Voorhis, 2012; Trautwein, Niggli, Schnyder and Lüdtke, 2009), and (2) the provision of feedback on homework (Trautwein, Lüdtke, Schnyder and Niggli, 2006; Núñez, Suárez, Rosário, Vallejo, Cerezo and Valle, 2015). Designing homework requires teachers to reflect on the purposes, format and other elements of assignments that will engage students and help them succeed. In addition to teachers' subject knowledge, assignments reflect their understanding of the skills, abilities and needs of their students (Epstein and Van Voorhis, 2001). The challenge for all teachers is to create homework assignments that students are motivated to complete and that enhance student emotional responses, especially given research findings that demonstrate that students can experience negative emotions when undertaking homework tasks (Trautwein, Niggli, Schnyder and Lüdtke, 2009).

The notion of quality homework assignments rather than the quantity of homework or the time needed to do it has received increasing attention from researchers. Epstein and Van Voorhis (2012) argued that teachers should endeavour to design high-quality homework so that students benefit from completing homework tasks. It is important that students fully understand the concepts and have the skills needed to complete homework. Requiring students to complete mathematics problems for homework, for example, when they have not fully understood them in class is likely to discourage and frustrate them (Marzano, Pickering, and Pollock, 2001). Other researchers have commented on the lack of research on the quality of homework assignments, the relationship between quality and student achievement and the connection between subject and homework assignment (Dettmers, Trautwein, Lüdtke, Kunter and Baumert, 2010; Liang, 2010; Strandberg, 2013).

What factors do teachers consider when planning and setting homework? To be effective homework should be planned as an integral part of teaching and learning (Earle, 1992; MacBeath and Turner, 1990; Epstein and Van Voorhis, 2012; Buijs and Admiraal, 2013). However, the evidence suggests that teachers' concern with the planning and setting of homework may not always be optimal. There are indications that teachers often feel under pressure, regardless of the stage of work that has been reached in class, to set homework on the appointed day in order to keep to the stated timetable and maintain a positive school image for parents (Le Métais, 1985).

In the Medlife study of 1,000 US teachers, many reported that they 'very often or often' assigned homework because they ran out of time in class (Markow, Kim and Liebman, 2007, p. 30). In practice, instructions about homework are often given hurriedly, with insufficient guidance and inadequate opportunities for students to ask questions and seek clarification (MacFarlane, 1987; Grotenhuis, 1984).

The small-scale study reported by Buijs and Admiraal (2013) (see also Chapter 3) illustrates how teachers can be innovative in the design of homework tasks. This intervention explicitly sought to devise homework assignments that promoted homework and class participation to challenge student disengagement. Four different assignments were adopted: preparing analytical skills, fragmented assessment (spread over six lessons), jigsaw assignment, and student choice. The jigsaw assignment and the preparation of analytical tasks increased time on task and class participation.

An area that has received little consideration in research concerns the contribution that pre-service teacher-training programmes make to the development of homework design and feedback practices in beginning teachers. Tas, Vural and Öztekin (2014), in a study of 168 middle school (grades 6–8) science teachers in Turkey, asked whether or not they thought they were given sufficient education about homework practices during their pre-service teacher-training programme. Over half (N=97, 58.8 per cent) reported that they had not received sufficient training in how to prepare homework properly and only 20 teachers (12 per cent) had participated in in-service training in homework practices. Concerns about the lack of preparedness of new teachers in effective homework practices have been raised by others (Kronberg, 2014).

Overall, we know very little about the ways teachers plan, set and explain homework to their pupils. As these will clearly have a major impact on pupils' ability to undertake homework and on its effectiveness in relation to academic learning outcomes, this is an area in which research would seem to be urgently needed.

Teachers' views of homework with different groups of pupils

There are suggestions that secondary school teachers place less emphasis on developing good study habits (e.g., managing homework time) than their elementary counterparts (Xu and Wu, 2013; Gu and Kristoffersson, 2015). Teachers tend to view boys as having more negative attitudes to homework and more homework problems than girls (Hong, Wan and Peng, 2011).

In mainstream schools, evidence from studies of ability grouping indicates that some teachers assign students in low-ability classes less homework or less interesting assignments than students in advanced classes, or convey low expectations that slower students will do the work (Epstein and Van Voorhis, 2001; Hallam and Ireson, 2003). Some teachers perceive that students who have difficulty with their studies will ignore homework (Gu and Kristoffersson, 2015). Among Normal Technical education students – those in the lowest track in secondary education in Singapore – Heng and Atencio (2017) found that the setting of homework was not commonplace for these students, this despite Singapore's high global ranking for time spent on homework.

Some evidence suggests that the amount of homework feedback provided by teachers is related to the students' age (Katz, Kaplan and Gueta, 2010; Xu and Wu, 2013; Núñez, Suárez, Rosário, Vallejo, Cerezo and Valle, 2015). Students in higher grades perceived less teacher support related to homework than more junior-grade students in relation to the teachers' interest in the students' understanding of the homework, the degree of individual adaptation of homework assignments to the students' needs, and involvement in mistakes.

Setting homework for students who have special education needs or learning difficulties can be challenging for teachers. As discussed in Chapter 3, teachers often set the same homework tasks for all pupils regardless of different needs (Costa, Cardoso, Lacerda, Lopes and Gomes, 2016; Kukliansky, Shosberger and Eshach, 2016). Yet teachers need to be mindful that students with disabilities may need adjustments to the way homework is organized and structured for it to be effective (Carr, 2013). See Chapter 3.

Teacher feedback

Feedback is an important source of information that can improve academic performance (Nicol and Macfarlane-Dick, 2006; Shute, 2008; Duijnhouwer, Prins and Stokking, 2012). Effective feedback informs students of gaps between their performance and achievement outcomes and can also guide the learner on what to do next to improve (Black and Wiliam, 2003; Hattie and Timperley, 2007; Sadler, 2005).

Research has demonstrated a consensus that homework must be monitored and marked if students are to take it seriously (Austin and Austin, 1974; Small, Holtan and Davis, 1967; O'Connor, 1985; Austin, 1976; Stewart and White, 1976; DES, 1987; Berliner and Casanova, 1985; Coulter, 1985; Natriello and McDill, 1986). It has also been acknowledged that marking homework is time-consuming and that if teachers doubt the value of that marking, or indeed the homework they are setting, they will not be motivated to take the time to do this (Le Métais, 1985).

In the UK most teachers do regularly assign, collect and grade homework (Johnson and Pontius, 1989; MacBeath and Turner, 1990). The way in which this is undertaken varies in relation to the kind of feedback that teachers give: a mark or grade, a written evaluative comment, e.g. 'good work', or instruction on ways the assignment could have been more accurately or better completed, teachers' perceptions of the purpose of feedback, the quality of the feedback, and whether it is carried out with the pupils themselves.

Teachers agree that feedback is essential for homework to be effective. However, their practice does not always seem to reflect this (MacBeath and Turner, 1990). Pupils perceive that some teachers do not provide feedback very regularly. Keys, Harris and Fernandes (1995) found that 57 per cent of primary school pupils and 36 per cent of secondary school pupils said that their teacher always marked their work. Forty per cent of primary and 59 per cent of secondary said that the teacher usually marked their work, while 2 per cent at primary and 5 per cent at secondary said that the teacher hardly ever marked their work. Further, pupils did not always see teacher comments as helpful (MacBeath and Turner, 1990). Teachers were seen as assessors in relation to homework. Parents were often seen as more helpful, although the older the pupil the more he or she relied on the teacher rather than parents for support and feedback about homework. Teachers suggested that in some cases, where homework was verbal, or contributed to group work it could not be 'marked' (MacBeath and Turner, 1990).

Feedback is a two-way process between the teacher and the pupil and yet pupils do not always understand or appreciate the feedback provided (MacBeath and Turner, 1990; Weeden, Winter, Broadfoot *et al.*, 1999; Weeden, Winter and Broadfoot, 2000). Effort and attainment grades are confused by some pupils. Pupils reported that teachers did not always give sufficient attention to their work, and that, often, feedback did not give guidance as to how improvement could be made in the future. Poor-quality feedback was perceived as demotivating, and particularly critical feedback could reduce motivation and self-esteem. Pupils felt that face-to-face feedback from the teacher was the best form as long as it was given soon after the work was handed in. That teachers provide appropriate, constructive and supportive feedback is important, as there is some evidence that boys respond to a lack of or poor feedback by ceasing to do homework (Warrington and Younger, 1999).

Since the study by MacBeath and Turner there has been a marked increase in research efforts to understand how assessment can best contribute to student learning. Central to this has been the importance attached to formative assessment or feedback. Hattie and Timperley (2007), using a review of 2000 articles, reported that feedback is one of the most powerful influences on learning and achievement, with the caveat that the impact could be positive or negative. As early as 1998, Black and Wiliam (1998b) argued that formative assessment practices can raise standards, but suggested that such practices were only weakly developed in classrooms. Since then there has been a plethora of research into formative assessment in schools. Work in Scotland, for example, as part of the Assessment is for Learning programme, indicated that where formative assessment strategies were adopted in the classroom and involved pupils as well as teachers there was a marked improvement in pupil motivation, commitment to work and metacognitive skills (Hallam, Kirton, Robertson, Stobart and Peffers, 2003).

Feedback is central to maximizing the positive effect of homework (Walberg and Paik, 2000) and yet according to most research on homework feedback continues to be used by teachers as a way of exerting control.

International perspectives on teacher feedback

International research has confirmed the importance of teacher feedback by reporting statistically significant positive relationships between teacher feedback and homework effort, emotions, motivation, interest, time, time management and completion (Katz, Kaplan and Gueta, 2010; Trautwein and Lüdtke, 2009; Trautwein, Lüdtke, Kastens and Köller, 2006; Trautwein, Schnyder, Niggli, Neumann and Lüdtke, 2009; Walberg, 1991; Xu, 2011). Katz, Kaplan and Gueta (2010) argued that the level of teacher support significantly affected the quantity and quality of students' motivation to do homework.

Rosário, Núñez, Vallejo, Cunha, Nunes *et al.* (2015), using a quasi-experimental design, explored the impact of five homework follow-up practices among 26 teachers of school-age students of English as a Foreign Language. Teachers were assigned to one of the following forms of homework feedback: checking homework completion, answering questions about homework, checking homework orally, checking homework on the board, and collecting and grading homework. When the content of the homework was considered (by checking homework orally, checking it on the board, or collecting and grading it) there was a positive impact on students' performance.

The study raises two areas for consideration. Firstly, across many studies, checking whether students have completed their homework – homework control – is the practice adopted by most teachers across elementary and middle schools (Trautwein, Niggli, Schnyder and Lüdtke, 2009; Kaur, 2011; Kukliansky, Shosberger and Eshach, 2016). Checking homework completion means that the quality of the homework isn't checked, and neither is any explicit feedback given (see Kukliansky, Shosberger and Eshach, 2016). It has been suggested that teachers adopt this approach for fear that if they didn't check, students wouldn't do the homework (Rosário, Núñez, Vallejo, Cunha, Nunes *et al.*, 2015). Questions then arise as to the efficacy of this form of feedback: it is unlikely that simply checking whether homework has been completed will enable students to progress their understanding.

The second issue relates to the use of grading homework. Some studies indicate that giving grades seems to be effective (Austin and Austin, 1974) and that students prefer to receive grades for their homework (e.g. Peterson and Irving, 2008), possibly since they provide evidence of their work for parents and hence other opportunities for praise from parents and peers (Núñez, Suárez, Rosário *et al.*, 2015). Students might also value graded homework more than other types of homework. Small, Holtan and Davis (1967) and O'Connor (1985) indicated that the type of grading given seemed to make little difference to the learning outcomes. By contrast, Vatterott (2011) suggests that grading homework does not always make students focus on the learning objectives and may be detrimental to learning. Trautwein, Niggli, Schnyder and Lüdtke (2009) raised further concerns that over-controlling teachers who set graded homework might generate unacceptable behaviour in students, who may become so focused on achieving positive outcomes that they simply copy the work of higher-achieving peers (p. 185).

Who, though, should be responsible for grading homework, since grading or marking homework may include the teacher, the student or a teacher–student combination?

In the US study by Snead and Burris (2016) of 118 middle school teachers, 21 per cent of homework was graded as a combined effort between students and teachers, 10 per cent was graded solely by students and only 6 per cent of the grading was carried out by the teacher alone. Sixty-three per cent of all teachers did not grade or provided no indication as to how homework was graded. Where homework was graded as a combined effort both the teacher and student graded homework assignments. Examples given included the teacher calling out the correct answer or the student being called on to give his or her answer to the class. Other teachers described combination grading as a student holding up a homework paper, which allowed the teacher to visibly determine if the assignment was adequately completed. In this latter instance the quality of feedback was poor. Most often in student grading, students swapped papers with each other so that no student graded his or her own assignment, and answers were provided by the teacher. Grading by the teacher alone provided evidence of student participation and completion.

Overall, the evidence indicates that feedback on homework is an essential part of the student learning experience and impacts on student effort and motivation. There is wide variation in the type of feedback given to students and the use of grading for homework. If checking homework completion is the only feedback given, it is unlikely to facilitate students' learning.

Motivating students to complete homework

Teachers can provide reinforcement for completion, accuracy or quality of homework or punishment for non-completion. In the USA, non-verbal incentives, e.g. sweets or early dismissal from school, were sometimes used. Fink and Nalven (1972), studying economically disadvantaged children, found that verbal praise and rewards of sweets produced more homework completion than did no feedback or verbal praise alone. Harris and Sherman (1974) explored the effects of using candy or early finishing times for completion of homework, and keeping pupils in for non-completion. In Canada teachers have adopted several strategies to encourage homework, including rewards (Deslandes, 2009). Similarly, in England many schools use verbal praise, rewards systems including certificates, merits and stickers, and also letters home to parents to encourage homework completion.

MacBeath and Turner found that a range of sanctions were imposed in the UK, such as extra work, the writing of lines and double the amount of homework. Most teachers favoured the use of sanctions when homework was not completed. However, there were differences between schools (MacBeath and Turner, 1990). Some schools placed more emphasis on persuasion than on punishments. The whole issue of sanctions relating to homework creates dilemmas for teachers, as some children may not have completed homework because they found it too difficult or because of home circumstances (Le Métais, 1985). To ensure that children are not unfairly penalized, teachers need to have an understanding of their circumstances. The provision of homework clubs, where pupils can work in an appropriately supportive environment, with help on hand if they need it, can resolve some of these issues (see Chapters 3, 5 and 6).

It is likely that the setting of quality homework is more important than rewards, as is the value that pupils perceive their teachers to place on the homework completed and the quality of feedback provided (see Chapter 5). Quality homework, in which the activities align with the classroom learning and are set at an appropriate level, promotes student motivation and self-regulation (Corno and Xu, 2004; Trautwein, Schnyder, Niggli, Neumann and Lüdtke, 2009; Núñez, Suárez, Rosário *et al.*, 2015). There are indications, too, that students are more likely to do homework if they start it in class (Wilson and Rhodes, 2010).

Conclusions

Teachers' views, beliefs and practices are very influential on the development of students' homework effort, homework emotions, and achievement. While teachers are generally positive about the role of homework in pupils' learning they do not always treat it as seriously as work undertaken in the classroom. To be effective, homework needs to be aligned to classroom learning in terms of relevance, challenge level and meaningfulness, so that students are encouraged to do homework. Students need to understand how to do the work, and the directions provided by the teacher. If they do not, they not only will reject assigned homework tasks but also may resent the broader notion of homework in general (Carr, 2013).

Homework needs to be marked speedily and pupils given constructive feedback on how to improve their work in the future. At secondary level teachers can support pupils in the scheduling of their homework across different subjects, so that multiple deadlines do not fall at the same time. Such an approach would reward students for completing their homework in addition to enhancing future attainment. Involving pupils in formative assessment procedures, including those relating to homework, is a very effective means of increasing their commitment, metacognitive skills and attainment. There is room for greater use of dialogic formative assessment to provide feedback to the teacher on pupils' understanding as a prelude to rethinking classroom learning.

Approaches to setting homework tasks are explored in Chapters 3 and 7.

CHAPTER 4: KEY POINTS

Teachers' views, beliefs and practices about homework are very influential on students' engagement with homework.

Most teachers regularly assign homework to extend learning beyond the classroom.

Teachers see the main purpose of homework as mastery of the curriculum.

Teachers' attitudes towards homework reflect current cultural, social and economic factors.

Little research has explored how teachers design and plan homework. To be effective, homework needs to be planned as an integral part of teaching and learning.

Evidence suggests that the quality of homework assignments may be more important than the time they take or the quantity of homework set.

Most teachers provide feedback on homework. However, there is wide variation in how this is undertaken.

Too often, homework feedback is used as an element of control by teachers, rather than as an opportunity to engage in formative, dialogic feedback to maximize learning.

Chapter 5

Pupils' perspectives on homework

This chapter sets out the research evidence on the length of time pupils report spending on homework, their attitudes towards homework, and the strategies and approaches they adopt when they undertake homework. Consideration is given to how students manage their homework and whether doing homework develops wider skills such as responsibility and independent study. Attention is given to how homework may be mediated by gender and individual pupil characteristics. The influence of extra-curricular activities, employment, homework resources and the homework environment is discussed.

How long do pupils spend doing homework?

International perspectives

In 2012, across OECD countries, on average 15-year-old students reported that they spent almost five hours per week doing homework (OECD, 2014). The time varied significantly between countries. For instance, in Ireland, Italy, Kazakhstan, Romania, the Russian Federation and Singapore, students reported that they spent seven hours or more per week on average doing homework, while in Shanghai students reported that they spent 14 hours per week on average. In contrast students in Finland and Korea reported that they spent less than three hours per week doing homework. Overall, since the previous survey undertaken in 2003, the amount of reported homework had declined by one hour. More recent studies identify averages within this range: for example, Kalenkoski and Pabilonia (2017) in the USA reported 6.4 hours of total homework per week; Fernández-Alonso, Suárez-Álvarez and Muñiz (2015) in Spain found 70 minutes a day.

Research in the USA (Markow, Kim and Liebman, 2007), drawing on 2,101 public school students in grades 3 to 12, found that three-quarters of the students (77 per cent) spent at least 30 minutes doing homework on a typical school day, 45 per cent of the students spent at least 1 hour and 27 per cent of the students spent at least one and a half hours. Only 6 per cent of the students did not spend any time on homework.

In a study of 128 primary school pupils in Portugal, Costa, Cardoso, Lacerda, Lopes and Gomes (2016) found that 47.7 per cent of pupils reported homework taking up to 30 minutes, 41.1 per cent taking between 30 minutes and one hour and

10.9 per cent taking between one and two hours. The teachers in this study reported that students should be spending 30 minutes to one hour.

The amount of homework set by teachers is not necessarily a good indication of how long students spend completing that homework. For instance, research in France has shown that the time spent on the same homework varies enormously between pupils, at both primary and secondary level. Some children take twice as long as others to do the same homework (Larue, 1995). The 2000 cycle of the Programme for International Student Assessment (PISA) (OECD, 2001) obtained homework data relating to 15-year-olds from 32 countries. The reported amount of time spent on homework in mathematics, the home language and natural sciences ranged from 2.9 hours in Japan to 7.0 hours in Greece and included 4.6 hours in the USA and 4.5 hours in Germany.

In the UK

MacBeath and Turner (1990), working in Scotland, found that in a typical evening primary pupils and their parents agreed that they had homework of less than an hour. At secondary level just over 40 per cent said less than an hour was spent on homework and just under 50 per cent said 1 to 2 hours. There was an increase in time spent on homework from early primary to upper secondary school, but within this there was considerable variation from school to school, class to class and teacher to teacher. Keys, Harris and Fernandes (1995) reported that 43 per cent of primary-aged children claimed they were not usually given homework, 24 per cent were given half an hour or less and 16 per cent about an hour. Eleven per cent claimed to be given more than an hour. At secondary level 20 per cent said that they were given half an hour or less, 39 per cent about an hour, 19 per cent about an hour and a half and 13 per cent more than two hours. Farrow, Tymms and Henderson (1999) found that pupils at primary school reported doing homework in reading more than once a week, in mathematics once a week and in science not at all. Among 310 high-achieving pupils from two single-sex schools in England students reported undertaking homework for between 3.5 hours and 35 hours each week, with a mean of 11.80. Just one pupil reported doing 35 hours' homework each week, this being due mainly to 10 hours each for art and design technology. Most pupils completed between 7.5 and 12.5 hours' homework weekly (Rogers and Hallam, 2006).

Overall, there continues to be wide variation in the amount of homework set by schools and the amount completed by individual pupils. However, time spent does not necessarily equate with effort or interest. Pupils may need different amounts of time to complete homework tasks, and when pupils spend more time on homework this could be due to poor homework management strategies (Suárez, Regueiro, Epstein *et al.*, 2016; Rogers, 2013a).

Pupils' attitudes to homework

Pupils' attitudes towards homework are often influenced by peer group and community factors (Cooper, 1989a, 1989b; Ulrich, 1989; Murphy and Decker, 1989, Reetz, 1991; Pratt, Green, MacVicar and Bountrogianni, 1992; Chen and Stevenson, 1989). They often report that homework has little relationship to the work in hand, is poorly set or unclear or is marked late, and that there is a lack of pupil–teacher interaction, which results in poor feedback (Le Métais, 1985; Heller, Spooner, Anderson and Mims, 1988; Rosenberg, 1989; Ulrich, 1989; Bechler, 1991; Hodapp and Hodapp, 1992; Wilson and Rhodes, 2010; Maharaj-Sharma and Sharma, 2016). Despite these apparently negative attitudes towards homework, students seem to view teachers as more effective when they set daily homework (Dudley and Shawver, 1991; Hong, Wan and Peng, 2011). There also seem to be relationships between time spent on homework and positive attitudes towards school (Keys and Fernandes, 1993). Pupils who like school are more likely to believe in the importance of homework than those who dislike school (Lapointe, Mead and Askew, 1992; Keys, Harris and Fernandes, 1995; Leung, 1993). MacBeath and Turner (1990) found that a range of factors affected pupils' attitudes towards doing their homework, including motivation, mood, well-being, family circumstances, the weather, and the quality and quantity of homework assigned. Pupils resented work set above or below their ability, criticized teachers who catered to the lowest common denominator, and felt that good teachers individualized homework. Cooper, Jackson, Nye and Lindsay (2001) demonstrated that students' attitudes towards homework did not predict homework completion or classroom grade.

Pupils in the UK and the USA believe that homework helps them to do well at school (Black, 1990; Keys, Harris and Fernandes, 1995) and that they sometimes learn a lot from it (MacBeath and Turner, 1990), although 8 per cent of primary and 13 per cent of secondary pupils indicated that they did not learn a lot from homework. Most pupils said that they enjoyed homework at least sometimes, but a sizeable proportion from primary (26 per cent) and secondary (30 per cent) schools reported that they never enjoyed it. The proportion enjoying it only sometimes increased from primary to secondary school, while the proportion of those always enjoying it declined from primary to secondary school. Some pupils viewed homework as unacceptable in principle (MacBeath and Turner, 1990).

Black (1990), exploring attitudes towards homework in two secondary schools in the USA, suggested that pupils held unfavourable attitudes towards homework because it was tedious, boring and amounted to 'busy work'. They wanted something that was individualized, creative and challenging. In the UK, earlier research (DES, 1987) suggested that pupils enjoyed imaginative and challenging homework but held negative attitudes towards low-level work, particularly copying from textbooks. Harris and Rudduck (1994) reported that students did not like doing homework that they perceived did not contribute to or consolidate their learning. Not understanding what was expected of them also generated negative attitudes (Ofsted, 1995).

At primary level, when asked what was the best thing about homework, most pupils specified a particular subject. A sizeable proportion, which increased with age, stated that homework helped you understand or learn, but some felt that the best thing about homework was finishing it, 'when you didn't get any', or 'nothing'. Some also said that it could be interesting or fun (MacBeath and Turner, 1990). The worst things about homework were its interference with other activities, having to do it at all, the amount, and the time it took. These responses occurred across all age levels. Some said that they found homework boring or difficult to understand. At primary level, English, mathematics and having too much writing were also cited as amongst the worst things. Homework was perceived as easier if it was well explained, if there was less of it, if it was more interesting, if there was more time to do it, and if there was someone to help. In addition, at secondary level, better timetabling was mentioned. Another factor perceived as making homework easier, unrelated to school, was concentration. This response was the highest in the first two years of secondary school. Other factors mentioned included being able to borrow books from the library, having shorter exercises, it not only involving writing, and being able to do it with friends (MacBeath and Turner, 1990).

As pupils progressed through school the proportion who did homework to get through it as quickly as possible decreased from 38 per cent to 22 per cent. Perhaps as important examinations draw closer it becomes more meaningful, although the percentage of pupils who said that they sometimes got through homework as quickly as possible increased from 38 per cent to 52 per cent. High percentages of pupils claimed that they took time over homework and thought about what they were doing, that is, 61 per cent at primary level increasing to 77 per cent at the highest secondary ages, with a dip at transfer to secondary school. Asked if they did more homework than they had to because they were interested in it 57 per cent at secondary level responded 'sometimes'. Once again there was large variation between schools (MacBeath and Turner, 1990).

Homework quality

More recent research has focused on pupils' interest in homework and their perceptions of homework quality. Homework quality is the extent to which students perceive assignments to be well prepared, how they integrate with the lessons and their level of challenge and difficulty. High homework quality requires careful selection and preparation of appropriate and, to some extent, interesting tasks that reinforce classroom learning (Trautwein and Lüdtke, 2007) (see Chapters 3 and 5). Among 511 grade 8 and 9 students, Trautwein and Lüdtke (2009) demonstrated that homework quality as perceived by students was positively associated with homework motivation and homework effort. In a study involving 3,283 German students in grades 9 and 10, homework quality was positively associated with homework motivation and achievement. Interesting assignments were perceived as being valuable and offering a high expectancy of success. This resulted in more effort being expended (Dettmers, Trautwein, Lüdtke, Kunter and Baumert, 2010). Other research has observed that students considered homework interesting if it was connected to a topic or skill relevant to their lives or if they understood the purposes of the specific exercise (Xu, 2007, 2009). Of relevance is that homework interest is positively linked with homework environment management, at both the individual and the class level (Xu, 2012). Not surprisingly, when students are unclear about the reasons for doing homework and the extent to which it will be beneficial, they tend not to value it (Akioka and Gilmore, 2013; Bembenutty, 2010).

The influence of teachers' control over homework

The extent to which teachers control homework and the feedback they provide seems to influence the level of students' effort when they do their homework (Natriello and McDill, 1986; Trautwein, Niggli, Schnyder and Lüdtke, 2009).

Students who perceive their teachers to be supportive of autonomy, as opposed to controlling, tend to show more motivation towards and invest more effort in schoolwork, and consequently earn better grades. A controlling homework style, by contrast, has been negatively associated with homework effort and homework emotions (Trautwein, Niggli, Schnyder and Lüdtke, 2009). Hagger, Sultan, Hardcastle and Chatzisarantis (2015), using data from 220 high school students, indicated that the extent to which students perceived that they were receiving support for their autonomous learning in mathematics class activities was positively related to them being independently motivated in relation to those classes. In turn, this was positively related to intrinsic motivation, the frequency of doing homework, homework completion and homework grades. What is less clear is whether teachers' autonomy support regarding homework can be empirically distinguished from other aspects of teacher involvement with homework (e.g. homework quality and feedback quality) (Xu, 2016).

Regarding feedback, if teachers do not grade homework and return it quickly, students report feeling they have wasted their time on that activity (Wilson and Rhodes, 2010). Students consider limited feedback an impediment to homework completion, and recognize teachers' feedback as supporting their completion of homework (Bang, Suárez-Orozco and O'Connor, 2011). Núñez, Suárez, Rosário, Vallejo, Cerezo and Valle (2015) demonstrated that students' perceptions of teachers' homework feedback was positively and significantly related to the amount of homework completed and the perceived quality of homework time management. It was not related to the amount of time spent on homework. Other studies have identified a positive relationship between students' perceptions of homework feedback provided by teachers and (1) students' interest in homework (Xu, 2008), (2) students' homework management (Xu, 2012; Xu and Wu, 2013), and (3) students' homework completion (Xu, 2011).

Where students perceived that teachers assigned too much homework on the same evening, 77 per cent of students reported that they would do more homework if teachers in different subjects would set it on different nights (Wilson and Rhodes, 2010).

Overall, pupils consider that:

- homework should be clearly related to ongoing classroom work;
- there should be a clear pattern to classwork and homework;
- homework should be varied;
- homework should be manageable;
- homework should be challenging but not too difficult;
- homework should allow for individual initiative and creativity;
- homework should promote self-confidence and understanding;
- there should be recognition or reward for work done;
- there should be guidance and support.

These are sensible and reasonable demands. The challenge for educators is to find ways of satisfying them.

Homework and attitudes towards school and particular subjects

There is evidence that there are relationships between positive attitudes towards homework and positive attitudes towards school (Chen and Stevenson, 1989; Keys, Harris and Fernandes, 1995; Leung, 1993). These are both likely to be related to success at school. There are also cultural differences.

Farrow, Tymms and Henderson (1999), in England, found that frequency of doing homework was related to positive attitudes to school among Year 6 pupils, but that these data did not hold at the level of the school. Assessment of pupils' self-concept also showed some relationship with the reported amounts of homework completed. Keys and Fernandes (1993) also reported that the more time pupils spent on homework in Years 7 and 9 the more positive attitudes they had towards school. However, the amount of variance explained by time spent on homework was very small. Evidence from studies on ability grouping suggests that teachers tend to give more homework to the more able pupils, who also have more positive attitudes towards school. Ability may therefore be a mediating factor between attitudes towards school and the amount of homework undertaken (Hallam, Kirton, Robertson, Stobart and Peffers, 2003).

Farrow, Tymms and Henderson (1999) also found that those pupils who reported doing most homework showed the most positive attitudes towards the particular subject concerned. This association was least marked in mathematics and most marked in reading and science, more so in the former. For reading, 'once a month' homework was associated with a lower attitude rating. These findings may simply indicate that pupils who like a particular subject spend more time doing homework for that subject. Where homework is open-ended or flexible, e.g. reading, this is likely to be the case. In mathematics, where a certain amount of work is set, even those who enjoy mathematics will limit the amount of time they spend on it, while those who find it difficult and may enjoy it less may take longer to complete it.

International evidence indicates that American pupils have less positive attitudes towards homework than pupils in Japan and China, although they spend less time doing it (Chen and Stevenson, 1989; Hong, Wan and Peng, 2011). These differences are mediated by cultural attitudes. In Japan and China, there is a much greater emphasis on effort in learning, rather than on ability. This is reflected in the finding that teachers in the USA put less emphasis on the importance of homework than their counterparts in the other countries.

Some studies have reported students' preferences for certain types of homework according to subject. Deveci and Önder (2013) studied science and technology homework among 1,584 7th- and 8th-grade students at middle schools in Turkey. Most students indicated that they preferred experimental homework assignments that enabled them to use their creativity and were hands-on. Among primary school students, while the most frequent types of homework were exercises from textbooks and numerical operations (43.0 per cent and 41.4 per cent respectively), the pupils indicated that they would like teachers to set homework based on group work (mentioned by 69.5 per cent of pupils), as well as on research on the internet (51.6 per cent of pupils) (Costa, Cardoso, Lacerda, Lopes and Gomes, 2016).

Homework styles and strategies

The way students undertake their homework has been explored as a means of explaining differences in achievement. De Jong, Westerhof and Creemers (2000) reported that only three variables of a range relating to student study characteristics were related to achievement. The first two applied to students in lower-ability groups: being told to start homework by parents and finding problems doing their homework. The other variable related to students who reported watching television while doing homework. Differences in study strategies themselves were not related to achievement. Hong and Lee (2000) explored the relationships between homework styles and academic attainment in Chinese students in Hong Kong. They found that similar and different patterns of preferred homework styles were reported by both high- and low-achieving students. In other words, the patterns adopted did not relate to the students' ability. However, motivational patterns, particularly relating to responsibility and persistence, were significantly different between the high and low achievers. Students in high-achieving groups were more self-motivated, persistent and responsible in doing their homework. For students with high levels of self-perceived homework achievement and positive attitudes towards homework, motivation was influenced by parents and teachers. No consistent perceptual sensitivity elements relating to homework (auditory, visual, tactile, kinaesthetic) distinguished high- and low-achieving students, which suggests that these preferences are unrelated to attainment (Hong and Lee, 2000; Hong, 1998). Low-achieving students often had a greater preference for eating, drinking and moving about while doing homework than their high-achieving peers, while students who perceived their homework achievement level as high tended to prefer a well-lit room and formal design and organization of furniture. They also preferred to work with structured homework instructions, organize an order for working on assignments and use the same spot in the house. These differences did not impact on achievement as rated by teachers.

Approaches to homework

More recent research has looked at students' approaches to homework and the process of doing homework. Through factor analysis, Rogers (2013b) identified five factors or perceptions of studying among 826 16-year-old students: self-management, anxiety, understanding, ambivalence and wider interest. Relevant is that these factors mirrored those consistently identified among higher-education students (Tait and Entwistle, 1996) particularly in relation to the distinction between deep, surface and strategic approaches to learning. Two factors – understanding (deep) and self-management (strategic) – were positively related to reported homework hours each week. Where students perceived studying for their GCSEs to be about understanding or about managing their resources, there was an increase in reported homework hours. In considering the interplay between the different factors, attainment at GCSE and homework, a positive relationship held with GCSE attainment and homework hours when previous attainment was taken into account.

The use of statistical approaches that enable a person-centred approach to understanding student perceptions and approaches to homework has enabled more nuanced understandings of homework patterns and learning experiences. Flunger, Trautwein, Nagengast *et al.* (2015), through the application of latent profile analyses to a longitudinal data set with 1,915 8th-grade students, showed that some students benefited more than others from doing homework. For high-effort learners, large amounts of homework tended to have a positive impact on attainment. Differences in students' learning types were also reflected in students' agentic and emotional engagement, and in the amount of homework attempted.

Rogers (2013a), through the technique of cluster analysis, classified 826 Year-11 students into six groups based on different metacognitive, effort- and time-management strategies, task value and self-regulatory strategies. Clusters were identified of students who had become disengaged with their studies, in contrast to clusters of hard-working students, who valued the task and adopted a variety of strategies. Clusters were identified of students with poor time-management strategies, use of planning and organizational strategies. Not all hard-working students held positive perceptions of studying; some were driven by a sense of anxiety. The clusters differed in relation to attainment and the amount of homework they reported completing. Reported homework hours were not consistently predictive of academic success as measured by GCSE scores. Students in one of the high-attaining clusters reported completing the least amount of homework, despite adopting effective self-checking strategies. It seemed that successful strategy use, together with prior attainment, contributed to success, rather than working long hours. Students in one of the lower-attaining clusters reported working long hours but without task-management control. It appeared students in this cluster, although willing to work long hours, lacked sufficient metacognitive awareness to employ a variety of strategies effectively.

Both Rogers (2013a) and Flunger, Trautwein, Nagengast *et al.* (2015) drew attention to the importance of study intervention strategies that target groups of struggling learners and the need for further research in this area. To support students in their studies, teachers need to give attention to the development of thinking skills and self-regulated learning strategies (Núñez, Rosário, Vallejo and González-Pienda, 2013; Rosário, Gonzalez-Pienda, Cerezo *et al.*, 2010).

Group homework

Ma (1996) considered the effects of co-operative homework on mathematics achievement, taking into account team characteristics. The findings showed that three-member teams were preferable for organizing co-operative learning for mathematics homework. Teams of two, four or five were less successful. Middle and low achievers all benefited from co-operative work, whereas high achievers did not, although they still maintained their top position in mathematics. It may be that in heterogeneous groups they spent time helping those less able than themselves and that in homogeneous high-ability groups the work was not sufficiently challenging. Overall, the findings suggest that doing homework in teams can improve achievement for most students.

Students' management of homework

One of the challenges of completing homework is the management of time. This is not straightforward: it includes an individual's efforts to budget time to meet homework deadlines (e.g. creating study schedules and allocating time for different activities), from time planning to monitoring and regulating time use (Xu, 2010b). It involves setting priorities and planning ahead, scheduling regular time to do homework in the midst of other after-school activities, and pacing oneself to complete several assignments with different due dates. It also involves keeping track of what remains to be done and being aware of how much time is left.

Given the inconclusive evidence surrounding academic gains and the time spent on homework (see Chapter 2), some research has focused on the use of homework-management strategies and how the quality of homework management relates to time spent on homework, completion of homework, and attainment. Studies have shown that the use of homework-management strategies is positively associated with homework completion and academic achievement (Ramdass and Zimmerman, 2011; Xu, 2009).

Xu (2007) studied 194 US students in grades 5 and 6. Girls, and students who received family help, more frequently reported that they managed their homework. Interest in homework and affective attitude were positively related to the use of homework-management strategies. Intrinsic reasons, such as doing homework for reinforcement of school learning and the development of self-regulatory attributes, were positively associated with the use of homework-management strategies. There was no relationship between time spent on homework and the use of homework-management strategies.

In a larger study involving 633 rural and urban US students in grade 8, Xu (2009) identified five homework-management strategies: (1) setting an appropriate work environment, (2) managing time, (3) handling distraction, (4) monitoring motivation, and (5) controlling negative emotion. High-achieving students reported more frequently than low-achieving students that they worked to manage their workspace, plan their time, handle distraction, monitor motivation and control emotion while doing homework. Urban students reported more than rural students being self-motivated during homework.

Later research demonstrated a positive relationship between students' grade level, an organized environment and homework time management (Xu, 2010a). Homework management may be influenced by several variables, including goal orientation, task value, task interest, affective attitude, the influence of others and background variables (Xu, 2013). Drawing on data from 866 8th-grade and 745 11th-grade students, Xu and Wu (2013) demonstrated that homework management was positively associated with learning goals, affective attitude, self-reported assessment, family homework help, homework interest, teacher feedback and issues related to adults. Núñez, Suárez, Cerezo *et al.* (2015) found, among 454 students aged between 10 and 16 from three Spanish schools, that effective homework time management positively affects the amount of homework done and, consequently, academic achievement. This relationship was stronger for elementary students than for students in high school. Homework time management was a crucial variable for determining students' academic achievement – more important than the quantity of homework completed or the quantity of time spent doing homework. No relationship was found between gender and the perceived quality of homework time management.

These studies reiterate the importance of using self-regulated learning strategies while managing homework time. Indeed, homework is frequently viewed as an important vehicle for developing good study habits and desirable self-regulatory strategies (Xu, 2009). Furthermore, it appears that adolescents need to take a more proactive role in homework management. Teachers can support this through the promotion of mastery approaches to learning and by setting tasks that foster the development of self-regulatory strategies. Other researchers (e.g. Trautwein, Lüdtke, Schnyder and Niggli, 2006; Zimmerman and Kitsantas, 2005) have established connections between self-regulated learning and homework completion.

Does homework develop responsibility and independent study?

While parents and teachers both argue that homework should develop a sense of responsibility in pupils (Heller, Spooner, Anderson and Mims, 1988; Epstein, 1988; McCaslin and Murdock, 1991; Xu, 1994), there is little research to assess whether it does and the conditions under which this might best be achieved. Some authors have suggested that homework can encourage the transition from being motivated by a desire to please the teacher to a position in which work becomes intrinsically satisfying (Jünger, Feider and Reinert, 1990), whereas others have suggested that through the process of doing homework pupils develop self-regulation strategies to motivate themselves, set goals, manage time, monitor progress and evaluate homework outcomes (Bembenutty, 2011; Ramdass and Zimmerman, 2011). Others still argue that homework does not improve study skills or promote self-discipline and responsibility (Kohn, 2006)

In an early study, Hudson (1965) reported that homework inculcated better study habits and time management than supervised study. However, MacFarlane (1987) reported that no development appeared to take place in the pupils' understanding of the role of homework, or in their ability to cope with independent study. This may be because they did not appear to have been taught how to organize their study time, instructions about homework were given hurriedly with insufficient guidance, there were inadequate opportunities to ask questions or seek clarification, and assignments were often unrelated to classwork. Students repeatedly indicated that these factors were causes of difficulties.

Warton (1997) interviewed primary-aged children about homework and their understandings of its functions in order to establish if there was any development of responsibility. The sample were Australian middle-class children from grades 2 (aged 7/8), 4 (aged 9/10) and 6 (aged 11/12). The results indicated few age differences in reported practices in undertaking homework but an age-related shift in ideas from being regulated by others to being regulated by themselves by grade 6. Responses concerning whether homework was their responsibility fell into three categories: identification, introjection (for which responses referred to letting other people down) and external (for example, 'The teacher wouldn't like it'). The findings suggested that pupils develop understanding of their responsibilities in relation to homework as they get older. Given the limited nature of the sample, which comprised middle-class children whose parents might be expected to be supportive of their learning, it would be unwise to generalize these findings, particularly as, in a further study, Warton found that 47 per cent of mothers felt that one of the purposes of homework was to encourage responsibility and self-discipline. Despite this, remembering to do homework was seen by the mothers as a responsibility shared between them and their children, although as the children became older they were expected to take more responsibility.

In another small-scale study, in the USA, Xu and Corno (1998) observed the homework behaviour of six 3rd-grade pupils, also from middle-class backgrounds. The pupils adopted strategies such as self-talk to keep themselves motivated and to prevent themselves becoming too frustrated while they were doing homework. They also used a variety of strategies to help themselves follow through on homework, including arranging the environment, managing time and monitoring their attention, motivation and emotions. Some of these strategies were similar to those adopted by their parents and had probably been learned through modelling. Their strategies to monitor motivation and emotion appeared less sophisticated and more variable than those adopted to manage the environment, which may indicate that these are more difficult to learn. However, these children, as young as 8, had begun to manage their approaches to homework, which suggests that quite young children can acquire self-regulatory strategies while doing homework with their parents. However, the sample consisted of pupils likely to receive the highest levels of support from their parents in optimal learning environments. For this reason, the findings may not generalize across other populations.

An interesting intervention study carried out by Stoeger and Ziegler (2008) in Germany explored how 219 4th-grade students could be taught to develop self-regulatory strategies when doing homework. The 17 teachers and the students were assigned to a training or a control group. Those in the training group received a five-week in-class programme delivered by the teachers to develop self-regulated learning. Students self-evaluated and monitored their learning abilities, set specific, attainable goals with the guidance of the teacher and used appropriate strategies to achieve them. Students then implemented the strategy, monitored their work and engaged in self-reflection to evaluate their learning. Pupils in the training group reported improved time-management skills and reflection on their own learning in comparison to the control group. The reported self-efficacy of these pupils also increased during training, as did their motivation.

There are suggestions that pupils who engage in self-regulatory processes while doing homework are more motivated and achieve more highly than those who do not (Bembenutty, 2009; Bempechat, 2004). Critical are the ways in which students set goals, and their motives for doing homework. Research has demonstrated that students who value learning and show an intention to learn and improve their skills are likely to use deep learning strategies (Suárez Riveiro, Gonzalez Cabanach and Valle Arias, 2001; Rogers, 2013b). Furthermore, there are suggestions that learning-goal-oriented students are likely to self-regulate their learning process (Valle, Núñez, Cabanach *et al.*, 2015), make an effort to learn, and assume control of their learning processes (Rosário, Núñez, Vallejo, Cunha, Azevedo *et al.*, 2016). They persist longer when faced with difficult and challenging tasks.

Gender differences

International perspectives on gender differences

Many studies internationally have commented on gender differences in relation to homework. Girls tend to spend longer doing their homework (Featherstone, 1985; Chen and Ehrenberg, 1993; Keys, Harris and Fernandes, 1995; Harris, Nixon and Rudduck, 1993; MacBeath and Turner, 1990; Bonyun, 1992; Chen and Stevenson, 1989; Farrow, Tymms and Henderson, 1999; Rogers and Hallam, 2006; OECD, 2015), be more positive in their responses to it (Bonyun, 1992; Chen and Stevenson, 1989; Harris, Nixon and Rudduck, 1993; Keys, Harris and Fernandes, 1995; Xu, 2010a) and be more committed to doing homework than boys (Younger and Warrington, 1996; Xu, 2006, 2007, 2010a; Cavas, 2011). Boys are more likely than girls to report lack of interest in homework as a reason for not completing mathematics homework (Peng, Hong, Li *et al.*, 2010). Xu (2014) found that boys were less likely than girls to take initiatives to manage homework time.

Hong and Lee (2000) found no gender differences in the homework styles of 5th- and 7th-grade Chinese students in Hong Kong, although there were gender differences between US and Korean 7th-grade students (Hong and Milgram, 1999). More females than males reported that they liked doing their homework in a brightly illuminated home environment and that they organized their assignments in a certain order. More males than females reported that they did their homework with an adult figure present.

Among 426 US students in grades 9–12, girls more frequently reported working to manage their workspace, budget their time and monitor their emotion. Girls also reported more time spent doing homework and were less likely to come to class without homework (Xu, 2006). Similarly, in a study of 685 African American students from the 8th and 11th grades, girls more frequently reported working to manage their workspace, monitor motivation and control emotion (Xu, 2010a). Peng, Hong, Li, Wan and Long (2010), in a study of mathematics homework among 525 Chinese students in grade 10, also found that boys reported having more homework problems than girls. Girls homework difficulty more highly as their reason for failure to complete homework.

Although studies have indicated that girls experience more stress due to homework, girls also report better ability to control stress; that is, girls are more likely than boys to report that they 'frequently' use emotional regulation techniques such as 'calming myself down' when stressed during homework (Xu and Corno, 2006). In a study by Kackar, Shumow, Schmidt and Grzetich (2011), girls, regardless of age, reported greater stress when doing homework alone, and lower stress when doing it with friends. High school girls reported lower interest than middle school boys when doing homework alone.

In contrast, in a study of Turkish students, İflazoğlu and Hong (2012) reported no gender differences in homework motivation, attitudes and achievement. Trautwein, Lüdtke, Schnyder and Niggli (2006) revealed that boys expressed more expectancy of success and more concentration than girls; however, girls spent more time on homework than boys. In relation to time management, Núñez, Suárez, Cerezo *et al.* (2015), among 454 Spanish students, and Xu (2010a), among 685 African American students, found no relationship between gender and homework time management. Gender differences existed in other areas among the African American students, however: girls were more likely to manage the homework environment and control emotion (Xu, 2010a).

Gender differences in England

In England, there are suggestions that girls adopt a more conscientious approach towards homework, and produce work that is neat, well planned and shows evidence of effort (Warrington, Younger and Williams, 2000). Boys appear to dislike homework, spending less time on it than girls. There has been some concern that girls, in learning to conform to the conventions of school education, that is, handing work in on time and remaining on task, complete excessive amounts of homework in response to school demands. This may be detrimental to them in the long term because of the extreme pressures that they put themselves under (Murphy and Elwood, 1998; Weston, 1999). Both boys and girls believe that homework is important in helping them to do well in school, although this tendency is stronger at primary level in girls. Primary school girls also tend to perceive that teachers always mark their work (Keys, Harris and Fernandes, 1995).

Harris, Nixon and Rudduck (1993) have suggested that some of the reported gender differences regarding homework are related to peer and community factors. In the communities where their research was undertaken, men tended to maintain a clearer distinction between time at work and time off work, when they relaxed. This distinction did not apply to women who, while holding a job, still worked in the domestic role at home. These images were reflected in the way that students did homework. For boys, there was a strong distinction between school and homework, while girls were more ready to do schoolwork at home and to discuss work with their peers. Out of school, boys tended to spend more time in larger groups involved in sport whereas girls spent more time with a single close friend, which might involve working with them on homework. Girls were more ready to plan their time and cope with their responsibility in an orderly fashion (Harris, Nixon and Rudduck, 1993) and were more likely than the boys to report reading for pleasure outside school (Keys, Harris and Fernandes, 1995).

Among high-achieving Year 10 and 11 pupils, Rogers and Hallam (2006) found that girls reported higher levels of stress about homework, while boys reported more positive affect towards it. The boys more frequently reported taking breaks when doing their homework, and more often reported doing the minimum if they felt that the homework was not important. They also reported doing less homework than the girls. Findings suggested that, overall, high-achieving boys have better studying strategies than high-achieving girls. They achieve high standards while doing less homework (Rogers and Hallam, 2006).

In a larger-scale study by the same authors, involving 644 students, boys and girls alike reported trying to plan homework so that it was manageable, planning what they needed to complete for the next day and taking regular breaks when doing homework (Rogers and Hallam, 2010). Boys and girls sometimes had to work long hours to complete homework and found that the variation in homework made it difficult to plan their work. Girls reported fewer difficulties when working at home.

While many studies internationally and in England have identified gender differences in relation to homework management and organization, time spent, and stress, these do not hold consistently across research. The evidence does, though, draw attention to the powerful impact of different cultures on gendered approaches to homework.

Homework and individual pupil characteristics

There has been little systematic research that has considered individual differences in pupil characteristics in relation to the amount of homework completed. In the

USA, Keith and Benson (1992) and Mau and Lynn (1999) found that students from Asian backgrounds spent more time on homework than students from other ethnic groups. At primary school, Farrow, Tymms and Henderson (1999) found that the amount of homework undertaken was related to cultural capital. Those children with significantly higher values for cultural capital, that is, with more educationally oriented and supportive home backgrounds, tended to do more homework.

Ability

The relationship between ability and the amount of homework set varies. While higher-ability groups in secondary school tend to be set more homework, at primary level Farrow, Tymms and Henderson (1999) reported that there was almost no correlation between the amount of homework reported by pupils and their non-verbal ability. The more able children did no more work than the less able. While several studies suggest that lower-achieving pupils and those with special needs should have homework assignments tailored to their needs, a study of pupils at secondary level in the USA, which took the pupils' perspective, suggested that pupils did not necessarily support this idea, because being given assignments that were different from the rest of the class tended to have a negative impact on self-esteem (Nelson, Epstein, Bursuck, Jayanthi and Sawyer, 1998). The amount and type of homework set for pupils of different abilities almost certainly depends on the way they are grouped within school. Where classes are mixed-ability the homework that is set is likely to be similar for all pupils. Where pupils are grouped by ability homework is likely to be differentiated.

The cluster analysis undertaken by Rogers (2013a) reported earlier in this chapter provides further insight into high- and low-achieving student characteristics and homework. Of the higher-achieving clusters, cluster 2, with high anxiety, reported completing the most homework each week, followed by cluster 5. Students in cluster 5 worked long hours, but had an effective array of study strategies so that anxiety was not detrimental to success. Students in these clusters reported completing more than 11 hours of homework each week. Students in cluster 4, who displayed many self-checking strategies, reported completing a mean of 9.75 homework hours. Their reported homework time may have been spent more effectively. Clusters 3 and 6 reported the least amount of homework and were characterized by minimal effort in the use of strategies. Cluster 1 students, with little control over task demands, reported completing over 10.5 homework hours each week. When controlling for prior attainment, significant differences remained between the clusters in relation to success and reported homework hours, although prior attainment accentuated the differences between the clusters in relation to GCSE success.

Age

While research indicates that as pupils get older they do more homework, this contrasts with the evidence that students' motivation for school tasks declines among older students (Hong, Peng and Rowell, 2009). Little research, though, has explored changes in pupils' attitudes towards homework.

Warton (1997) demonstrated that older pupils held more negative attitudes towards homework and gave different reasons for doing it, while Cooper, Lindsay, Nye and Greathouse (1998) found that when greater amounts of homework were assigned by teachers they were associated with negative attitudes to homework among younger children (aged 3–5) but not those in the later years of secondary education. Older students regard homework as boring, expend less effort on it and are less motivated to do it (Trautwein, Lüdtke, Kastens and Köller, 2006). Among 7th–11th-grade Chinese students, Hong, Peng and Rowell (2009) found that older students reported being less engaged, persisted less and enjoyed doing homework less than their younger colleagues. Studies in Spain (Núñez, Suárez, Cerezo *et al.*, 2015) and Turkey (İflazoğlu and Hong, 2012) have reported similar findings.

Personality

Lubbers, van der Werf, Kuyper and Hendriks (2010), in a study of approximately 9,000 Dutch secondary students, demonstrated that personality influences homework behaviour. The analysis controlled for cognitive ability, ability group, gender and ethnic minority status. Three types of learning strategies were revealed: critical strategy (a tendency to do more work than is required and to form one's own opinions), integrative strategy (a tendency to try to grasp the meaning of the material by relating and structuring), and memorizing and rehearsal. Conscientious students spent more time on homework, procrastinated less, and used all learning strategies more than less conscientious students. A similar pattern was observed for Agreeableness, although this was not related to critical strategy use. Extraverts used more surface strategies and less critical strategies than introverts and procrastinated less. There was no difference in homework time between extraverts and introverts. Emotionally stable students spent less time on homework than neurotic students, and procrastinated more. Their strategy use revealed that they used their time more efficiently than neurotic students. Autonomous students procrastinated more and used all strategies more than less autonomous students.

Overall, research suggests that many factors at the level of the individual contribute to approaches to homework, whether in relation to age, ability or personality. What is less clear is how pupils' attitudes to homework change, and the interrelationship between these different factors.

The homework environment

The advice usually given in relation to studying is to work in a quiet place where disturbance will be minimal; however, this advice is rarely taken and the evidence suggests that for some pupils it may be not only impossible but inappropriate. Many children do their homework with music or the TV playing (MacBeath and Turner, 1990; Patton, Stinard and Routh, 1983; Wober, 1990, 1992; Kotsopoulou and Hallam, 2010). Pupils have reported that these provide companionship and help overcome the loneliness of doing homework. More commonly, pupils said that they found it easier to concentrate with music in the background because it either shut out other distractions or 'built a wall of sound behind which they were able to retreat'. Some teachers have been sufficiently convinced of the value of music for enhancing their pupils' concentration that they have allowed them to listen to music in class. Teachers reported that this was beneficial for pupils who were easily distracted by what was going on around them (MacBeath and Turner, 1990). Some pupils said that watching TV helped them to concentrate, but for many it provided an intermittent distraction because it 'eased the pain' (MacBeath and Turner, 1990). These findings are supported by Patton, Stinard and Routh (1983). TV can also act to occupy someone else who might otherwise be distracting (Wober, 1990). Controlled studies of the effects on studying of listening to music or the radio have had mixed results. While verbal material often acts as a distraction (Mitchell, 1949), the effect of music can be positive (Miller, 1947; Mitchell, 1949), but complex multifaceted models are necessary to account for its effects (Hallam and MacDonald, 2016).

MacBeath and Turner (1990) established that pupils adopt different patterns of doing homework. Some children do homework as soon as they get home, others pace the work, starting, taking a break to watch TV, then doing more homework, others need a break when they get home and do homework later in the evening or the next morning. Primary school children tend to do their homework as soon as they get in from school or in the early evening. As pupils progress through secondary school the time of starting work tends to be later. Late evening is most popular in mid-secondary (around age 13–14). During the 1990s in the UK there was little tradition of working with friends in doing homework, although phone calls might be made to clarify issues (MacBeath and Turner 1990; MacBeath, 1996). Hong and Milgram (1999) suggest that pupils cannot always work in the way they prefer because of physical or parental constraints.

There also seem to be cultural and gender differences in preferences for different working environments. Hong and Milgram (1999) found that US secondary students preferred more informal conditions for homework, including music, refreshments, learning with adults present and auditory learning, while students in Korea preferred more formal conditions. This is supported by Kotsopoulou and Hallam (2010), who found cultural differences between Greek, US, UK and Japanese students in their preferences for listening to background music while studying. Overall, the Japanese students listened to the least music, the Greeks the most. A key finding from this research was that, with age, students became better able to identify when music was distracting them from their work and were more inclined to take steps to remove the music. Among Turkish students, older students who preferred to complete homework in a quiet area rated themselves more highly on homework achievement than students who preferred background music did (İflazoğlu and Hong, 2012). In a study of low-income students, Bempechat, Li, Neier, Gillis and Holloway (2011) reported that most students did their homework alone, listening to either music or the television, in their rooms (on their beds, at their desks, or on the floor), or in their kitchens or living rooms.

In 1990, apart from time spent on homework the most common leisure activity reported by school pupils in the UK was watching TV. This was followed by going out, playing with friends, taking part in sports, listening to music, reading, or playing with a computer (MacBeath and Turner, 1990). Some studies suggest that watching TV does not prevent pupils from doing homework (Keith, Reimers, Fehrmann, Pottebaum and Aubey, 1986; Holmes and Croll, 1989; MacBeath and Turner, 1990; Epstein, 1988). However, Cooper, Valentine, Nye and Lindsay (1999) found a significant negative association between time spent watching TV and test scores in mathematics and English, and Xu and Wu (2013) demonstrated that homework management was negatively associated with time spent watching television. Keith, Keith, Troutman *et al.* (1993) found an indirect effect. Secondary students who spent more time on homework spent less time watching TV, and time spent on homework was related to test scores, but TV viewing and test scores were not directly related. Aksoy and Link (2000) found that extra daily minutes spent in mathematics classes and in doing homework increased students' mathematics test scores, while extra hours per day of watching television impacted negatively on test scores. However, the number of hours spent on maths each week was not statistically significant, only daily minutes per class period were.

Overall, the evidence from studies regarding watching TV and doing homework is mixed.

Homework resources

Historically, research demonstrated that where students had a desk, a dictionary and a computer at home they tended to have higher test scores (Martin, Mullis, Beaton *et al.*, 1997; Mullis, Martin, Beaton *et al.*, 1997). Some pupils in English and Welsh secondary schools reported, however, that they had insufficient books at home to support their learning (M. Johnson, 1999), although in 1999 Weston reported that 57 per cent of Key Stage 3 pupils had access to a home computer.

More recently, Kitsantas, Cheema and Ware (2011), drawing on analysis of the USA PISA 2003 data for mathematics among 5,200 15-year-olds, found that students' having more homework resources was associated with higher academic achievement. Homework resources included a desk, a room of their own, a quiet place to study, a computer for schoolwork, internet access, a calculator, books to help with their homework, and dictionaries. On average, White students had 10 per cent more homework support resources than Black students, 13 per cent more homework support than Hispanic students, and 4 per cent more homework support than students who identified themselves as belonging to multiple/other races. Asian (Chinese and Japanese) students had approximately 11 per cent more homework support than Black students and 14 per cent more homework support than Hispanic students. It seemed that more support resources increased self-efficacy in students (Kitsantas, Cheema and Ware, 2011). As with earlier research, these findings may simply reflect the economic and educational status of the family, a known strong predictor of educational attainment, rather than indicating that this equipment of itself will assist students to increase their attainment. It is also known that children from disadvantaged homes may attend under-resourced schools (Harper and Anglin, 2010).

Perceptions of a digital divide have raised concerns that students from disadvantaged families are further disadvantaged by having no computers at home. To an extent the emergence of Web 2.0 technologies and mobile devices has changed this, since even the very disadvantaged have mobile phones (Walsh, Lemon, Black, Mangan and Collin, 2011); however, there remain many parts of the world where students lack reliable high-speed internet connections, or where the one mobile phone or computer is shared by many members of the family. Among low- and middle-income families in the USA many parents and their children are under-connected (Rideout and Katz, 2016). Where families were living below the median income level, one in five connected to the internet only through a mobile device. As Rideout and Katz point out, this is a clear hindrance for students trying to research and write papers or complete online work.

Across OECD countries, the average amount of time that students spend online during a typical weekend day does not differ across socio-economic groups. Indeed, in some countries students from poorer families spend more time online than students from wealthier families. What is notable, and relevant in the use of technology for homework, is that a digital divide persists in the way in which students use technology. Advantaged students are more likely than disadvantaged students to search for information or read news online (OECD, 2016).

The differential access of students to books, mobile phones and high-speed internet connections at home may limit the extent to which some students can gain the most benefit from completing their homework. Students themselves report difficulties in accessing the internet outside school to complete their homework

(Project Tomorrow, 2015), and there are numerous reports in the news of students using hotspots in cafes or outside school to try to do their homework. Homework clubs and study centres can address some of these resource issues (see Chapter 3).

Technology, multitasking and homework

The significant increase in the use of technology, including games and social media, means that these activities form a regular part of the home environment for many students. The number of televisions and personal computers per household has grown, the growth of broadband access has increased computing potential on home computers, mobile phones and other devices, and the options for devices on which to listen to music, as well as access to different types of music, have expanded (Pabilonia, 2015). While access to the internet has become for many students a prerequisite for homework completion, in terms of searching for information, accessing school-hosted virtual learning environments and seeking help, it also forms a fundamental part of the way in which young people lead their lives and engage in socializing and entertainment. It isn't just the level of access that has changed. Kenyon (2008), using UK time use data, has shown that the internet has changed how we use our time – both in the choice of activities and in the extent to which we multitask. As early as 2006, a study of diary recordings from 694 3rd–12th grade US students showed that they were frequently (65 per cent of the time) doing something else when their main activity was doing homework on the computer (Foehr, 2006).

Pabilonia (2015), using time-diary data, further demonstrated the prevalence of multitasking while doing homework. Interestingly, while girls spent more time doing homework than boys, they spent more of that time doing simultaneous activities than boys. Rosen, Carrier and Cheever (2013) showed that students who used Facebook while doing homework had lower grade point averages. Dividing attention between homework and other activities, especially electronic media activities such as watching TV or using a computer for leisure purposes, may have negative consequences for students' academic success (Pabilonia, 2015). Among Turkish students, those who spent less time watching TV or videos or playing computer games during a week had more positive behaviour and a better attitude towards homework practices than those who spent more time on these out-of-school activities (Deveci and Önder, 2015).

An aspect that has received little attention to date is how students engage in social networking sites (SNS) as part of homework practices. Asterhan and Bouton (2017), using two surveys of Israeli, Hebrew-speaking teenagers (N1 = 206 and N2 = 515), have demonstrated how teenagers are using SNS technology for academic purposes rather than just for socializing and entertainment. The students in this study regarded online peer-to-peer knowledge sharing positively and believed that it improved their academic performance. The study materials most frequently shared were administrative messages, snapshots, handouts and peer assistance. Sharing of content summaries was less frequent. Although solved homework assignments were shared (copied) the least, more than a quarter of the students in both studies reported doing this very frequently.

Homework distraction

Other researchers have explored homework distraction, particularly in relation to technology. Given that homework is characterized by less supervision, structure and specified time than class-based study (Xu, 2015; Wolters, 2011), it is hardly surprising that pupils are often distracted from homework tasks. Distraction has an adverse effect on task completion, knowledge acquisition, application and academic performance (Jacobsen and Forste, 2011; Junco and Cotten, 2011). The rise in new media and its increased functionality and ease of operation means that such devices present an easy outlet for coping with the boredom and negative experiences associated with homework (David, Kim, Brickman, Ran and Curtis, 2015). In the study by Foehr (2006), for example, when computer-based homework was the main activity, 50 per cent of the time students were using other media (e.g. text messaging, surfing websites, using e-mail, and playing computer games and video games).

Xu (2010b), drawing on survey data from 969 US 8th- and 11th-grade students, demonstrated that at the individual level homework distraction was negatively related to affective attitude, homework environment, academic achievement, learning goals and issues related to adults. Interestingly, given the consideration of gender differences earlier in this chapter, boys reported statistically lower levels of homework distraction than girls. Students who spent more time on television, extra-curricular activities and paid jobs reported that they were more likely to be distracted while doing homework. At the class level, older students were more likely to be distracted while doing homework than their younger, 8th-grade, students. Gender differences were also revealed in a study of 1,799 10th- and 11th-grade students (aged 15–16) in China regarding mathematics homework (Xu, 2015). Here the research distinguished between conventional and tech-related distractions and through factor analysis argued that these are factorially distinct. Girls were more likely to be side-tracked by conventional and tech-related distractions (Xu, 2015).

While distraction has an adverse effect on task completion, knowledge acquisition, application and academic performance, it is important to recognize that some distractions (e.g. listening to music) may have beneficial qualities as a motivational or emotional aid.

Extra-curricular activities and homework

The timing of homework, as something that takes place after school, means that it is subject to competition from other activities, e.g. television, music, sport and other extra-curricular activities, many of which could be said to be more appealing than homework. Pupils, in undertaking homework, inevitably give up other possible activities, and this can cause conflict (Black, 1990).

Extra-curricular activities, including sports, clubs, music, art and drama, have many positive effects on education, including better behaviour, better grades, school completion, characteristics that help them to become successful adults. They also have a social aspect (Massoni, 2011). Participating in activities has been linked to greater school attachment and sense of belonging, better academic achievement, higher academic aspirations, and less risky behaviours such as alcohol and drug use or dropping out of school (Darling, 2005; Eccles and Barber, 1999; Fredricks and Eccles, 2008).

Cooper, Valentine, Nye and Lindsay (1999), in a study in the USA, supported these findings. Exploring the relationships between five after-school activities and academic achievement, they reported that pupils who spent more time on extra-curricular activities and less time watching TV or in employment achieved significantly higher test scores and better teacher-assigned grades. These relationships held even when background factors were controlled for, for example gender, ethnicity, age, and eligibility for free school meals. Also in the USA, Mahoney, Harris and Eccles (2006) found that young people who participated in extra-curricular activities demonstrated healthier functioning on indicators ranging from academic achievement, school completion, psychological adjustment and lowered rates of smoking and drug use to the quantity and quality of interactions with their parents.

An Australian survey of 1,504 adolescents from 26 diverse secondary schools indicated that adolescents from low-socio-economic-status schools who participated in extra-curricular activities had a more positive general self-worth and social self-concept than adolescents from similar socio-economic schools who did not participate in any extra-curricular activities (Blomfield and Barber, 2011). It is plausible to suggest that by engaging in structured extra-curricular activities students are being provided with opportunities to reinforce skills that relate to homework, for instance self-regulation, concentration, collaboration and goal-directed behaviour.

The evidence suggests that students may benefit from involvement in a wide range of activities, not only doing homework. There are indications that extra-curricular activities can be especially beneficial to students from low-SES schools in the development of self-worth and social self-concept. It may also be that students who become involved in many extra-curricular activities are those who are already high attainers and simply seek out new challenges and activities.

Employment

As students get older, part-time work becomes an important activity, competing with homework. There are suggestions that part-time work can have a serious impact on study time and motivation to study (MacBeath and Turner, 1990). Although Holmes and Croll (1989) indicated that undertaking part-time employment was not related to time spent on homework, more recent research among high school students has shown it to reduce the time spent on homework (DeSimone, 2006; Kalenkoski and Pabilonia, 2009, 2012). While employment offers students valuable work experience, working long hours is associated with lower achievement. It also decreases the time that students can spend on other extra-curricular activities. Using time-diary data from the American Time Use Surveys, Kalenkoski and Pabilonia (2009) examined the effects of high school students' employment on the time they spend on other major activities. Being employed reduced a student's daily homework time on a school day by 45 minutes, a substantial amount given that the average daily time spent on homework across the entire sample of students was 49 minutes. Employment also reduced screen time (TV, computer use for leisure, internet surfing, chat and video games).

Conclusions

Students generally seem to believe that homework is important in helping them do well at school. Many, though, especially older students, find homework boring, are unclear about what is required and feel that it is not always related to the work they are doing in class. Research into students' approaches to homework has revealed different homework patterns and learning experiences, and drawn attention to the importance of developing study strategies, thinking skills and self-regulation when undertaking homework. Studies have also demonstrated that effective homework management is associated with academic achievement.

There remains a wealth of research exploring gender differences in relation to homework. While evidence often suggests that girls adopt a more conscientious approach to homework and spend more time on it, this is not always the case, since cultural influences and ability are influential here.

Extra-curricular activities and employment provide other opportunities for children and young people to develop new skills and support their emotional and social development. Schools need to be confident when setting homework that it is of real value in supporting learning and increasing attainment.

Rapid expansions in technology mean that many children multitask when completing homework. New areas of research are looking specifically at traditional and tech-based homework distraction. While technology has many affordances for new avenues of engaging homework tasks and support for students, many children and their families remain under-connected to high-speed access.

CHAPTER 5: KEY POINTS

There is wide variation in the amount of homework set and the amount completed by individual pupils.

Time spent on homework may not equate with interest or effort, since individual pupils may need different amounts of time to complete homework tasks.

Where students regard homework quality as high, value the tasks set and are provided with meaningful feedback, these characteristics are associated with greater effort.

To support students with homework, teachers need to give attention to the development of thinking skills and self-regulated learning strategies to assist students in the management of homework and to support them in developing resilience when faced with challenging tasks.

Students' attitudes, engagement and approaches to homework are mediated by multiple factors, including age, ability, gender, personality, local differences and cultural influences.

The home environment remains an important place for students to complete homework.

Technological developments have changed the way in which young people engage in homework completion.

The availability of resources to assist with homework completion is important. In setting homework, teachers need to be mindful that different students have different access to digital technologies.

Chapter 6

Parents' perspectives on homework

This chapter considers the role that parents play in homework. It considers the evidence relating to the impact of parental support for homework on attainment, the different types of parental support, the approaches to homework that parents adopt, and the impact of children's characteristics on the way that parents interact with them in relation to homework. First the issues pertaining to homework in primary and secondary schools are considered, and then homework and family relationships, parental insecurities, issues for particular groups of parents, parents' perceptions of the purpose of homework, international perspectives, school–home relationships and home tutoring.

There has been much interest over the years, from researchers, parents, politicians and the media, in parental involvement in children's education (Dearing, Kreider, Simpkins and Weiss, 2006; Desforges and Abouchaar, 2003; Epstein and associates, 2009; Fan and Chen, 2001; Hill and Chao, 2009; Hoover-Dempsey, Battiato, Walker *et al.*, 2001; Sheldon and Epstein, 2002). There is a further literature documenting the connection between parenting, parental involvement and children's academic achievement (e.g. Hill and Wang, 2015; McGill, Hughes, Alicea and Way, 2012; Silinskas, Niemi, Lerkkanen and Nurmi, 2013). Most parents want to support their children's academic development. This support can take many forms. It can involve having high aspirations, discussing educational issues, attending parents' meetings, participating in school activities and supporting children in doing their homework. Overall, parents have an important role to play in their child's motivation for education and personal development. Where parents support their children's intellectual development, the kinds of activities that they share can accustom children to the kinds of tasks that they will face in school (Grolnick and Slowiaczek, 1994). In adolescence, taking part in academically enriching practices at home is an important predictor of progress. Parents' negative attitudes towards school and homework can have a detrimental impact on their children's attitudes and behaviour (Sylva, Melhuish, Sammons *et al.*, 2014). Across the age range, children's attitudes towards homework are positively associated with those of their parents (Cooper, Lindsay, Nye and Greathouse, 1998).

To summarize, the strongest relationship between parental engagement and attainment occurs in relation to parental aspirations. The weakest relationship is with homework. Overall, parents' aspirations and expectations of their child's learning have a greater influence on their child's academic attainment than specific activities related to homework (Fan and Chen, 2001; Jeynes, 2007).

The impact of parental support for homework on attainment

Most parents do try to ensure that their children complete homework (Keys, Harris and Fernandes, 1995). However, the evidence regarding the impact of parental support for homework is mixed. Some research has suggested that parental help with homework improves achievement (Brooks, 1916; Maertens and Johnston, 1972; Keith, Reimers, Fehrmann *et al.*, 1986; Chen and Stevenson, 1989; Bowen and Bowen, 1998; Chen and Uttal, 1988; Cooper, Jackson, Nye and Lindsay, 2001; Pomerantz and Eaton, 2001), while other research suggests that the impact of parental involvement is inconclusive or that the effects are negligible (Rankin, 1967; Hinckley, 1979; Epstein, 1983, 1988; Miller and Kelley, 1991; Wolf, 1979; Levin, Kevy-Shiff, Appelbaum-Peled *et al.*, 1997; Dumont, Trautwein, Lüdtke *et al.*, 2012). For instance, Hill and Tyson (2009), focusing on middle school pupils, carried out a meta-analysis of 50 studies published between 1985 and 2006. Overall, there was a positive relationship between parental involvement and academic achievement; academic socialization (expectations, aspirations, learning strategy discussion, planning for the academic future) had the most significant impact. A weaker relationship was found between school-based involvement and some home-based activities, but this relationship did not include assisting children with homework, although providing an appropriate structure, environment and material conducive to learning did have a statistically significant impact. Similarly, in a meta-synthesis, Wilder (2014) concluded that there was no positive relationship between homework assistance and student academic achievement, and that in some cases homework assistance was negatively correlated with achievement. Parental aspirations were positively related with achievement across different grade levels and ethnic groups, but the strength of that relationship depended on the type of assessment used to measure student achievement. Parents' aspirations seemed to operate through mediating students' self-efficacy beliefs, intrinsic motivation and behavioural engagement in school, and these effects were moderated by ethnic group (Fan, Williams and Wolters, 2012). The mixed results regarding assistance with homework may be mediated by the type of involvement that parents have with their children's homework.

Types of parental support for homework

Several ways in which parents can support homework have been suggested. Le Métais (1985) and MacBeath and Turner (1990) proposed three main roles: monitoring, support and help. Cooper, Lindsay and Nye (2000) also suggested three dimensions, a suggestion based on a survey of over 700 parents in three school districts in the USA:

support for pupils' autonomy, direct involvement in homework, and elimination of distractions. For secondary school pupils a further dimension, which was called parental interference, emerged. This included interventions to speed up the process of doing homework, helping with homework that was supposed to be completed independently and involvement that, counterproductively, made the task harder.

Pomerantz and colleagues (Pomerantz, Grolnick and Price, 2005; Pomerantz, Moorman and Litwack, 2007) distinguished four forms of parental involvement:

- autonomy support vs control (parents support children in developing their own schedules for doing homework as opposed to making decisions without children's input);
- process vs person focus (parents help their children focus on the process as opposed to emphasizing achievement);
- positive vs negative affect (parents establish a sense of connectedness with children by maintaining positive affect as opposed to being hostile and critical when checking students' homework; and
- positive vs negative beliefs about children's potential (parents trust their children's capabilities to do well as opposed to focusing on avoiding failure).

Lorenz and Wild (2007) also proposed four dimensions: autonomy support practices, control, structure and emotional involvement.

Five styles of homework support were identified by Solomon, Warin and Lewis (2002) in interviews with 58 families with teenagers aged 11–16: no particular help (16 per cent), praise and unconditional support (7 per cent), promoting autonomy but being available when needed (parents as responsive helpers) (48 per cent), homework support as proactive involvement (encouragement and guidance) (17 per cent), and monitoring and parental control (12 per cent).

Adopting a different approach, Hoover-Dempsey, Battiato, Walker *et al.* (2001) suggested that support could take many forms, ranging from establishing structures for undertaking homework to teaching for understanding and developing student learning strategies. They proposed that parent behaviours influenced students largely through the psychological mechanisms of encouragement, modelling, reinforcement and instruction, and that these influenced success because they supported student attributes related to achievement, for instance perceptions of personal competence and self-regulatory skills. Dotterer and Wehrspann (2016) supported the finding that parental involvement was positively associated with the behavioural and cognitive engagement of their children in school. This in turn was associated with their children having more positive experiences in school, greater self-esteem and academic competence, and higher grades. Overall, it seems that there are a range of different parental approaches to homework and that these mediate its effectiveness (Darling and Steinberg, 1993).

While researchers have conceptualized parents' support for homework in slightly different ways, there is general agreement that parents can adopt a range of approaches that range from extreme control to support of autonomous learning. The key issue is whether different kinds of parental involvement have an impact on attainment. The next section sets out the evidence that explores which parental behaviours are most effective.

The impact of parents' homework style on the relationship with attainment

The exact process by which parental involvement influences student outcomes in terms of achievement is not fully understood. However, there is evidence that parental expectations and some types of support for homework are important in determining the time spent doing homework (Natriello and McDill, 1986; Holmes and Croll, 1989; MacBeath and Turner, 1990; M. Chen and Ehrenberg, 1993). One research approach assumes that there is a direct link between parental involvement and pupil achievement and uses the reported beliefs of parents to predict student outcomes (e.g. X. Fan and Chen, 2001; Jeynes, 2007). Another strand assumes that it is students' perceptions of parental involvement that are important (e.g. Ibañez, Kuperminc, Jurkovic and Perilla, 2004). The relationship between these different measures may vary, depending on the particular aspect of involvement being assessed. For instance, Trautwein and Kropf (2004) reported that ratings of motivation made by parents and their children were similar, but that there was greater difference in relation to homework behaviour.

Different forms of parental support for homework have different impacts on attainment, particularly in secondary education (e.g. Cooper, Lindsay and Nye, 2000; Dumont, Trautwein, Lüdtke *et al.*, 2012; Pomerantz, Grolnick and Price, 2005). Overall, regardless of grade level, where parents adopt controlling behaviours relating to homework and offer help when it is not wanted there is a negative relationship with homework motivation, effort and achievement. Children are particularly vulnerable to negative comments from parents when they are struggling with homework and their emotional well-being may suffer (Offer, 2013). Karbach, Gottschling, Spengler, Hegewald and Spinath (2013) found that academic achievement in mathematics and German was negatively associated with parental control and parents structuring homework activities, and in particular with excessive control and pressure on children to complete assignments as well as rules about homework and schoolwork. Supporting this, Núñez, Suárez, Rosário, Vallejo, Valle and Epstein (2015) showed that perceived parental homework control was directly and negatively related to academic achievement, particularly for pupils in secondary education. Dumont, Trautwein, Nagy and Nagengast (2014) also reported a negative effect of perceived parental homework control on academic achievement, although in middle school this was indirectly affected by homework procrastination, in other words by the children putting off doing their homework. They argued that parental control as perceived by children was detrimental to children's motivation and academic achievement. Overall, where the parental approach is based on control, there are no effects or negative effects on attainment. Higher control is linked to lower performance (Pomerantz, Grolnick and Price, 2005). In addition, Donaldson-Pressman, Jackson and Pressman (2014) argue that parents' engagement in a high degree of correction and instruction in the early grades can lead to a pattern of dependency that persists throughout the child's school career. In such circumstances, assistance from parents can be academically and behaviourally detrimental.

In contrast, when parents support children to become autonomous learners there tends to be a positive association with homework outcomes (Hoover-Dempsey, Battiato, Walker *et al.*, 2001; Niggli, Trautwein, Schnyder, Lüdtke and Neumann, 2007; Pomerantz, Grolnick and Price, 2005; Pomerantz, Moorman and Litwack, 2007; Warton, 2001; Gonida and Cortina, 2014). Parents who are involved positively with homework, allowing their children to take the initiative to solve their own problems, focusing on the pleasure of learning and only helping when needed, tend to have higher-achieving children (Pomerantz, Moorman and Litwack, 2007). Parental responsiveness and the provision of some structure during homework involvement predicts less homework procrastination and more effort and achievement (Dumont, Trautwein, Nagy and Nagengast, 2014). It also supports positive motivation towards completing homework (Dumont, Trautwein, Lüdtke *et al.*, 2012).

In a videotaped study of 61 elementary school children in interactions with their mothers in a homework-like task related to reading achievement, Doctoroff and Arnold (2017) found that children displaying higher task engagement performed better and that support for autonomy was a significant predictor of child task engagement when other parenting values were controlled for. Further, Pomerantz, Ng and Wang (2006) found that the mother's positive approach during homework buffered children from adopting a helpless orientation towards their schoolwork. Early research also suggested that authoritative parenting (Baumrind, 1971, 1989) was associated with more effective scaffolding of children's learning and led to superior learning outcomes in mathematics homework (Pratt, Green, MacVicar and Bountrogianni, 1992). Parental support seems to foster positive engagement with school and greater intrinsic motivation for homework (d'Ailly, 2003). It also encourages persistence when coping with challenging situations, particularly in children at secondary school (Nolen-Hoeksema, Wolfson, Mumme and Guskin, 1995). Explaining to students that they can overcome difficulties may help them to improve their intrinsic motivation and defeat procrastination (Katz, Kaplan and Buzukashvily, 2011; Katz, Eilot and Nevo, 2014). Unfortunately, there are some children, particularly from minority groups, who may believe that they cannot turn to their parents for help as they will not be able to help them. Such children are vulnerable to negative academic outcomes (Martinez, 2011).

It seems that the way parents engage with homework influences student success primarily because it supports student attributes related to achievement, e.g. perceptions of personal competence and self-regulatory skills. Parents can encourage and model important learning skills, reinforce behaviours and attitudes related to learning and instruct their children about ways to enhance learning. This can also have a positive impact on mental health (Kenney-Benson and Pomerantz, 2005) and behaviour (Grolnick and Slowiaczek, 1994).

Student characteristics mediate parents' expectations and students' relationships with homework. For instance, in Singapore, using data from 2,648 secondary school students, Luo, Ng, Lee and Aye (2016) found that students' mathematics self-efficacy, values and achievement emotions mediated parental expectations and students' homework effort positively and had a negative impact on distraction. Trautwein, Lüdtke, Kastens and Köller (2006) also found that parental involvement in student learning was positively associated with students' expectancy and value beliefs about homework.

Family help is positively related to students' ability to manage their homework and negatively to them becoming distracted (Xu, 2010b; Xu and Wu, 2013). Xu and Corno (2006) and Xu (2007) found that girls and those students who received family help reported using self-motivation strategies more frequently during homework (Xu, 2007).

Closely linked with parental control of homework is the way parents have an influence on the homework environment, for instance in stipulating when and where children can do homework. Cooper, Lindsay and Nye (2000) described this as the 'elimination of distractions' and included making pupils complete homework before undertaking other activities, placing limits on TV viewing and checking that homework had been completed. Keith, Keith, Troutman *et al.* (1993) conceptualized this as a distinctive parental approach that was not related to other aspects of parental involvement in doing homework, for instance autonomy, direct involvement in homework, discussion about homework, or involvement in school activities.

Parents may inhibit pupils' efficacy in doing homework by controlling the environment. Some researchers have suggested that parents should identify their children's learning preferences and help them adapt the environment to suit these (E. Hong and Milgram, 1999; Perkins and Milgram, 1996). For instance, Hong and Milgram (1999) found that the greater the gap between the student's preferred and actual conditions of homework the lower the level of achievement. Preference was divided into four sub-categories, organizational, surroundings, perceptual-physical (auditory, visual, tactile, kinaesthetic, intake and mobility) and interpersonal (alone or with peers). Parental knowledge about their children's homework preferences was positively related to children having both high achievement and a positive attitude towards homework (Hong and Lee, 2000). Children who share an understanding of the preferred conditions for learning at home with their parents tend to have more positive attitudes towards homework than those who do not (Perkins and Milgram, 1996).

In summary, the most effective approach for parents to adopt in relation to homework is to support their children in becoming autonomous learners by being responsive to their needs and modelling and subsequently reinforcing effective studying strategies. This promotes motivation and active engagement with homework and avoids the development of a dependent learning style. The extent to which such an approach is possible may depend on their child's attitudes towards homework and the nature of their relationship. Some parents actively involve themselves in homework by intervening in the actual process or setting strict parameters for the homework environment. Both can have a negative impact. Environmental restrictions that do not match the preferences of their children can be counterproductive.

The impact of children's characteristics on parental involvement

The relationship between parental involvement and student achievement is reciprocal; that is, student performance elicits a particular type of parental involvement, which in turn affects future achievement (Silinskas, Niemi, Lerkkanen and Nurmi, 2013). For instance, Knollmann and Wild (2007) found that parents' effectiveness in supporting homework effort varied across student differences in motivational orientation. More intrinsically motivated students reported more positive affect when parents offered autonomy support during homework involvement, whereas more extrinsically motivated students reported more positive responses to relatively direct parental help with homework.

Students' perceptions of the kind of goals that their parents value have been found to predict children's personal goals and goal-related behaviour (Friedel, Cortina, Turner and Midgley, 2007). Parental emphasis on mastery goals has been linked with children's adoption of mastery goals and subsequent achievement (Madjar, Shklar and Moshe, 2016). Conversely, where parents emphasize performance goals, their children tend to adopt a personal performance approach and performance-avoidance goals which have been associated with many negative outcomes such as surface-level processing and low subjective well-being (Kaplan and Maehr, 2007). Performance goals can also lead to dissonance between home and school.

The ways in which parents support homework, such as setting rules regarding school and home activities, may be prompted by the low academic achievement of their children. Students who perceive high levels of parental control may be viewed by their parents as needing close monitoring of homework because of their low level of attainment (Núñez, Suárez, Rosário, Vallejo, Valle and Epstein, 2015; Dumont, Trautwein, Nagy and Nagengast, 2014). In an early study, Epstein (1983) found that the time parents spent helping their children with homework correlated negatively with the child's reading achievement and was positively associated with discipline problems. Teachers are more likely to ask parents to be involved with their children's homework when children are experiencing difficulties (Epstein, 1983), and more parental help is likely to be given (Levin, Kevy-Shiff, Appelbaum-Peled *et al.*, 1997; Chen and Stevenson, 1989; Epstein, 1988).

Students with learning difficulties or behaviour disorders have more problems with homework than other students and are more likely to ask their parents for help (Anesko, Schoiock, Ramirez and Levine, 1987; Bryan and Nelson, 1994; Epstein, Polloway, Foley and Patton, 1993; Salend and Schliff, 1989). Their parents face particular challenges in supporting the completion of homework. Kay, Fitzgerald, Paradee and Mellencamp (1994) found that parents of children with a range of difficulties felt ill-equipped to help their children with their homework and wanted greater communication with teachers and schools. These parents perceived as the most appropriate kind of homework that based on 'real life' tasks that were individualized to meet the needs of pupils. Where parents were able to support their children, there were positive outcomes. Deslandes, Royer, Potvin and Leclerc (1999), in a comparison of pupils in mainstream classes and those educated separately, with learning difficulties or behavioural problems, found a positive relationship between parental monitoring of homework completion and the time pupils spent on homework, for children with special educational needs. Children of above average attainment can also experience problems with homework. For instance, Worrell, Gabelko, Roth and Samuels (1999) undertook a survey of the parents of gifted pupils and found that, while the children submitted homework on time, not all completed their homework successfully unless they had support. A substantial proportion had to be reminded to do homework, procrastinated and were easily distracted.

The way parents interact with lower- and higher-achieving students is different. Mayo and Siraj (2015), in a case study of 35 14–16-year-olds from low-income families, suggested a number of links between progress at secondary school and the home learning environment. Parents of boys who were not making progress at secondary school reported that they felt that they had missed an opportunity to develop positive attitudes to school and learning when their sons were at primary school. At secondary school, the way they supported their sons changed. Regulation in terms of time or routines disappeared and there was less direct help as work became more challenging. However, for pupils who achieved beyond what was predicted at primary school support at home was markedly different: it involved frequent conversations about school, regulation and routines around homework and leisure, and positive feedback, not just on achievements but also on behaviour that was perceived to demonstrate a positive attitude to learning.

The approach parents adopt to homework is, to a great extent, determined by their children's motivation to do homework and the extent to which they are capable of completing it unaided. Where children are struggling academically or lack focus when studying parents may have no alternative but to adopt a relatively controlling approach. It is easier to support and facilitate homework completion when children are well motivated and in control of the work that they are doing.

Parental involvement at primary and secondary school

In general, parents have more involvement in their child's schooling at primary level, and parental involvement in their child's education seems to have an impact regardless of grade level (Jeynes, 2007; Patall, Cooper and Robinson, 2008). The association between parental engagement with homework and student achievement is mediated by grade level (Skaliotis, 2010), involvement becoming less frequent as young people progress through school (Epstein and Lee, 1995; Hoover-Dempsey and Sandler, 1997; Gonida and Cortina, 2014; MacBeath and Turner, 1990). This may be because parents have a better mastery of subjects in the early grades and feel more able to offer help. Certainly, parents of elementary school children tend to help their children for longer and feel more confident in helping with reading and mathematics than do parents of older students (Dauber and Epstein, 1993). Older students may also seek greater independence. Indeed, Patall, Cooper and Robinson (2008) suggest that parents helping or providing guidelines for homework at secondary level may be counterproductive.

Cooper, Lindsay and Nye (2000) found that some parents interfered with homework when their children were in secondary school. This was particularly evident for girls and students in high grades. At elementary school, boys received more direct involvement from parents, while at secondary level the situation was reversed. Cooper and colleagues suggested that this was because older boys were expected to be more autonomous than females, although it may be that girls requested more support because of their anxiety about homework. Unsurprisingly, parents of younger children reported more direct involvement with homework, whereas older children were given more support for autonomy. In contrast, children's perceptions of parental involvement in homework and academic achievement were found to be related in junior high and high schools but not in elementary schools. The reason for this counter-intuitive finding may be that there is less variation in parents' approach to supporting homework at elementary level, or that young children are unable to perceive differences in parenting styles (Núñez, Suárez, Rosário, Vallejo, Valle and Epstein, 2015).

Overall, parents tend to engage with their children's homework more at primary level. The nature of homework tends to differ between primary and secondary school. Tasks set at primary school, for instance reading, and learning tables and spellings, may be more amenable to parental involvement, which may promote higher levels of engagement. If children enjoy doing homework and are given work matched with their current level of attainment, parents may be able to support autonomous learning even in young children. If this is not the case they may feel that they need to adopt a more controlling approach to ensure that homework is completed. Older children are expected to work more independently, so parental engagement with homework may be less, although this will depend on a range of factors related to the characteristics of the child and to the parents' aspirations for that child.

Family relationships and homework

There are considerable differences in the ways families approach homework. There are differences in physical arrangements, time organization and attention paid to procedural matters. Some families find it difficult to integrate homework into family life, while others find it easy to balance homework and social activities (McDermott, Goldman and Varenne, 1984). Typically, parents believe that it is their responsibility to support their children in doing homework (Epstein and Van Voorhis, 2012). However, homework presents a complex, multidimensional set of tasks for parents. They may feel ill-prepared to support their children with homework because of limitations in their knowledge and competing demands for their time and energy (Hoover-Dempsey, Bassler and Burow, 1995). Despite this, some parents believe that homework can support the development of strong bonds between them and their children and provide a vehicle for communication (MacBeath and Turner, 1990), although homework can also take up time that might be spent in more pleasurable family activities. When the latter occurs children's and parents' well-being may be affected negatively (Katz, Buzukashvili and Feingold, 2012; Offer, 2013).

While homework can offer a range of benefits, supporting academic learning, self-efficacy and motivation, it can also have negative consequences, including the generation of parent–child conflict (Cooper, Steenbergen-Hu and Dent, 2012). When parents help children with their homework there may be negative feelings, even if they are not openly articulated (Goodnow and Collins, 1990). This is particularly the case when parents are attempting to support children whose performance is less than optimal. In this situation, tensions are more likely to develop, which may lead to frustration and disappointment. This can be counterproductive to the child's functioning in school and to their general well-being (Cowan, Traill and McNaughton, 1998; Weston, 1999; Xu and Corno, 1998; Symeou, 2009). One study in the USA found that 50 per cent of parents surveyed said that they had had serious arguments with their children over homework, while 34 per cent indicated that it was a source of struggle and stress (Bennett and Kalish, 2006).

A study in the USA focused on family stress, in the context of the amount of homework that primary school children were set (Pressman, Sugarman, Nemon *et al.*, 2015). Family stress increased as homework load increased and as parents' capacity to assist decreased. Primary school children, up to about 3rd grade, were given about three times the recommended daily load of homework, which is ten minutes multiplied by the child's grade level (Cooper and Valentine, 2001; Cooper, 2007).

As parents and other caregivers perceived their efficacy in helping their children to be declining they were more likely to see homework as having a negative impact on their family. Children who disliked homework were more likely to be in homes that experienced high stress and tension.

Exploring the relationships between middle-class parents and their children in relation to homework, Cowan, Traill and McNaughton (1998) found that parents tended to construct their perception of their children in terms of which aspects of their child's behaviour resembled their own and which their partner's. Parents viewed aptitudes for subjects and attitudes to homework as part of their child's nature, made comparisons between siblings and experienced different emotions and homework scenarios with different siblings. The parents seemed to be trying to make sense of their children's development in relation to their progress at school and their own experiences of trying to help them. Homework served to heighten tensions in relationships, or it could be fun and rewarding. This did not necessarily depend on the child's progress at school but seemed to be related more to parental expectations. Xu and Corno (1998) carried out a similar study which suggested that middle-class parents, their 3rd-grade children and teachers shared similar views about the complex purposes of doing homework. It was seen as a challenge for parents and children, as taking time from other activities and, often, as emotionally draining. Parents reported providing guidance and adopting a range of strategies, including keeping their child on track and ameliorating difficult emotions. The children also adopted a variety of strategies to help them complete homework, including arranging the environment, managing time and monitoring their attention, motivation and emotions. Some of these strategies were similar to those adopted by their parents and had probably been learned through modelling. The strategies adopted to monitor motivation and emotion were less sophisticated and more variable than those for managing the environment. Learning to control emotions and motivation can be problematic. Despite this, some quite young children demonstrated that they were capable of managing their own homework.

In contrast to the studies described above, Chandler, Argyris, Barnes, Goodman and Snow (1983) observed the interactions of 32 low-income parent–child dyads and found the interactions generally to be positive, co-operative, productive and strikingly similar to those which would occur at school between teacher and pupil, which reflects Epstein's (1986) conceptualization of school-like families. Whether the lack of reported tension in these relationships reflected parenting styles different from those adopted by middle-class parents, or was related to a lack of high expectations and an acceptance of their children's limitations, is an open question.

At secondary level homework plays a central role in the relationships between some teenagers and their parents, some families experiencing considerable conflict. Goodnow and Collins (1990) and Hoover-Dempsey, Bassler and Burow (1995) reported that parents' theories about their children's abilities played a substantial part in their handling of homework. Parenting style depended on the history of individual parent–child relationships. Differences between siblings suggest that effective homework support is not just a question of effective parenting. Homework takes place within the context of the existing parent–child relationship (Dunn and Plomin, 1990; Dunn, 1993).

There has been little work on the influence of siblings on homework. McNaughton (1995) suggested that 4-year-olds were influenced by older siblings, who, by bringing books from school to read and doing written work, seemed to provide models of emerging literacy. Research from the literature on practising a musical instrument has shown that successful children often reported sibling influence as inspirational, leading to modelling. Other young musicians reported that siblings had bullied them into working with positive effects (Davidson, Howe and Sloboda, 1997).

Overall, it is clear that homework can be a source of extreme family stress. This may be because of the time it takes and the way that it can interfere with other family activities, the reluctance of some children to do their homework and the pressure that this puts on parents to ensure that it is completed, or the difficulties that parents experience when their children are struggling and they are trying to help. These stresses seem to be greater in higher-socio-economic-status families, which may have higher aspirations for the academic success of their offspring.

Parents' insecurities in relation to homework

Some parents report that they are inadequately equipped to help their children with homework because of their own limited education (MacBeath and Turner, 1990; Hoover-Dempsey, Bassler and Burow, 1995). Solomon, Warin and Lewis (2002) found that 31 per cent of parents were confident about the support they gave, 29 per cent felt that they were acting on behalf of the school, 20 per cent felt that they were acting on behalf of the child, and 20 per cent reported that they did not feel really capable. For 53 per cent homework was seen as part of their identity as a parent, for 14 per cent it was embedded in the parent–child relationship and represented enjoyment and closeness, while 25 per cent expressed anxiety about their child's future and 8 per cent identified conflicts over homework. Mothers, who are more frequently involved in homework than fathers (Gouyon, 2004), are sometimes afraid, especially in working-class families, of getting something wrong (Glasman, 1992). They may also worry that their children may not respect them if they cannot help them do their homework (Thin, 2008). The proportion of parents who feel insecure about helping with homework tends to increase as children progress through school. This can lead to a lack of interest and a failure, mainly on the part of the parents but sometimes also on that of the children, to place any importance on homework completion (Heller, Spooner, Anderson and Mims, 1988; Cooper, 1989a, 1989b; Toomey, 1989). Socio-economic and educational differences are important here. The more formal education parents have had, the more time their children spend on homework, particularly where the parents also have high aspirations (MacBeath and Turner, 1990). A home curriculum, which includes informed parent–child conversations, encouragement and discussion of leisure reading, deferral of immediate gratification to accomplish long-term goals, expressions of affection and interest in the child's progress at school and personal growth, is more likely to be in evidence where parents are well educated (Natriello and McDill, 1986). Parents who themselves have problems with literacy or numeracy tend to have children with similar problems, which suggests that homes can act as mediators for the transmission of intergenerational difficulties with literacy through the lack of an appropriate home curriculum (Adult Literacy and Basic Skills Unit, 1993).

Overall, homework can be a source of anxiety for parents, particularly when they feel they have insufficient skills to support their children. For parents who themselves have difficulties with literacy, supporting their children's development of literacy skills may be especially challenging. As children progress through school, parents tend to feel more insecure about helping with homework. This is exacerbated when they themselves have lower levels of education. Well-educated, middle-class parents tend to be advantaged in the ways in which they can support their children's education.

Homework issues for particular groups of parents

Parents of lower SES report being less able to provide appropriate accommodation for doing homework (Cooper, Lindsay and Nye, 2000), and they face more obstacles to participating in homework than their middle-class counterparts (Finders and Lewis, 1994; Lareau, 2000; Reay, 1998; Symeou, 2001, 2002; Vincent, 1996). Better-educated parents spend more time helping their children with homework (Guryan, Hurst and Kearney, 2008; Rønning, 2011), while lower-income parents are less likely to help with homework. They are just as likely as middle-class parents to monitor homework completion (Richards, Garratt, Heath, Anderson and Altintaş, 2016), and are more likely to interfere in relation to homework than to support their child's developing autonomy (Cooper, Lindsay and Nye, 2000). Single parents are particularly likely to experience difficulties in supporting homework (Reay, 1998; Maclachlan, 1996).

Strand (2011) notes an ethnic dimension to homework practice: British Indian pupils are more likely to spend time on homework, regardless of their SES. This may explain why these pupils seem to be better insulated from poverty's effect on progress than their peers from other British Asian backgrounds. A study in China that included 10,959 elementary school students found generally high levels of homework, as effort, not ability, is seen as key to improving attainment. Some parents and students from disadvantaged families approached homework as a way of compensating for an unprivileged background, and parents themselves assigned homework for their children to complete. Learning performance improved when a moderate amount of homework was assigned in this way. Despite this, middle-class children still had higher educational attainment (Zhao, Valcke, Desoete and Verhaeghe, 2017). Generally, parents from ethnic minorities and of low SES report that school practices frequently exclude them (Crozier, 1997; Reay, 1998; Bastiani, 1997).

While middle-class parents tend to be better able to support their children with their homework, there is evidence that those of lower SES do engage with their children in relation to homework, albeit in a different way. Despite this, homework does tend to maintain socio-economic differences in academic attainment. There are cultural differences in perceptions of the role of homework. In some cultures, effort is seen to underpin attainment, not ability. Where this is the case, more importance tends to be attached to homework.

Parents' perceptions of the purpose of homework

In the UK, parents' views of the purposes of homework tend to reflect those of teachers. Reinforcement and consolidation are seen as important functions, particularly at secondary level. Parents tend to emphasize reading and mathematics at primary level, while mathematics and English are considered most important at secondary level. Parents acknowledge a range of other purposes of homework, including increasing general knowledge, broadening outlook, doing something practical, establishing good study habits, improving communication, developing critical thinking skills and increasing family interaction. The kinds of homework cited as most useful to them as parents included: homework which 'keeps me in touch'; 'anything I can help with'; projects; 'anything of benefit to the child'; things that promote family discussion; practice in weak areas; research; encouraging out of school interests; listening; and encouraging self-discipline (MacBeath and Turner, 1990).

Not all parents believe that homework has a clear purpose. In one US survey, 40 per cent of parents reported that some homework was just 'busy work'. Families were critical when teachers failed to explain assignments to students in class, when assignments did not relate to classwork, and when students were unsure how to complete work. Sometimes they tried to motivate students by making the work more interesting (Markow, Kim and Liebman, 2007).

Overall, parents perceive the same value for homework as teachers do. Their preferences for homework cover a wide range of different types. They are sometimes critical of the homework that their children are given as they think it does not always reflect the purported aims and could be more motivating. They are also critical when they believe that it has not been explained clearly.

International perspectives on homework

The previous sections in this chapter have drawn on a range of international research. This section provides examples of how parents perceive homework in a sample of different countries around the world. Focusing on homework in Brazil, De Carvalho (2009) reported high levels of homework, with much school time spent on the collective correction of past homework, and the setting of new homework. Mothers in Brazil on the one hand expressed positive views of homework, understanding that it builds responsibility and autonomy, but on the other had negative experiences because their children did not want to complete it. This caused stress. To alleviate this, some mothers sought help from other children, neighbours or relations, as they felt that they were blamed by the school when homework was not completed.

In Cyprus, Symeou (2009) undertook 86 individual interviews and 18 focus groups with Greek Cypriot parents and found that primary-aged children had a lot of homework on a daily basis and that homework was viewed as extremely stressful. Parents complained about anxiety, shouting and reprimands, and the deprivation of social life because of lack of time. Parents of higher SES most frequently complained about the quantity of homework, while parents of rural and low-SES families faced most problems with the work set. Their children constantly sought their presence during homework, to give them confidence and encouragement and to ensure that the homework was completed. Their children generally had a negative attitude towards homework. The amount of homework was blamed on an overloaded curriculum and on constant changes in textbooks and teaching approaches. Mathematics was most often referred to as problematic, as parents did not understand how to help. Homework was often raised in teacher–parent meetings as parents sought advice on how to help their children. Those of moderate or high SES saw the value of homework as developing good study habits and preparing children for high school. Most of these parents had high-achieving children and were well educated themselves. Low-SES and rural parents saw homework as a medium for conversation with their children, as a means of communication with the school and as a way of assessing their child's progress and attainment. They supported homework, although it was disruptive to home life, as they believed that it was essential in any programme of education. Overall, parents saw homework as important and valuable.

In France, Safont-Mottay, Oubrayrie-Roussel and Lescarret (2009) studied 62 parent–child dyads in which the child was aged 6 or 9. Parents were more positive about homework than their children, but the children seemed to believe more in the benefits of homework than their parents. However, by the 3rd grade children were losing confidence in the usefulness of homework, whereas parents were more convinced of its utility. There were also opportunities for private tuition, which meant that some parents did not need to help with homework. In some working-class districts volunteers helped with homework (Glasman, 2009).

In Canada, Cameron and Bartel (2008), in a survey of 1,094 parents, revealed that over 28 per cent of 1st-grade and 50 per cent of 2nd-grade children were doing more than 20 minutes of homework a day. The type of homework most often set was drill and practice. Parents indicated that they helped a lot with homework and also that their children had a great many other activities that competed with homework and family time. Similarly, Deslandes, Royer, Potvin *et al.* (1999) surveyed parents and children in the 1st and 4th grades. Over 85 per cent of parents and 65 per cent of children stated that they were in favour of homework, although by the 4th grade the children were beginning to develop negative attitudes (Deslandes, 2009). Parents indicated that the most frequent types of homework were evaluation, memorization, exercises and continuation of work begun in class.

There are cultural differences in the extent to which parents believe that they should help their children with their homework. Completion of homework was considered to be solely the child's responsibility by 43 per cent of Japanese and 32 per cent of Chinese mothers compared with only 8 per cent of mothers in the USA (Chen and Stevenson, 1989). While the participating mothers from each country felt able to help with mathematics and reading homework, they differed in the extent to which they felt that they should help.

Internationally, parents share many similar concerns about homework. While they value homework, some find difficulty in getting their children to complete it and this causes stress in the family. Many feel inadequate to help their children, particularly those from low-SES families. There are also cultural differences in the extent to which parents feel that they should help with homework. These may be mediated by the extent to which other resources to support their children are available, for instance home tutoring and various types of group support (see Chapter 3).

Relationships between home and school

Parental involvement with homework means that a dialogue needs to develop between home and school. Communication between home and school can be problematic (Brown, 1993), and parents are often dissatisfied with the way schools set homework and the lack of information and guidance that they are given (Kibble, 1991; MacBeath and Turner, 1990). Parents are sometimes concerned that practices are not consistent in schools. At primary level, schools may not specify the time to be spent on homework and pupils may spend more time on their homework than the school suggests (Ofsted, 1995). Parents often feel that homework has little relation to the work in hand and is poorly set and marked late, and that there is a lack of pupil–teacher interaction, which results in poor feedback for the pupil (Heller, Spooner, Anderson and Mims, 1988; Rosenberg, 1989; Ulrich, 1989; Bechler, 1991; Hodapp and Hodapp, 1992; MacBeath and Turner, 1990). Parents believe that teachers are not always aware of how long it takes to do particular pieces of homework (Kibble, 1991). Schools often fail to explain homework to parents and do not consult them about the amount of homework. While expecting parents to support their children, they often do not wish to involve parents in developing their homework policy (Timperley, McNaughton, Parr and Robinson, 1992; Beresford and Hardie, 1996; MacBeath, 2000), thus ensuring that educational power is retained within the school (McNaughton, 1995). However, recent technological developments are making it easier for schools to communicate with parents about homework. These will be discussed in Chapter 7.

Home tutoring

In the latter part of the twentieth century, internationally, there was a considerable growth in out-of-school educational activities which were meant to supplement formal schooling (Baker, Akiba, LeTendre and Wiseman, 2001; Bray, 1999). This includes one-to-one tutoring taking place in the child's home. In England, Ireson and Rushforth (2014) explored why parents employed private tutors, collecting survey data from 1,170 parents and carrying out interviews with 58 parents. The most home support was provided for students in Year 6 as they were reaching the end of primary school and taking tests that would affect their educational opportunities at secondary school. Parents with higher educational levels who tended to value educational achievement and self-regulation were typically those providing higher levels of home support. For these parents, the employment of a private tutor was seen as part of their role. The need for a tutor was assessed against the family's existing resources to help. The parents wanted to increase their child's confidence, improve their understanding in particular subjects and help them with the tests. Chapter 3 explores the role of out-of-school tutoring at the individual or group level.

Conclusions

Most parents want to support their children in their education. There are many different ways in which they can do this, including support for homework, but it is parental aspirations that have the greatest impact on children's attainment. Despite this, many parents invest considerable time and effort into supporting homework. They are driven by concerns about their child's future. Some parents take a controlling approach to homework, which creates a climate of pressure to succeed. There can then be a cost in terms of the quality of the relationship between parent and child. The most effective way in which parents can help is by supporting their children to become autonomous learners. The extent to which this occurs depends on complex personal interactions that in part, depend on the characteristics of the child and their attitudes and aptitudes in relation to academic work. Family tensions can be created or exacerbated by children not wanting to do homework or struggling with its completion. In such circumstances, parental help with or supervision of homework may be counterproductive, inducing such resentment in offspring that homework is deliberately not completed. Parental help may also develop dependency or helplessness in the child.

Parents tend to be more involved in their child's homework at primary level, showing less engagement as they move on to secondary school. Many parents feel anxious about supporting homework, even at primary level, as they feel that they do not have sufficient knowledge or skills. This is particularly the case for parents from low-SES families and some minority groups. These and other concerns about homework tend to be shared internationally, although there are some cultural differences in the extent to which additional learning support is available at the individual or group level out of school time. Overall, many parents would like more information and help from schools on how they can support homework.

CHAPTER 6: KEY POINTS

Most parents want to support their children in their education.

Parental engagement with education can take many forms.

Parents' aspirations for their children have the strongest relationship with attainment. Supporting homework has a weaker effect than aspirations.

There are different kinds of parental involvement in homework, ranging from a controlling approach to support for autonomous learning. A controlling approach tends to have a negative impact on attainment, particularly at secondary level.

The approach to homework that parents adopt is related to the characteristics of their child.

Parents tend to be more involved with their child's homework at primary level.

Homework can lead to conflict and stress in families.

Some parents feel that they do not have the necessary knowledge and skills to help their children with their homework.

Homework is particularly challenging for parents from low socio-economic groups and some minority groups.

Parents tend to see the purposes of homework in a similar way to teachers.

While there are cultural differences, parents around the world share many of the same perceptions and concerns regarding homework. There are differences in the extent to which parents see homework as the child's responsibility.

Homework provides opportunities for links between home and school. Most parents would like more support from schools with homework.

Internationally, there has been an increase in home tutoring and other forms of extra-curricular support for learning.

Future directions

This chapter provides an overview of the key issues relating to homework, with particular reference to the roles of schools, teachers, children and young people, and parents. It also sets out advances in the use of technology in relation to homework, and other innovative ways of supporting homework. It concludes with a section that sets out the implications for different groups.

This review of the evidence relating to homework has attempted to cast light on issues that have caused controversy for almost a hundred years. It has demonstrated that there is no universally accepted perception of whether homework should be set, particularly for younger children, and that internationally there are a wide range of different policies and practices. In the UK, where homework policy and practice are entirely the responsibility of the school, there are opportunities for teachers to consider seriously how homework can enable full coverage of the curriculum and support students in their development of autonomous learning skills, thus enhancing their attainment.

Research on homework can only be understood within the historical and cultural context in which it is undertaken. Perceptions of the importance of homework are highly influenced by the economic, political, social and educational circumstances pertaining at the time. The relative advantages and disadvantages of homework take on lesser or greater importance depending on these circumstances.

If there is a coherent societal agenda that relates to education in general and homework in particular, then the amount of homework set, the age of the children for which it is set and the nature of that homework can be tailored to the aims of that agenda. For instance, if the aim is to promote independent learning in students, homework schedules can be devised that provide interesting tasks at a level that provides appropriate challenge to pupils, while ensuring success in order to provide intrinsic rewards for undertaking and completing the homework. If the aim is to engage parents with their children's homework, tasks can be devised that will require no expert knowledge on the part of the parents but which their life experiences will enable them to support. If the aim is to improve examination performance, homework can be designed to prepare children for examinations. Combinations of aims can be met over time through providing variety in homework. Unfortunately, in practice homework is rarely given this level of scrutiny. It is routinely given to satisfy school requirements or meet curriculum needs without sufficient consideration of its purpose or of the need to align tasks with aims.

Impact on attainment

The contribution made by homework to achievement is small compared with that made by prior knowledge and skills. Assessing the specific impact of homework on attainment is extremely difficult, as there are many confounding factors, relating not only to the individual student but also to the quality of the teaching, the nature of the homework set and the human and material resources that may be available to the student at home. High-attaining students tend to be set more homework, and they achieve at higher levels; homework makes some contribution, but their prior knowledge and skills account for much of the variance. At the individual level, there tends to be a negative relationship between attainment and the amount of time spent doing homework, which reflects the fact that those with less prior knowledge take longer to complete homework. While at secondary level homework does contribute to attainment, there may be a curvilinear relationship, moderate levels of homework being the most effective. Homework could be used to enable lower-attaining students to lessen the gap between their knowledge and that of their higher-attaining peers, but this rarely occurs. At primary level, there is much less evidence that homework is effective in raising attainment. One reason for this is that children who are struggling with the acquisition of basic skills in literacy and numeracy are encouraged to do more work at home with the support of their parents. In this case, research that examines the relationship between time spent doing homework and attainment will not show that more homework leads to greater attainment. It is also possible that many activities undertaken by parents with primary school children make a major contribution to their learning but are not counted as homework, such as playing games that require number or vocabulary skills, encouraging reading, enhancing general knowledge through family trips, and discussing educational issues.

The role of schools in homework

Schools are the source of homework and as such have responsibilities to ensure that its setting, monitoring and marking are undertaken in a way that optimizes its effectiveness and enhance the learning of those undertaking it. Schools also need to ensure that homework given for different subjects is balanced across the school week so that the workload for individual students is manageable. This means that schools need to have clear policies in relation to homework. However, there is a danger that such policies may be implemented inflexibly, with teachers setting homework because they feel they are required to do so even if it has no meaningful relationship with current aims in terms of the curriculum or required skills.

To support teachers in relation to homework, schools should provide training for their staff in how to make homework more effective. This is particularly the case where students have learning difficulties, since the evidence suggests that teachers need support to develop strategies to adapt homework to the needs of individual students. Teachers, at the start of their careers in schools, may lack the experience to set quality homework and provide quality feedback. As part of in-school training, they may benefit from collaborative approaches to designing homework and linking it with classroom learning. Schools should also ensure that there are appropriate technological resources to support homework. Homework clubs provide a vital resource here providing access to technology that students might not have at home. Other resources include online homework systems, interactive computer programs, educational apps and resources for flipped learning. It is important that the adoption of digital technologies does not disadvantage students from poorer backgrounds.

Young people might also benefit from schools giving them opportunities to discuss general issues relating to the management of homework. These could include strategies for planning and monitoring homework completion, how to use resources most effectively (books, materials, the internet), how to use self-testing in preparation for examinations, and how taking the time to really understand what is being learned supports memory.

If homework is important, it is important for all pupils. It should not be reserved for high achievers but used across the school as an integral part of the learning process. The provision of homework clubs or study centres where students can make use of a wide range of resources, with support from a teacher or another adult with relevant expertise, is particularly valuable for students who require additional support or who have inappropriate learning environments at home. Such centres have been shown to make an important contribution to student motivation, engagement and subsequent attainment.

Homework provides opportunities for links between home and school, but these are not always strong and most parents would like more support in relation to homework. At primary school, particularly for the youngest students, the involvement of parents in completing homework is crucial. Schools need to either offer parents guidance on how to support their children in completing homework or provide tasks that require no expert knowledge. Initiatives to support parents as they help their children to do their homework are most effective when the children are young and when parents are taught how to teach their children.

Teachers

The influence of teachers on the importance pupils attach to homework cannot be overestimated. The amount they set, whether it is collected in and the type of feedback given will all have an impact on the motivation of the pupils to complete it and the seriousness with which it is viewed by parents and carers. Schools typically do not reward students for completing homework. It is assumed that pupils will routinely complete it and will receive punishment if they do not. If teachers provide no constructive feedback on work or do not mark it at all there is no incentive for pupils to carry out the work. How well homework is done also depends on the clarity of the instructions given and the planning and thought put into its development. While homework can be seen as a way of ensuring that the curriculum is covered, it offers much wider opportunities. Teachers need to consider carefully what homework approaches will best meet the learning needs of their students. They need to be clear about why they are setting homework in general and about the exact purpose of each homework task. The quality of the thinking required of the pupil may be particularly important in this respect. In addition, encouraging pupils to evaluate their own work and increase their metacognitive skills will have long-term benefits. This can be achieved through adopting formative assessment techniques in the classroom and actively engaging students in their own learning and that of their peers.

Requiring students to do ever increasing amounts of homework has no real impact on their attainment. There is an optimal level beyond which increased effort will make little or no difference. Although research on the quality of the homework that is set is minimal, it is likely that quality is as important in raising attainment as the amount of time spent. From the pupil's perspective homework tasks need to be relevant. If they can be made interesting they are more likely to be completed. Teachers might consider offering pupils a choice of homework topics. Interactive computer homework packages that offer instant feedback may be particularly attractive to boys and may serve to reduce the disparity between boys and girls in time spent doing homework.

Overall, when teachers set homework it should have clearly specified aims that are aligned with the overall curriculum and with what students need to learn, and be designed to meet those needs. Students need to be made aware of the aims and purposes of particular pieces of homework and to be given clear instructions and guidance as to what they are to do. In order to motivate pupils to complete homework, teachers need to monitor its completion, mark it and provide constructive feedback, so that students know what to do to improve their learning in the future.

Children and young people

Pupils value homework as they see it as a means to enhance their attainment and future prospects. At the same time, they see it as an encroachment on their leisure time. They would like teachers to plan homework so that it is clearly related to ongoing classroom work, varied, manageable, and challenging but not too difficult. They believe that it should allow for individual initiative and creativity, and promote self-confidence and understanding. They would like schools to provide guidance and support and also recognize and reward completed work.

Students have responsibilities regarding homework. They may feel that it reduces the time that they have for their leisure pursuits, but they can take steps to become more efficient in completing homework. Approaching homework with a positive attitude, understanding how they learn best, ensuring that their environment supports that and making sure that they are clear about what they have to do will support homework efficiency. Learning to manage negative emotions and frustration is an important life skill that can be acquired through managing homework.

Parents

Most parents want to support their children in their education. The strongest impact that parents can have on attainment is through aspirations, not homework. Parents do not involve themselves with homework in the same ways. Some adopt a controlling approach, while others support autonomous learning. A controlling approach has a negative impact on homework outcomes and attainment. Supporting the development of autonomous learning has the most positive effect. The latter may be difficult when children are experiencing difficulties with homework, and it can lead to conflict and stress in families. Some parents feel that they do not have the necessary knowledge and skills to help their children with their homework and those from low socio-economic and some minority groups perceive homework as particularly challenging. Parents around the world share many of the same perceptions and concerns regarding homework. While homework provides opportunities for links between home and school, most parents would like more support with homework from schools.

Approaches to homework that can enhance learning outcomes

The rapid expansion of digital technologies means that schools worldwide are exploring how the use of technology by children and young people may influence and change the time, place and mode of completion of homework.

Flipped learning

Flipped learning, or flipped classrooms (see Chapter 3), requires students to undertake preparatory reading, watch videos, engage with other media or undertake research at home. In the USA and Canada, flipped learning is often associated with students watching a video of their teacher giving a lecture, but other approaches are evolving (see Box 7.1). Used effectively, flipped learning can enable teachers to use their analysis of homework responses to differentiate more effectively in class, enable teachers to focus on higher-order skills if routine facts have been understood by pupils before the lesson, and be used to introduce and stimulate initial questions and ideas before starting a topic.

Box 7.1: Flipped learning as a homework strategy to raise attainment

Shireland Collegiate Academy in England introduced flipped learning as a homework strategy to boost attainment. Central to their approach is that homework is being used by pupils to prepare for lessons rather than as a follow-up to the lesson. This means that children are more familiar with the topics to be covered and so can participate more confidently in class. Children are set well-crafted homework tasks, which they complete before a lesson. The children are directed to different websites, videos and resources, often placed on the schools' learning gateway. The teacher looks at the responses to homework and is able to modify the lesson to the children's understanding. Homework completion has increased, as has attainment, and behaviour has improved. More importantly, this approach enables the teacher to differentiate learning in the classroom and to prepare well-planned lessons.

(OCR and Shireland Collegiate Academy, n.d.)

Online resources to support homework

There has been a massive growth in resources, either freely available or on subscription, that schools and students are using to support homework. BBC Bitesize, for example (www.bbc.co.uk/education), is a free online study support resource for primary and secondary students across the UK. It is available on any device that can access the web, including mobile phones. Resources include video clips, activities and tests. Hegarty Maths (www.hegartymaths.com), originating in the UK and inspired by Khan Academy (see Box 7.2), provides videos and resources for all aspects of the mathematics curriculum. There are free and paid versions.

Box 7.2: Khan Academy: Online resources to support learning

Khan Academy, founded in 2006, describes its mission as providing 'a free world-class education for anyone, everywhere'. From its starting point in video instruction, Khan Academy has expanded its resources to provide a range of problems and exercises for students to complete to practise and develop their learning of concepts. These exercises are delivered using an 'adaptive' approach, which responds to students' performance and alters the questions according to their previous answers. The system records and tracks students' activities and performance to provide information for teachers on what they are doing and how well they are progressing. This identifies students who need help from their teacher with specific topics. The reporting functions indicate whether a student has viewed a video and how many problems they have attempted. This information can help teachers to pinpoint conceptual misunderstandings and behavioural or confidence issues.

(Straw, Quinlan, Harland and Walker, 2015)

Online homework systems

In addition to virtual learning environments there has been a growth in online tools to support teachers, students and parents with homework. Mostly they consolidate homework information and resources in one place and are accessible to teachers, parents/carers and students. Examples include Doddle, Edmodo, Firefly and Show My Homework (see Box 7.3). These systems work across the web and mobile and tablet devices.

BOX 7.3: ONLINE HOMEWORK SYSTEMS

Show My Homework, a web-based initiative, is a centralized resource that hosts all the information on homework relating to a class or school. The task, assignment details, resources, timing and deadlines are clearly displayed to pupils, parents/carers and other teachers. Teachers use it to set homework and parents/carers and students can see the details of homework tasks that students have been set. Automated notifications are sent before homework is due. Findings from 20 case studies provide evidence of clarity and consistency and show a reduction in confusion about homework and improvements in homework submission rates. More important was the emergence of new ways of teaching and learning, in that teachers, parents/carers and students felt more accountable for their role in ensuring that homework had successful outcomes.

(Preston, Gohil and Langan, 2014)

Individual online support for homework

There is endless availability of apps worldwide that have been developed for homework. Some support students in the scheduling of homework, others provide platforms for helpline support. For example, The Homework App, myHomework Student Planner and My Study Life support students in the organization and scheduling of homework. Many of these apps have a free version and an optional charged account with additional features. MyHomework Basic enables students to track assignments, projects and tests, to track classes to receive due date reminders, and to sync between devices, and provides widgets for dealing with upcoming homework. MyHomework Premium, which has a small cost, includes no advertisements, all themes, file attachments, enhanced app widgets and external calendar access.

By contrast, Got It is a mobile tutoring platform that offers help for students who need to solve mathematics and chemistry problems. Through a sophisticated system of algorithms, this app connects students with expert tutors from around the world. Students take a photo of their problem, printed or handwritten, and are instantly matched with an expert and provided with step-by-step explanations to solve their problems. Communication is through written, text-based chat. This platform is not free. Another example is StudyRoom, which is aimed at those at university or about to apply. It has over 1.8 million subscribers and enables discussion of a very wide range of topics.

In addition to these open-access systems, there are examples of online support established as part of a Ministry of Education initiative (see Box 7.4).

BOX 7.4: MATHEMATICS HOMEWORK HELP FOR ONTARIO STUDENTS

Through the TVOntario Independent Learning Centre, the Ontario Ministry of Education provides Homework Help to Ontario students. The focus is on help in mathematics for students in grades 7 to 10. Students have access to both guided and independent learning in a unique environment that combines technology and personal interaction. Tutors are Ontario-certified teachers. Interactions focus on understanding and comprehension. Students are engaged in the process and learn how to find the answer; it is not given to them. Resources include Ask A Tutor Chat Rooms, Listen and Learn presentations with certified teachers, Interactive Tutorials, and Best Sessions.

(Ontario Ministry of Education, 2012)

Overcoming disadvantage

In devising different approaches to homework to interest students, schools and teachers are increasingly using digital resources and tools. However, many students lack access to high-quality broadband and hence the internet, and there are concerns that this digital inequity has created a homework gap, whereby some students are unable to complete the homework assigned by teachers. In the USA, for example, in 2015, Barack Obama, the then President, launched ConnectHome, an initiative undertaken by communities, the private sector and federal government to expand high-speed broadband to more families across the country (US Office of the Press Secretary, 2015). At the time, it was estimated that half of low-income students had no internet access at home. The two case study examples (see Boxes 7.5 and 7.6) provide examples of initiatives to reduce the digital gap.

BOX 7.5: CLOSING THE HOMEWORK GAP: MOBILE DEVICES AND WIRELESS CONNECTIVITY

Alvin Dunn Elementary School in California used Ipads with 6th-grade students as part of classroom activities, but they were not taken home. Fifty-nine per cent of the students reported not having access to high-speed broadband at home. Thirty-eight per cent reported difficulties completing homework assignments due to the challenges of internet access outside school. As part of this project the students were provided with tablets with mobile broadband access off site. The aim was to see how anytime, anywhere internet access impacted on the students' learning opportunities, their homework assignments and their curriculum choices.

Following the implementation of the initiative, teachers reported being able to think more creatively about setting projects and assignments for the students, knowing that all of them had internet access. Parents of the mainly (89%) Hispanic or Latino students began emailing teachers using the child's tablet, which created stronger connections between school and home. Using a multilingual vocabulary app through the tablets, the students were able to develop their academic English and practise their Spanish. Many students reported using the app with their parents. Students' technology and research skills improved, as did their engagement with learning.

(Project Tomorrow, 2015)

Box 7.6: Homework goes mobile

A trial project in Lesotho, in southern Africa, sends lessons and quizzes to children via mobile phone and enables teachers to monitor progress. The project is supported by the Vodacom Foundation, which is paying for the airtime for the trial, the Ministry of Education and the local teachers' union. Via Sterio.me, children are sent homework on basic phones. Internet access is not required. The Sterio.me team generates homework and quizzes for teachers, with content relevant to what students will be learning in the next term. The teachers approve the content before the school year starts. Students receive a call covering the day's work. A text-to-speech programme reads out several multiple-choice questions that the pupil can answer using the phone's keypad. Teachers can see the data in real time, check which students have completed assignments and monitor their progress.

(Griliopoulos, 2015)

In addition to solutions for students lacking sufficient access to technology to do their homework, examples of innovative approaches to overcoming disadvantage can be seen in the Family Meal and Homework Clubs in Glasgow (see Box 7.7). In contrast to homework clubs where engagement with parents/carers is minimal, these clubs were designed for the family from the start. This initiative is part of an intensive neighbourhood approach in Glasgow called Thriving Places.

Box 7.7 Family meal and homework club

Established through the Thriving Places initiative, the Bridgeton Family Meal and Homework Club is open to families from both the Dalmarnock and Sacred Heart primary schools. The club offers parents/carers the chance to learn how to cook healthy family meals under the guidance of a qualified community chef. They prepare a two-course meal for everyone attending the club. Parents/carers who don't cook sit with children during homework time and can ask school staff questions about homework and observe new techniques for helping their children learn. The children receive homework support from school staff and when the homework is completed they take part in active play sessions. When the homework, play and cooking are finished everyone sits down together to enjoy the meal that the parents/carers have created. In addition to supporting homework, the club has enabled children and parents to make new friends and to build up support networks.

(Thriving Places, 2017)

A further expansion to the role of homework clubs (see Chapter 3) can be seen in the increase in the provision of university-supported clubs. Staffed in part by volunteers drawn from the university student body, many of these clubs are seeking to raise aspirations among children and young people from disadvantaged communities to inspire them to go to university (see Box 7.8).

Box 7.8 Homework clubs and widening participation

The Homework Club, Adamsdown Resource Centre, Cardiff, supports each week around 70 children and young people, aged 6–18 years, from a range of different ethnic backgrounds. Eight students from Cardiff University deliver these sessions, supported by approximately 12 community volunteers. A deliberate attempt has been made to recruit volunteer university students from Black and ethnic-minority backgrounds and those who are the first in their family to go to university, to help raise further the aspirations of the children involved in the club. The programme includes visits to the university, also to raise the children's aspirations. Other learning opportunities include visits to the theatre and trips during the school holidays. Central to the success of this initiative is the partnership between Cardiff University Widening Access Team and STAR Communities First.

(Paul Hamlyn Foundation, 2015)

Implications for research

Recent UK research on homework is limited. Given the major changes in the educational system in the twenty-first century that may have impacted on homework, this needs to be addressed. There is a particular need for research that focuses on the areas described below.

Schools

- The approaches that schools, primary and secondary, are currently taking to homework;
- the kinds of homework policies that schools have;

- the amount of homework that they envisage learners doing over the course of a week;
- the impact of 'no homework' policies;
- whether the amount of homework is differentiated by structured ability grouping;
- the way schools manage the allocation of homework between subjects and days of the week;
- the extent to which they monitor the homework practices of teachers;
- the amount of homework currently being undertaken by students;
- what provision they have for supporting homework;
- the extent to which technology is used in relation to homework;
- an understanding of the quality of the formative feedback provided and how this impacts on students;
- how teachers make use of feedback from pupils as part of their planning;
- digital literacy and the use of technology for homework;
- the perceived wider skills benefits of homework;
- examples of innovative approaches to homework and their effectiveness.

Teachers

- How important they think homework is;
- the kinds of homework they set, differentiated by subject;
- the extent to which they differentiate homework to meet the needs of learners;
- the extent to which they monitor homework completion and give feedback;
- the extent to which they use technology to support homework and give feedback.

Learners

- Where and how they do their homework (school, home, alone, with friends, on the move);
- the challenges they face doing homework;
- the amount of time they spend doing homework;
- whether they get feedback on their homework;
- what kinds of homework they are given and which they perceive as the most useful or enjoyable.

Parents/carers

- Their attitudes towards homework;
- the extent to which they help their children with homework;
- the challenges that homework presents;
- the extent to which homework interferes with family life;

- what support they get for understanding homework and helping their child with it.

Conclusions

Homework has been a part of school life since compulsory schooling began. The controversies which surround it have not changed in almost a hundred years. The debate will only move on if schools take the lead in redefining the homework agenda and putting student learning at its centre. This requires a focus on the purpose and quality of homework, not its amount. The relationship between homework and attainment is complex and, as was set out in Chapter 1, depends on a range of factors that interact. Schools need to devise policies and practices that take account of this complexity if they wish to maximize the positive impact of homework.

Schools also need to take advantage of the major advances in technology of recent years. These can offer a range of support for homework, some providing direct feedback to students, others offering opportunities to discuss issues with other learners in chat rooms. Historically, schools have been reluctant to embrace technological support for learning. The first teaching machine was devised by Sidney Pressey (1927) in the 1920s. It was a relatively simple device, which offered learners multiple-choice responses to a question. If their response was incorrect they were given the opportunity to make an alternative choice until they selected the correct answer. In the late 1950s, Skinner (1958) strongly advocated the use of teaching machines to support learning. These opportunities for using technology in an educational context were not implemented at the time, perhaps in part because of the simplicity of the systems and the limited learning opportunities that they offered. Now, new developments in technology have the potential to revolutionize the way children and young people learn and how they complete homework. Interactive programs that can provide detailed feedback when processes or answers are incorrect offer individualized support for learning. Such programs are particularly useful for subjects in which problems have correct answers or factual recall is required. When learners are required to develop critical arguments, chat rooms in which they can discuss issues with peers and be guided by teachers are invaluable. The provision of information about homework and feedback through technology can also support learning and offer guidance to parents. Some teachers are already making extensive use of such opportunities, but more training is needed if the whole profession is to develop the necessary skills to make learning rather than teaching the focus in schools.

CHAPTER 7: KEY POINTS

Homework can make a small but important contribution to student attainment.

Schools have the responsibility to ensure that homework policies and practices are effective.

Schools can:

- improve the effectiveness of homework by providing training for teachers;
- provide electronic resources to support homework;
- set up homework clubs or study centres;
- set up support for parents of young children.

Teachers need to:

- ensure that homework tasks have value and contribute to the curriculum or the development of specific student skills;
- allow sufficient time for explaining homework;
- monitor homework completion and give constructive feedback to students.

Students should approach homework positively and develop homework-management skills in order to increase their efficiency and free time for other pursuits.

To support high levels of achievement parents should have high aspirations for their children and support them in becoming autonomous learners.

References

Adult Literacy and Basic Skills Unit (1993) *Parents and Their Children: The intergenerational effect of poor basic skills*. London: Adult Literacy and Basic Skills Unit.

Akioka, E. and Gilmore, L. (2013) 'An intervention to improve motivation for homework'. *Australian Journal of Guidance and Counselling*, 23 (1), 34–48.

Aksoy, T. and Link, C.R. (2000) 'A panel analysis of student mathematics achievement in the US in the 1990s: Does increasing the amount of time in learning activities affect math achievement?'. *Economics of Education Review*, 19 (3), 261–77.

Anesko, K.M. and O'Leary, S.G. (1982) 'The effectiveness of brief parent training for the management of children's homework problems'. *Child and Family Behavior Therapy*, 4 (2–3), 113–26.

Anesko, K.M., Schoiock, G., Ramirez, R. and Levine, F.M. (1987) 'The homework problem checklist: Assessing children's homework difficulties'. *Behavioral Assessment*, 9 (2), 79–185.

Apsler, R. (2009) 'After-school programs for adolescents: A review of evaluation research'. *Adolescence*, 44 (173), 1–19.

Asterhan, C.S.C. and Bouton, E. (2017) 'Teenage peer-to-peer knowledge sharing through social network sites in secondary schools'. *Computers and Education*, 110, 16–34.

Austin, J.D. (1976) 'Do comments on mathematics homework affect student achievement?'. *School Science and Mathematics*, 76 (2), 159–64.

Austin, J.D. (1979) 'Homework research in mathematics'. *School Science and Mathematics*, 79 (2), 115–21.

Austin, J.D. and Austin, K.A. (1974) 'Homework grading procedures in junior high mathematics classes'. *School Science and Mathematics*, 74 (4), 269–72.

Baker, D.P., Akiba, M., LeTendre, G.K. and Wiseman, A.W. (2001) 'Worldwide shadow education: Outside-school learning, institutional quality of schooling, and cross-national mathematics achievement'. *Educational Evaluation and Policy Analysis*, 23 (1), 1–17.

Baker, D.P., LeTendre, G.K. and Akiba, M. (2005) 'Schoolwork at home? Low-quality schooling and homework'. In Baker, D.P. and LeTendre, G.K. (eds) *National Differences, Global Similarities: World culture and the future of schooling*. Stanford, CA: Stanford University Press, 117–33.

Balli, S.J. (1995) 'The Effects of Differential Prompts on Family Involvement with Middle-Grades Homework'. Unpublished PhD thesis, University of Missouri.

Balli, S.J., Demo, D.H. and Wedman, J.F. (1998) 'Family involvement with children's homework: An intervention in the middle grades'. *Family Relations*, 47 (2), 149–57.

Balli, S.J., Wedman, J.F. and Demo, D.H. (1997) 'Family involvement with middle-grades homework: Effects of differential prompting'. *Journal of Experimental Education*, 66 (1), 31–48.

Bang, H.J. (2012) 'Promising homework practices: Teachers' perspectives on making homework work for newcomer immigrant students'. *High School Journal*, 95 (2), 3–31.

Bang, H.J., Suárez-Orozco, C. and O'Connor, E. (2011) 'Immigrant students' homework: Ecological perspective on facilitators and impediments to task completion'. *American Journal of Education*, 118 (1), 25–55.

Bang, H.J., Suárez-Orozco, C., Pakes, J. and O'Connor, E. (2009) 'The importance of homework in determining immigrant students' grades in schools in the USA context', *Educational Research*, 51 (1), 1–25.

Barber, B. (1986) 'Homework does not belong on the agenda for school reform'. *Educational Leadership*, 43 (8), 55–7.

Barber, M., Myers, K., Denning, T., Graham, J. and Johnson, M. (1997) *School Performance and Extra-Curricular Provision*. London: Department for Education and Employment.

Barrett, D.E. and Neal, K.S. (1992) 'Effects of homework assistance given by telephone on the academic achievement of fifth grade children'. *Educational Research Quarterly*, 15 (4), 21–8.

Baş, G., Şentürk, C. and Ciğerci, F.M. (2017) 'Homework and academic achievement: A meta-analytic review of research'. *Issues in Educational Research*, 27 (1), 31–50.

Bastiani, J. (ed.) (1997) *Home–School Work in Multicultural Settings*. London: David Fulton.

Baughman, M.D. and Pruitt, W. (1963) 'Supplemental study for enrichment vs supplemental study for reinforcement of academic achievement'. *Bulletin of the National Association of Secondary School Principals*, 47 (281), 154–7.

Baumrind, D. (1971) *Current Patterns of Parental Authority* (Developmental Psychology Monograph, 4 (1) Part 2). New York: American Psychological Association.

Baumrind, D. (1989) 'Rearing competent children'. In Damon, W. (ed.) *Child Development Today and Tomorrow*. San Francisco: Jossey-Bass, 349–78.

Beaton, A.E., Martin, M.O., Mullis, I.V.S., Gonzalez, E.J., Smith, T.A. and Kelly, D.L. (1996) *Science Achievement in the Middle School Years: IEA's Third International Mathematics and Science Study (TIMSS)*. Chestnut Hill, MA: Center for the Study of Testing, Evaluation, and Educational Policy, Boston College.

Beaton, A.E., Mullis, I.V.S., Martin, M.O., Gonzalez, E.J., Kelly, D.L. and Smith, T.A. (1996) *Mathematics Achievement in the Middle School Years: IEA's Third International Mathematics and Science Study (TIMSS)*. Chestnut Hill, MA: Center for the Study of Testing, Evaluation, and Educational Policy, Boston College.

Bechler, P. (1991) 'Homework as an element of learning'. *English Teachers' Journal (Israel)*, 42, 56–61.

Bembenutty, H. (2009) 'Academic delay of gratification, self-regulation of learning, gender differences, and expectancy-value'. *Personality and Individual Differences*, 46 (3), 347–52.

Bembenutty, H. (2010) 'Homework completion: The role of self-efficacy, delay of gratification, and self-regulatory processes'. *International Journal of Educational and Psychological Assessment*, 6 (1), 1–20.

Bembenutty, H. (2011) 'Meaningful and maladaptive homework practices: The role of self-efficacy and self-regulation'. *Journal of Advanced Academics*, 22 (3), 448–73.

Bembenutty, H. and White, M.C. (2013) 'Academic performance and satisfaction with homework completion among college students'. *Learning and Individual Differences*, 24, 83–8.

Bempechat, J. (2004) 'The motivational benefits of homework: A social-cognitive perspective'. *Theory into Practice*, 43 (3), 189–96.

Bempechat, J., Li, J., Neier, S.M., Gillis, C.A. and Holloway, S.D. (2011) 'The homework experience: Perceptions of low-income youth'. *Journal of Advanced Academics*, 22 (2), 250–78.

Bennett, S. and Kalish, N. (2006) *The Case Against Homework: How homework is hurting our children and what we can do about it*. New York: Crown Publishers.

Beresford, E. and Hardie, A. (1996) 'Parents and secondary schools: A different approach?'. In Bastiani, J. and Wolfendale, S. (eds) *Home–School Work in Britain: Review, reflection and development*. London: David Fulton, 139–51.

Bergmann, J. and Sams, A. (2012) *Flip Your Classroom: Reach every student in every class every day*. Eugene, OR: International Society for Technology in Education.

Berliner, O. and Casanova, U. (1985) 'Why what you write on homework papers counts'. *Instructor*, 95 (4), 14–15.

Bhandarkar, S., Leddo, J. and Banerjee, M. (2016) 'Comparing the relative effects of homework on high aptitude vs average aptitude students'. *International Journal of Humanities and Social Science Research*, 2 (9), 59–62.

Birmingham, P., Keys, W. and Lee, B. (1999) *Headteachers' Main Concerns (Annual Survey of Trends in Education*, Digest No. 7). Slough: National Foundation for Educational Research.

Bishop, J.L. and Verleger, M.A. (2013) 'The flipped classroom: A survey of the research'. Paper presented at the American Society for Engineering Education (ASEE) Annual Conference, Atlanta, GA, 23–26 June 2013.

Black, P. (1990) 'Homework: The sixth day of instruction'. *ERS Spectrum*, 8 (2), 35–41.

Black, P. and Wiliam, D. (1998a) 'Assessment and classroom learning'. *Assessment in Education: Principles, Policy and Practice*, 5 (1), 7–74.

Black, P. and Wiliam, D. (1998b) *Inside the Black Box: Raising standards through classroom assessment*. London: King's College London.

Black, P. and Wiliam, D. (2003) '"In praise of educational research": Formative assessment'. *British Educational Research Journal*, 29 (5), 623–37.

Blackwell, W.R. (1979) 'An analysis of the Dial-A-Teacher Assistance Program (Dataline)'. Paper presented at the National Urban Education Conference, Detroit.

Blomfield, C.J. and Barber, B.L. (2011) 'Developmental experiences during extracurricular activities and Australian adolescents' self-concept: Particularly important for youth from disadvantaged schools'. *Journal of Youth and Adolescence*, 40 (5), 582–94.

Bloom, B.S. (1976) *Human Characteristics and School Learning*. New York: McGraw-Hill.

Board of Education (1937) 'Homework'. Educational Pamphlets, 110. London: HMSO.

Bonyun, R. (1992) *Homework: A review of reviews of the literature*. Ottawa: Ottawa Board of Education.

Bowen, N.K and Bowen, G.L. (1998) 'The mediating role of educational meaning in the relationship between home academic culture and academic performance'. *Family Relations*, 47 (1), 45–51.

Bradley, R.M. (1967) 'An Experimental Study of Individualized versus Blanket-Type Homework Assignments in Elementary School Mathematics'. Unpublished EdD thesis, Temple University.

Brandsma, H.P. and van der Werf, M.P.C. (1997) *Beschrijving van het onderwijspeil van leerlingen in het eerste leerjaar van het voortgezet onderwijs: Een analyse op de meting in het eerste leerjaar van het cohort VOCL'93.* [Description of the achievement level of students in the first year of secondary education]. Enschede/Groningen: OCTO/GION.

Bray, M. (1999) *The Shadow Education System: Private tutoring and its implications for planners.* Paris: UNESCO International Institute for Educational Planning.

Brink, W.G. (1937) *Directing Study Activities in Secondary Schools*. New York: Doubleday.

Brock, C.H., Lapp, D., Flood, J., Fisher, D. and Han, K.T. (2007) 'Does homework matter? An investigation of teacher perceptions about homework practices for children from nondominant backgrounds'. *Urban Education*, 42 (4), 349–72.

Brooks, E.C. (1916) 'The value of home study under parental supervision'. *Elementary School Journal*, 17 (3), 187–94.

Brown, A. (1993) 'Participation, dialogue and the reproduction of social inequalities'. In Merttens, R. and Vass, J. (eds) *Partnership in Maths: Parents and schools: The IMPACT Project.* London: Falmer Press, 190–213.

Bryan, T. and Burstein, K. (2004) 'Improving homework completion and academic performance: Lessons from special education'. *Theory into Practice*, 43 (3), 213–19.

Bryan, T. and Nelson, C. (1994) 'Doing homework: Perspectives of elementary and junior high school students'. *Journal of Learning Disabilities*, 27 (8), 488–99.

Bryan, T. and Sullivan-Burstein, K. (1997) 'Homework how-to's'. *TEACHING Exceptional Children*, 29 (6), 32–7.

Bryan, T. and Sullivan-Burstein, K. (1998) 'Teacher-selected strategies for improving homework completion'. *Remedial and Special Education*, 19 (5), 263–75.

Buijs, M. and Admiraal, W. (2013) 'Homework assignments to enhance student engagement in secondary education'. *European Journal of Psychology of Education*, 28 (3), 767–79.

Bursuck, W.D., Harniss, M.K., Epstein, M.H., Polloway, E.A., Jayanthi, M. and Wissinger, L.M. (1999) 'Solving communication problems about homework: Recommendations of special education teachers'. *Learning Disabilities Research and Practice*, 14 (3), 149–58.

Butcher, J.E. (1975) 'Comparison of the Effects of Distributed and Massed Problem Assignments on the Homework of Ninth-Grade Algebra Students'. Unpublished EdD thesis, Rutgers University.

Butler, A.C., Karpicke, J.D. and Roediger, H.L. (2007) 'The effect of type and timing of feedback on learning from multiple-choice tests'. *Journal of Experimental Psychology: Applied*, 13 (4), 273–81.

Callahan, K., Rademacher, J.A. and Hildreth, B.L. (1998) 'The effect of parent participation in strategies to improve the homework performance of students who are at risk'. *Remedial and Special Education*, 19 (3), 131–41.

Cameron, L. and Bartel, L. (2008) *Homework Realities: A Canadian study of parental opinions and attitudes*. Toronto: Ontario Institute for Studies in Education.

Cameron, L. and Bartel, L. (2009) 'The researchers ate the homework! Perspectives of parents and teachers'. *Education Canada*, 49 (1), 48–51.

Camp, J.S. (1973) 'The Effects of Distributed Practice upon Learning and Retention in Introductory Algebra'. Unpublished PhD thesis, Teachers College, Columbia University.

Cancio, E.J., West, R.P. and Young, K.R. (2004) 'Improving mathematics homework completion and accuracy of students with EBD through self-management and parent participation'. *Journal of Emotional and Behavioral Disorders*, 12 (1), 9–22.

Capper, L. (2000) '"Am I doing it right?": Share – a national parental involvement programme'. In Wolfendale, S. and Bastiani, J. (eds) *The Contribution of Parents to School Effectiveness*. London: David Fulton, 128–48.

Carr, N.S. (2013) 'Increasing the effectiveness of homework for all learners in the inclusive classroom'. *School Community Journal*, 23 (1), 169–82.

Carroll, J.B. (1963) 'A model of school learning'. *Teachers College Record*, 64 (8), 723–33.

Cartledge, C.M. and Sasser, J.E. (1981) 'The effect of homework assignments on the mathematics achievement of college students in freshman algebra'. Columbus College

Cavas, P. (2011) 'Factors affecting the motivation of Turkish primary students for science learning'. *Science Education International*, 22 (1), 31–42.

Chandler, J., Argyris, D., Barnes, W.S., Goodman, I.F. and Snow, C.E. (1983) 'Parents as teachers: Observations of low-income parents and children in a homework-like task'. Harvard University, Graduate School of Education.

Chang, C.B., Wall, D., Tare, M., Golonka, E. and Vatz, K. (2014) 'Relationships of attitudes toward homework and time spent on homework to course outcomes: The case of foreign language learning'. *Journal of Educational Psychology*, 106 (4), 1049–65.

Chavous, B.J. (1990) 'A study of teacher and student attitudes toward a program utilizing a calendar of homework activity'. *National Association of Laboratory Schools Journal*, 15 (1), 22–9.

Chen, C. and Stevenson, H.W. (1989) 'Homework: A cross-cultural examination'. *Child Development*, 60 (3), 551–61.

Chen, C. and Uttal, D.H. (1988) 'Cultural values, parents' beliefs, and children's achievement in the United States and China'. *Human Development*, 31 (6), 351–8.

Chen, M. and Ehrenberg, T. (1993) 'Test scores, homework, aspirations and teachers' grades'. *Studies in Educational Evaluation*, 19 (4), 403–19.

Cohen, J. (1992) 'Statistical power analysis'. *Current Directions in Psychological Science*, 1 (3), 98–101.

Cooper, H. (1989a) *Homework*. White Plains, NY: Longman.

Cooper, H. (1989b) 'Synthesis of research on homework'. *Educational Leadership*, 47 (3), 85–91.

Cooper, H. (1994) *The Battle over Homework: An administrator's guide to setting sound and effective policies*. Thousand Oaks, CA: Corwin Press.

Cooper, H. (2001) *The Battle over Homework: Common ground for administrators, teachers, and parents*. 2nd ed. Thousand Oaks, CA: Corwin Press.

Cooper, H., Jackson, K., Nye, B. and Lindsay, J.J. (2001) 'A model of homework's influence on the performance evaluations of elementary school students'. *Journal of Experimental Education*, 69 (2), 181–99.

Cooper, H., Lindsay, J.J. and Nye, B. (2000) 'Homework in the home: How student, family, and parenting-style differences relate to the homework process'. *Contemporary Educational Psychology*, 25 (4), 464–87.

Cooper, H., Lindsay, J.J., Nye, B. and Greathouse, S. (1998) 'Relationships among attitudes about homework, amount of homework assigned and completed, and student achievement'. *Journal of Educational Psychology*, 90 (1), 70–83.

Cooper, H., Robinson, J.C. and Patall, E.A. (2006) 'Does homework improve academic achievement? A synthesis of research, 1987–2003'. *Review of Educational Research*, 76 (1), 1–62.

Cooper, H., Steenbergen-Hu, S. and Dent, A.L. (2012) 'Homework'. In Harris, K.R., Graham, S. and Urdan, T. (eds) *APA Educational Psychology Handbook. Volume 3: Application to learning and teaching*. Washington, DC: American Psychological Association, 475–95.

Cooper, H. and Valentine, J.C. (2001) 'Using research to answer practical questions about homework'. *Educational Psychologist*, 36 (3), 143–53.

Cooper, H., Valentine, J.C., Nye, B. and Lindsay, J.J. (1999) 'Relationships between five after-school activities and academic achievement'. *Journal of Educational Psychology*, 91 (2), 369–78.

Corno, L. and Xu, J. (2004) 'Homework as the job of childhood'. *Theory into Practice*, 43 (3), 227–33.

Cosden, M., Morrison, G., Albanese, A.L. and Macias, S. (2001) 'When homework is not home work: After-school programs for homework assistance'. *Educational Psychologist*, 36 (3), 211–21.

Costa, M., Cardoso, A.P., Lacerda, C., Lopes, A. and Gomes, C. (2016) 'Homework in primary education from the perspective of teachers and pupils'. *Procedia: Social and Behavioral Sciences*, 217, 139–48.

Coulter, F. (1979) 'Homework: A neglected research area'. *British Educational Research Journal*, 5 (1), 21–33.

Coulter, F. (1980) *Secondary School Homework* (Cooperative Research Study Report 7). Perth: University of Western Australia.

Coulter, F. (1985) 'Homework'. In Husén, T. and Postlethwaite, T.N. (eds) *The International Encyclopedia of Education*. Oxford: Pergamon Press, 2289–94.

Cowan, R. and Hallam, S. (1999) *What Do We Know about Homework?* (Viewpoint 9). London: Institute of Education.

Cowan, R., Traill, D. and McNaughton, S. (1998) 'Homework for primary children: Ideals and reality'. *Psychology of Education Review*, 22 (2), 20–7.

Crozier, G. (1997) 'Empowering the powerful: A discussion of the interrelation of government policies and consumerism with social class factors and the impact of this upon parent interventions in their children's schooling'. *British Journal of Sociology of Education*, 18 (2), 187–200.

Dadas, J.E. (1976) 'A Study of the Effects of Assigning Spiral Exploratory Homework upon Achievement in and Attitude towards Mathematics'. Unpublished EdD thesis, New York University.

D'Ailly, H. (2003) 'Children's autonomy and perceived control in learning: A model of motivation and achievement in Taiwan'. *Journal of Educational Psychology*, 95 (1), 84–96.

Dandy, J. and Nettelbeck, T. (2002) 'The relationship between IQ, homework, aspirations and academic achievement for Chinese, Vietnamese and Anglo-Celtic Australian school children'. *Educational Psychology*, 22 (3), 267–75.

Danielson, M.L., Strom, B. and Kramer, K. (2011) 'Real homework tasks: A pilot study of types, values, and resource requirements'. *Educational Research Quarterly*, 35 (1), 17–32.

Darling, N. (2005) 'Participation in extracurricular activities and adolescent adjustment: Cross-sectional and longitudinal findings'. *Journal of Youth and Adolescence*, 34 (5), 493–505.

Darling, N. and Steinberg, L. (1993) 'Parenting style as context: An integrative model'. *Psychological Bulletin*, 113 (3), 487–96.

Dauber, S.L. and Epstein, J.L. (1993) 'Parents' attitudes and practices of involvement in inner-city elementary and middle schools'. In Chavkin, N.F. (ed.) *Families and Schools in a Pluralistic Society*. Albany: State University of New York Press, 53–71.

David, P., Kim, J.-H., Brickman, J.S., Ran, W. and Curtis, C.M. (2015) 'Mobile phone distraction while studying'. *New Media and Society*, 17 (10), 1661–79.

Davidson, J.W., Howe, M.J.A. and Sloboda, J.A. (1997) 'Environmental factors in the development of musical performance skill over the life span'. In Hargreaves, D.J. and North, A.C. (eds) *The Social Psychology of Music*. Oxford: Oxford University Press, 188–206.

Dearing, E., Kreider, H., Simpkins, S. and Weiss, H.B. (2006) 'Family involvement in school and low-income children's literacy: Longitudinal association between and within families'. *Journal of Educational Psychology*, 98 (4), 653–64.

DeBaz, T.P. (1994) 'A Meta-Analysis of the Relationship between Students' Characteristics and Achievement and Attitudes toward Science'. Unpublished PhD thesis, Ohio State University.

De Carvalho, M.E.P. (2009) 'Homework, gender, and family–school relations'. In Deslandes, R. (ed.) *International Perspectives on Student Outcomes and Homework: Family–school–community partnerships*. London: Routledge, 61–75.

Deci, E.L. and Ryan, R.M. (eds) (2002) *Handbook of Self-Determination Research*. Rochester, NY: University of Rochester Press.

De Jong, R., Westerhof, K.J. and Creemers, B.P.M. (2000) 'Homework and student math achievement in junior high schools'. *Educational Research and Evaluation*, 6 (2), 130–57.

De Kanter, A. (2001) 'After-school programs for adolescents'. *NASSP Bulletin*, 85 (626), 12–21.

DES (Department of Education and Science) (1987) *Homework: A Report by HM Inspectors* (Education Observed 4). London: Department of Education and Science.

Desforges, C. and Abouchaar, A. (2003) *The Impact of Parental Involvement, Parental Support and Family Education on Pupil Achievements and Adjustment: A literature review* (Research Report 433). Nottingham: Department for Education and Skills.

DeSimone, J. (2006) 'Academic performance and part-time employment among high school seniors'. *Topics in Economic Analysis and Policy*, 6 (1), Article 10, 1–34.

Deslandes, R. (2009) 'Elementary school teachers' views of homework and parents–school relations'. In Deslandes, R. (ed.) *International Perspectives on Student Outcomes and Homework: Family–school–community partnerships*. London: Routledge, 128–40.

Deslandes, R., Royer, É., Potvin, P. and Leclerc, D. (1999) 'Patterns of home and school partnership for general and special education students at the secondary level'. *Exceptional Children*, 65 (4), 496–506.

Dettmers, S., Trautwein, U. and Lüdtke, O. (2009) 'The relationship between homework time and achievement is not universal: Evidence from multilevel analyses in 40 countries'. *School Effectiveness and School Improvement*, 20 (4), 375–405.

Dettmers, S., Trautwein, U., Lüdtke, O., Kunter, M. and Baumert, J. (2010) 'Homework works if homework quality is high: Using multilevel modeling to predict the development of achievement in mathematics'. *Journal of Educational Psychology*, 102 (2), 467–82.

Deveci, İ. and Önder, İ. (2013) 'The students' views related to the given homeworks in the science and technology courses: A qualitative study'. *US–China Education Review (A)*, 3 (1), 1–9.

Deveci, İ. and Önder, İ. (2015) 'Views of middle school students on homework assignments in science courses'. *Science Education International*, 26 (4), 539–56.

DfEE (Department for Education and Employment) (1998a) *Extending Opportunity: A national framework for study support*. London: Department for Education and Employment.

DfEE (Department for Education and Employment) (1998b) *Homework: Guidelines for primary and secondary schools*. London: Department for Education and Employment.

Doctoroff, G.L. and Arnold, D.H. (2017) 'Doing homework together: The relation between parenting strategies, child engagement, and achievement'. *Journal of Applied Developmental Psychology*, 48, 103–13.

Donaldson-Pressman, S., Jackson, R. and Pressman, R.M. (2014) *The Learning Habit: A groundbreaking approach to homework and parenting that helps our children succeed in school and life*. New York: Penguin.

Dotterer, A.M. and Wehrspann, E. (2016) 'Parent involvement and academic outcomes among urban adolescents: Examining the role of school engagement'. *Educational Psychology*, 36 (4), 812–30.

Dudley, S. and Shawver, D.L. (1991) 'The effect of homework on students' perceptions of teaching effectiveness'. *Journal of Education for Business*, 67 (1), 21–5.

Duffett, A. and Johnson, J. (2004) 'All work and no play? Listening to what kids and parents really want from out-of-school time'. New York: Public Agenda and the Wallace Foundation.

Duijnhouwer, H., Prins, F.J. and Stokking, K.M. (2012) 'Feedback providing improvement strategies and reflection on feedback use: Effects on students' writing motivation, process, and performance'. *Learning and Instruction*, 22 (3), 171–84.

Dumont, H., Trautwein, U., Lüdtke, O., Neumann, M., Niggli, A. and Schnyder, I. (2012) 'Does parental homework involvement mediate the relationship between family background and educational outcomes?'. *Contemporary Educational Psychology*, 37 (1), 55–69.

Dumont, H., Trautwein, U., Nagy, G. and Nagengast, B. (2014) 'Quality of parental homework involvement: Predictors and reciprocal relations with academic functioning in the reading domain'. *Journal of Educational Psychology*, 106 (1), 144–61.

Dunn, J. (1993) *Young Children's Close Relationships: Beyond attachment*. Newbury Park, CA: SAGE Publications.

Dunn, J. and Plomin, R. (1990) *Separate Lives: Why siblings are so different*. New York: Basic Books.

Durlak, J.A., Mahoney, J.L., Bohnert, A.M. and Parente, M.E. (2010) 'Developing and improving after-school programs to enhance youth's personal growth and adjustment: A special issue of AJCP'. *American Journal of Community Psychology*, 45 (3–4), 285–93.

Durlak, J.A., Weissberg, R.P. and Pachan, M. (2010) 'A meta-analysis of after-school programs that seek to promote personal and social skills in children and adolescents'. *American Journal of Community Psychology*, 45 (3–4), 294–309.

Dustmann, C. and van Soest, A. (2007) 'Part-time work, school success and school leaving'. *Empirical Economics*, 32 (2–3), 277–99.

Earle, R.S. (1992) 'Homework as an instructional event'. *Educational Technology*, 32 (4), 36–41.

Eccles, J.S. and Barber, B.L. (1999) 'Student council, volunteering, basketball, or marching band: What kind of extracurricular involvement matters?'. *Journal of Adolescent Research*, 14 (1), 10–43.

Elbaum, B., Vaughn, S., Tejero Hughes, M. and Watson Moody, S. (2000) 'How effective are one-on-one tutoring programs in reading for elementary students at risk for reading failure? A meta-analysis of the intervention research'. *Journal of Educational Psychology*, 92 (4), 605–19.

Epps, M. (1966) *Homework*. Washington, DC: National Education Association.

Epstein, J.L. (1983) 'Homework practices, achievements, and behaviors of elementary school students' (Working Paper). Center for Social Organization of Schools, Johns Hopkins University.

Epstein, J.L. (1986) 'Toward an integrated theory of school and family connections' (Report 3). Center for Research on Elementary and Middle Schools, Johns Hopkins University.

Epstein, J.L. (1988) 'Homework practices, achievements, and behaviors of elementary school students (Report 26). Center for Research on Elementary and Middle Schools, Johns Hopkins University.

Epstein, J.L. (1998) 'Interactive homework: Effective strategies to connect home and school'. Paper presented at the American Educational Research Association (AERA) Annual Meeting, San Diego, 13–17 April.

Epstein, J.L. (2001) *School, Family, and Community Partnerships: Preparing educators and improving schools*. Boulder, CO: Westview Press.

Epstein, J.L. and associates (2009) *School, Family, and Community Partnerships: Your handbook for action*. 3rd ed. Thousand Oaks, CA: Corwin Press.

Epstein, J.L., Herrick, S.C. and Coates, L. (1996) 'Effects of summer home learning packets on student achievement in language arts in the middle grades'. *School Effectiveness and School Improvement*, 7 (4), 383–410.

Epstein, J.L. and Lee, S. (1995) 'National patterns of school and family connections in the middle grades'. In Ryan, B.A., Adams, G.R., Gullotta, T.P., Weissberg, R.P. and Hampton, R.L. (eds) *The Family–School Connection: Theory, research, and practice*. Thousand Oaks, CA: SAGE Publications, 108–54.

Epstein, J.L., Simon, B.S. and Salinas, K.C. (1997) 'Involving parents in homework in the middle grades' (Research Bulletin 18). Baltimore, MD: Johns Hopkins University, Center for Evaluation, Development and Research.

Epstein, J.L. and Van Voorhis, F.L. (2001) 'More than minutes: Teachers' roles in designing homework'. *Educational Psychologist*, 36 (3), 181–93.

Epstein, J.L. and Van Voorhis, F.L. (2012) 'The changing debate: From assigning homework to designing homework'. In Suggate, S. and Reese, E. (eds) *Contemporary Debates in Childhood Education and Development*. London: Routledge, 263–74.

Epstein, M.H., Munk, D.D., Bursuck, W.D., Polloway, E.A. and Jayanthi, M. (1999) 'Strategies for improving home–school communication about homework for students with disabilities'. *Journal of Special Education*, 33 (3), 166–76.

Epstein, M.H., Polloway, E.A., Foley, R.M. and Patton, J.R. (1993) 'Homework: A comparison of teachers' and parents' perceptions of the problems experienced by students identified as having behavioral disorders, learning disabilities, or no disabilities'. *Remedial and Special Education*, 14 (5), 40–50.

Eren, O. and Henderson, D.J. (2008) 'The impact of homework on student achievement'. *Econometrics Journal*, 11 (2), 326–48.

Eren, O. and Henderson, D.J. (2011) 'Are we wasting our children's time by giving them more homework?'. *Economics of Education Review*, 30 (5), 950–61.

Ericsson, K.A., Charness, N., Feltovich, P.J. and Hoffman, R.R. (eds) (2006) *The Cambridge Handbook of Expertise and Expert Performance*. Cambridge: Cambridge University Press.

Erion, J. (2006) 'Parent tutoring: A meta-analysis'. *Education and Treatment of Children*, 29 (1), 79–106.

Falch, T. and Rønning, M. (2012) *Homework Assignment and Student Achievement in OECD Countries* (Discussion Paper 711). Oslo: Statistics Norway.

Fan, H., Xu, J., Cai, Z., He, J. and Fan, X. (2017) 'Homework and students' achievement in math and science: A 30-year meta-analysis, 1986–2015'. *Educational Research Review*, 20, 35–54.

Fan, W., Williams, C.M. and Wolters, C.A. (2012) 'Parental involvement in predicting school motivation: Similar and differential effects across ethnic groups'. *Journal of Educational Research*, 105 (1), 21–35.

Fan, X. and Chen, M. (2001) 'Parental involvement and students' academic achievement: A meta-analysis'. *Educational Psychology Review*, 13 (1), 1–22.

Farrow, S., Tymms, P. and Henderson, B. (1999) 'Homework and attainment in primary schools'. *British Educational Research Journal*, 25 (3), 323–41.

Fashola, O.S. (1998) 'Review of extended-day and after-school programs and their effectiveness' (Report No. 24). Center for Research on the Education of Students Placed at Risk, Baltimore, MD.

Fashola, O.S. (2002) *Building Effective Afterschool Programs*. Thousand Oaks, CA: Corwin Press.

Faulkner, J. and Blyth, C. (1995) 'Homework: Is it really worth all the bother?'. *Educational Studies*, 21 (3), 447–54.

Featherstone, H. (1985) 'Homework'. *Harvard Education Letter*, 1, 1–4.

Felgate, R. and Kendall, L. (2000) *Headteachers' Main Concerns* (Annual Survey of Trends in Education, Digest No. 8). Slough: National Foundation for Educational Research.

Fernández-Alonso, R., Álvarez-Díaz, M., Suárez-Álvarez, J. and Muñiz, J. (2017) 'Students' achievement and homework assignment strategies'. *Frontiers in Psychology*, 8, Article 286, 1–11.

Fernández-Alonso, R., Suárez-Álvarez, J. and Muñiz, J. (2015) 'Adolescents' homework performance in mathematics and science: Personal factors and teaching practices'. *Journal of Educational Psychology*, 107 (4), 1075–85.

Fetler, M. (1984) 'Television viewing and school achievement'. *Journal of Communication*, 34 (2), 104–18.

Finders, M. and Lewis, C. (1994) 'Why some parents don't come to school'. *Educational Leadership*, 51 (8), 50–4.

Fink, S. and Nalven, F.B. (1972) 'Increasing homework motivation'. *Education*, 92 (3), 31–3.

Fleisher, G. and Ohel, S. (1977) 'Homework in the elementary school: Limitations and dangers'. *Studies in Education*, 17, 159–66.

Flunger, B., Trautwein, U., Nagengast, B., Lüdtke, O., Niggli, A. and Schnyder, I. (2015) 'The Janus-faced nature of time spent on homework: Using latent profile analyses to predict academic achievement over a school year'. *Learning and Instruction*, 39, 97–106.

Foehr, U.G. (2006) *Media Multitasking among American Youth: Prevalence, predictors and pairings*. Menlo Park, CA: Henry J. Kaiser Family Foundation.

Foley, R.M. and Epstein, M.H. (1993) 'Evaluation of the homework problem checklist with students with behavior disorders'. *Special Services in the Schools*, 7 (1), 79–90.

Foyle, H.C. (1984) 'The Effects of Preparation and Practice Homework on Student Achievement in Tenth-Grade American History'. Unpublished PhD thesis, Kansas State University.

Foyle, H. (1992) 'Homework: A historical perspective or the merry-go-round goes round and round!'. *Southern Social Studies Journal*, 17 (2), 15–24.

Foyle, H.C. and Bailey, G.D. (1988) 'Research. Homework experiments in social studies: Implications for teaching'. *Social Education*, 52 (4), 292–8.

Fredricks, J.A. and Eccles, J.S. (2008) 'Participation in extracurricular activities in the middle school years: Are there developmental benefits for African American and European American youth?'. *Journal of Youth and Adolescence*, 37 (9), 1029–43.

Friedel, J.M., Cortina, K.S., Turner, J.C. and Midgley, C. (2007) 'Achievement goals, efficacy beliefs and coping strategies in mathematics: The roles of perceived parent and teacher goal emphases'. *Contemporary Educational Psychology*, 32 (3), 434–58.

Friesen, C.D. (1979) 'The results of homework versus no-homework research studies'. University of Iowa (ED 167 508).

Gagné, R.M., Briggs, L.J. and Wager, W.W. (1988) *Principles of Instructional Design*. 3rd ed. New York: Holt, Rinehart and Winston.

Garner, B. (1991) 'Improving student grades in middle school mathematics through a homework policy involving automated daily parent contact'. MS. Nova Southeastern University.

Gennaro, E. and Lawrenz, F. (1992) 'The effectiveness of take-home science kits at the elementary level'. *Journal of Research in Science Teaching*, 29 (9), 985–94.

Gill, B. and Schlossman, S. (2000) 'The lost cause of homework reform'. *American Journal of Education*, 109 (1), 27–62.

Glasman, D. (1992) '"Parents" ou "familles": Critique d'un vocabulaire générique'. *Revue française de pédagogie*, 100, 19–33.

Glasman, D. (2009) 'Parents and children's homework in France'. In Deslandes, R. (ed.) *International Perspectives on Student Outcomes and Homework: Family–school–community partnerships*. London: Routledge, 39–46.

Goldstein, A. (1960) 'Does homework help? A review of research'. *Elementary School Journal*, 60 (4), 212–24.

Gonida, E.N. and Cortina, K.S. (2014) 'Parental involvement in homework: Relations with parent and student achievement-related motivational beliefs and achievement'. *British Journal of Educational Psychology*, 84 (3), 376–96.

Goodnow, J.J. and Collins, W.A. (1990) *Development according to Parents: The nature, sources, and consequences of parents' ideas*. Hove: Lawrence Erlbaum Associates.

Gorard, S. and See, B.H. (2013) 'Do parental involvement interventions increase attainment? A review of the evidence' (Nuffield Foundation Briefing Paper).

Gordon, P. (1980) 'Homework: Origins and justifications'. *Westminster Studies in Education*, 3 (1), 27–46.

Gouyon, M. (2004) 'L'aide aux devoirs apportée par les parents: Années scolaires 1991–1992 et 2002–2003'. *INSEE Première*, 996, 1–4.

Grant, E.E (1971) 'An Experimental Study of the Effects of Compulsory Arithmetic Homework Assignments on the Arithmetic Achievements of Fifth-Grade Pupils'. Unpublished EdD thesis, University of the Pacific.

Griliopoulos, D. (2015) 'Homework goes mobile for secondary school pupils in Lesotho'. *The Guardian*, 2 January. Online. www.theguardian.com/global-development/2015/jan/02/homework-goes-mobile-for-secondary-school-pupils-in-lesotho (accessed 15 September 2017).

Grolnick, W.S. and Slowiaczek, M.L. (1994) 'Parents' involvement in children's schooling: A multidimensional conceptualization and motivational model'. *Child Development*, 65 (1), 237–52.

Grossman, J.B., Walker, K. and Raley, R. (2001) 'Challenges and opportunities in after-school programs: Lessons for policymakers and funders'. April. Public/Private Ventures, Philadelphia, PA.

Grotenhuis, N.M.E. (1984) 'Huiswerk: tussen wal en schip'. *Ons A.V.O.-blad*, 8, 380–3.

Gu, L. and Kristoffersson, M. (2015) 'Swedish lower secondary school teachers' perceptions and experiences regarding homework'. *Universal Journal of Educational Research*, 3 (4), 296–305.

Guryan, J., Hurst, E. and Kearney, M. (2008) 'Parental education and parental time with children'. *Journal of Economic Perspectives*, 22 (3), 23–46.

Hagger, M.S., Sultan, S., Hardcastle, S.J. and Chatzisarantis, N.L.D. (2015) 'Perceived autonomy support and autonomous motivation toward mathematics activities in educational and out-of-school contexts is related to mathematics homework behavior and attainment'. *Contemporary Educational Psychology*, 41, 111–23.

Hall, R.W., Butler, L.G., McGuire, S.Y., McGlynn, S.P., Lyon, G.L., Reese, R.L. and Limbach, P.A. (2001) 'Automated, web-based, second-chance homework'. *Journal of Chemical Education*, 78 (12), 1704–8.

Hallam, S. (2010) 'Transitions and the development of expertise'. *Psychology Teaching Review*, 16 (2), 3–32.

Hallam, S. and Ireson, J. (2003) 'Secondary school teachers' attitudes towards and beliefs about ability grouping'. *British Journal of Educational Psychology*, 73 (3), 343–56.

Hallam, S., Kirton, A., Robertson, P., Stobart, G. and Peffers, J. (2003) *Interim Report of the Evaluation of Project 1 of the Assessment is for Learning Development Programme: Support for professional practice in formative assessment*. Edinburgh: Scottish Executive.

Hallam, S. and MacDonald, R. (2016) 'The effects of music in community and educational settings'. In Hallam, S., Cross, I. and Thaut, M. (eds) *The Oxford Handbook of Music Psychology*. 2nd ed. Oxford: Oxford University Press, 775–88.

Harding, R.C. (1979) 'The Relationship of Teacher Attitudes toward Homework and the Academic Achievement of Primary Grade Students'. Unpublished EdD thesis, Lehigh University.

Hargreaves, D.H. (1967) *Social Relations in a Secondary School*. London: Routledge and Kegan Paul.

Harper, S.N. and Anglin, M. (2010) 'Narrowing the gap in academic achievement: Homework clubs for students in low income neighbourhoods'. *Canadian Teacher Magazine*, January, 15.

Harris, S., Nixon, J. and Rudduck, J. (1993) 'School work, homework and gender'. *Gender and Education*, 5 (1), 3–15.

Harris, S. and Rudduck, J. (1994) '"School's great – apart from the lessons": Students' early experiences of learning in secondary school'. In Hughes, M. (ed.) *Perceptions of Teaching and Learning* (BERA Dialogues 8). Clevedon: Multilingual Matters, 35–52.

Harris, V.W. and Sherman, J.A. (1974) 'Homework assignments, consequences, and classroom performance in social studies and mathematics'. *Journal of Applied Behavior Analysis*, 7 (4), 505–19.

Hattie, J. (2009) *Visible Learning: A synthesis of over 800 meta-analyses relating to achievement*. London: Routledge.

Hattie, J. and Timperley, H. (2007) 'The power of feedback'. *Review of Educational Research*, 77 (1), 81–112.

Heller, H.W., Spooner, F., Anderson, D. and Mims, A. (1988) 'Homework: A review of special education practices in the southwest'. *Teacher Education and Special Education*, 11 (2), 43–51.

Heng, M.A. and Atencio, M. (2017) '"I assume they don't think!": Teachers' perceptions of normal technical students in Singapore'. *Curriculum Journal*, 28 (2), 212–30.

Hill, N.E. and Chao, R.K. (eds) (2009) *Families, Schools, and the Adolescent: Connecting research, policy, and practice*. New York: Teachers College Press.

Hill, N.E. and Tyson, D.F. (2009) 'Parental involvement in middle school: A meta-analytic assessment of the strategies that promote achievement'. *Developmental Psychology*, 45 (3), 740–63.

Hill, N.E. and Wang, M.-T. (2015) 'From middle school to college: Developing aspirations, promoting engagement, and indirect pathways from parenting to post high school enrollment'. *Developmental Psychology*, 51 (2), 224–35.

Hinckley, R.H. (ed.) (1979) *Student Home Environment, Educational Achievement, and Compensatory Education* (Study of the Sustaining Effects of Compensatory Education on Basic Skills Technical Report 4). Washington, DC: Office of Evaluation and Dissemination.

Hodapp, A.F. and Hodapp, J.B. (1992) 'Homework: Making it work'. *Intervention in School and Clinic*, 27 (4), 233–5.

Holmes, M. and Croll, P. (1989) 'Time spent on homework and academic achievement'. *Educational Research*, 31 (1), 36–45.

Holte, K.L. (2016) 'Homework in primary school: Could it be made more child-friendly?'. *Studia Paedagogica*, 21 (4), 13–33.

Holtzman, W.H. (1969) 'Study'. In Ebel, R.L. (ed.) *Encyclopedia of Educational Research*. 4th ed. New York: Macmillan, 1389–94.

Hong, E. (1998) 'Homework style, homework environment and academic achievement'. Paper presented at the American Educational Research Association (AERA) Annual Meeting, Montreal, April.

Hong, E. and Lee, K.-H. (2000) 'Preferred homework style and homework environment in high- versus low-achieving Chinese students'. *Educational Psychology*, 20 (2), 125–37.

Hong, E. and Milgram, R.M. (1999) 'Preferred and actual homework style: A cross-cultural examination'. *Educational Research*, 41 (3), 251–65.

Hong, E., Peng, Y. and Rowell, L.L. (2009) 'Homework self-regulation: Grade, gender, and achievement-level differences'. *Learning and Individual Differences*, 19 (2), 269–76.

Hong, E., Wan, M. and Peng, Y. (2011) 'Discrepancies between students' and teachers' perceptions of homework'. *Journal of Advanced Academics*, 22 (2), 280–308.

Hong, S. and Ho, H.-Z. (2005) 'Direct and indirect longitudinal effects of parental involvement on student achievement: Second-order latent growth modeling across ethnic groups'. *Journal of Educational Psychology*, 97 (1), 32–42.

Hoover-Dempsey, K.V., Bassler, O.C. and Burow, R. (1995) 'Parents' reported involvement in students' homework: Strategies and practices'. *Elementary School Journal*, 95 (5), 435–50.

Hoover-Dempsey, K.V., Battiato, A.C., Walker, J.M.T., Reed, R.P., DeJong, J.M. and Jones, K.P. (2001) 'Parental involvement in homework'. *Educational Psychologist*, 36 (3), 195–209.

Hoover-Dempsey, K.V. and Sandler, H.M (1997) 'Why do parents become involved in their children's education?'. *Review of Educational Research*, 67 (1), 3–42.

Huang, D. and Cho, J. (2009) 'Academic enrichment in high-functioning homework afterschool programs'. *Journal of Research in Childhood Education*, 23 (3), 382–92.

Huang, D., Gribbons, B., Kim, K.S., Lee, C. and Baker, E.L. (2000) 'A decade of results: The impact of the LA's BEST after school enrichment program on subsequent student achievement and performance'. University of California, Los Angeles, Center for the Study of Evaluation.

Huang, D., Wang, J. and the CRESST Team (2012) *Independent Statewide Evaluation of High School After School Programs: May 1, 2008–December 31, 2011*. Los Angeles: National Center for Research on Evaluation, Standards, and Student Testing.

Hudson, J.A. (1965) 'A Pilot Study of the Influence of Homework in Seventh Grade Mathematics and Attitudes toward Homework in the Fayetteville Public Schools'. Unpublished EdD thesis, University of Arkansas.

Hughes, C.A., Ruhl, K.L., Schumaker, J.B. and Deshler, D.D. (2002) 'Effects of instruction in an assignment completion strategy on the homework performance of students with learning disabilities in general education classes'. *Learning Disabilities Research and Practice*, 17 (1), 1–18.

Hughes, M. (1993) *Flexible Learning: Evidence examined*. Stafford: Network Educational Press.

Ibañez, G.E., Kuperminc, G.P., Jurkovic, G. and Perilla, J. (2004) 'Cultural attributes and adaptations linked to achievement motivation among Latino adolescents'. *Journal of Youth and Adolescence*, 33 (6), 559–68.

İflazoğlu, A. and Hong, E. (2012) 'Homework motivation and preferences of Turkish students'. *Research Papers in Education*, 27 (3), 343–63.

Incorporated Association of Assistant Masters in Secondary Schools (1928) *Report of the West Kent Branch on Homework in Secondary Schools*. London: Incorporated Association of Assistant Masters in Secondary Schools.

Ireson, J. and Rushforth, K. (2011) 'Private tutoring at transition points in the English education system: Its nature, extent and purpose'. *Research Papers in Education*, 26 (1), 1–19.

Ireson, J. and Rushforth, K. (2014) 'Why do parents employ private tutors for their children? Exploring psychological factors that influence demand in England'. *Journal for Educational Research*, 6 (1), 12–33.

Jacobsen, W.C. and Forste, R. (2011) 'The wired generation: Academic and social outcomes of electronic media use among university students'. *Cyberpsychology, Behavior, and Social Networking*, 14 (5), 275–80.

James-Burdumy, S., Dynarski, M. and Deke, J. (2008) 'After-school program effects on behavior: Results for the 21st Century Community Learning Centers program national evaluation'. *Economic Inquiry*, 46 (1), 13–18.

Jayanthi, M., Bursuck, W., Epstein, M.H. and Polloway, E.A. (1997) 'Strategies for successful homework'. *Teaching Exceptional Children*, 30 (1), 4–7.

Jeynes, W.H. (2005) 'A meta-analysis of the relation of parental involvement to urban elementary school student academic achievement'. *Urban Education*, 40 (3), 237–69.

Jeynes, W.H. (2007) 'The relationship between parental involvement and urban secondary school student academic achievement: A meta-analysis'. *Urban Education*, 42 (1), 82–110.

Jeynes, W. (2012) 'A meta-analysis of the efficacy of different types of parental involvement programs for urban students'. *Urban Education*, 47 (4), 706–42.

Johnson, J.K. and Pontius, A. (1989) 'Homework: A survey of teacher beliefs and practices'. *Research in Education*, 41 (1), 71–8.

Johnson, M. (1999) *Improving Learning: The use of books in schools*. Keele: Keele University Centre for Successful Schools.

Junco, R. and Cotten, S.R. (2011) 'Perceived academic effects of instant messaging use'. *Computers and Education*, 56 (2), 370–8.

Jünger, W., Feider, F.J. and Reinert, G.-B. (1990) 'Auf der Suche nach Hausaufgaben, die Spass machen' [In search of homework that's fun to do]. *Zeitschrift für Pädagogik*, 36 (2), 223–39.

Kackar, H.Z., Shumow, L., Schmidt, J.A. and Grzetich, J. (2011) 'Age and gender differences in adolescents' homework experiences'. *Journal of Applied Developmental Psychology*, 32 (2), 70–7.

Kahle, A.L. and Kelley, M.L. (1994) 'Children's homework problems: A comparison of goal setting and parent training'. *Behavior Therapy*, 25, 275–90.

Kalenkoski, C.M. and Pabilonia, S.W. (2009) 'Does working while in high school reduce US study time?'. *Social Indicators Research*, 93 (1), 117–21.

Kalenkoski, C.M. and Pabilonia, S.W. (2012) 'Time to work or time to play: The effect of student employment on homework, sleep, and screen time'. *Labour Economics*, 19 (2), 211–21.

Kalenkoski, C.M. and Pabilonia, S.W. (2017) 'Does high school homework increase academic achievement?'. *Education Economics*, 25 (1), 45–59.

Kaplan, A. and Maehr, M.L. (2007) 'The contributions and prospects of goal orientation theory'. *Educational Psychology Review*, 19 (2), 141–84.

Karbach, J., Gottschling, J., Spengler, M., Hegewald, K. and Spinath, F.M. (2013) 'Parental involvement and general cognitive ability as predictors of domain-specific academic achievement in early adolescence'. *Learning and Instruction*, 23, 43–51.

Katz, I., Buzukashvili, T. and Feingold, L. (2012) 'Homework stress: Construct validation of a measure'. *Journal of Experimental Education*, 80 (4), 405–21.

Katz, I., Eilot, K. and Nevo, N. (2014) '"I'll do it later": Type of motivation, self-efficacy and homework procrastination'. *Motivation and Emotion*, 38 (1), 111–19.

Katz, I., Kaplan, A. and Buzukashvily, T. (2011) 'The role of parents' motivation in students' autonomous motivation for doing homework'. *Learning and Individual Differences*, 21 (4), 376–86.

Katz, I., Kaplan, A. and Gueta, G. (2010) 'Students' needs, teachers' support, and motivation for doing homework: A cross-sectional study'. *Journal of Experimental Education*, 78 (2), 246–67.

Kaur, B. (2011) 'Mathematics homework: A study of three grade eight classrooms in Singapore'. *International Journal of Science and Mathematics Education*, 9 (1), 187–206.

Kay, P.J., Fitzgerald, M., Paradee, C. and Mellencamp, A. (1994) 'Making homework work at home: The parent's perspective'. *Journal of Learning Disabilities*, 27 (9), 550–61.

Keeble, R. (2016) *Effective Primary Teaching Practice 2016*. Teaching Schools Council. Online. www.tscouncil.org.uk/wp-content/uploads/2016/12/Effective-primary-teaching-practice-2016-report-web.pdf (accessed 11 February 2018).

Keeves, J.P. (1995) *The World of School Learning: Selected key findings from 35 years of IEA research*. The Hague: International Association for the Evaluation of Educational Achievement.

Keith, T.Z. (1982) 'Time spent on homework and high school grades: A large-sample path analysis'. *Journal of Educational Psychology*, 74 (2), 248–53.

Keith, T.Z. (1986) *Homework*. West Lafayette, IN: Kappa Delta Pi.

Keith, T.Z. (1987) 'Children and homework'. In Thomas, A. and Grimes, J. (eds) *Children's Needs: Psychological perspectives*. Washington, DC: National Association of School Psychologists, 275–82.

Keith, T.Z. and Benson, M.J. (1992) 'Effects of manipulable influences on high school grades across five ethnic groups'. *Journal of Educational Research*, 86 (2), 85–93.

Keith, T.Z. and Cool, V.A. (1992) 'Testing models of school learning: Effects of quality of instruction, motivation, academic coursework, and homework on academic achievement'. *School Psychology Quarterly*, 7 (3), 207–26.

Keith, T.Z., Keith, P.B., Troutman, G.C., Bickley, P.G., Trivette, P.S. and Singh, K. (1993) 'Does parental involvement affect eighth-grade student achievement? Structural analysis of national data'. *School Psychology Review*, 22 (3), 474–96.

Keith, T.Z., Reimers, T.M., Fehrmann, P.G., Pottebaum, S.M. and Aubey, L.W. (1986) 'Parental involvement, homework, and TV time: Direct and indirect effects on high school achievement'. *Journal of Educational Psychology*, 78 (5), 373–80.

Kelly, K., Heffernan, N., Heffernan, C., Goldman, S., Pellegrino, J. and Soffer Goldstein, D. (2013) 'Estimating the effect of web-based homework'. In Lane, H.C., Yacef, K., Mostow, J. and Pavlik, P. (eds) *Artificial Intelligence in Education: 16th International Conference (AIED 2013), Memphis, TN, USA, July 9–13, 2013 Proceedings* (Lecture Notes in Artificial Intelligence 7926). Heidelberg: Springer, 824–7.

Kenney-Benson, G.A. and Pomerantz, E.M. (2005) 'The role of mothers' use of control in children's perfectionism: Implications for the development of children's depressive symptoms'. *Journal of Personality*, 73 (1), 23–46.

Kenyon, S. (2008) 'Internet use and time use: The importance of multitasking'. *Time and Society*, 17 (2–3), 283–318.

Keys, W. and Fernandes, C. (1993) *What Do Students Think about School? Research into the factors associated with positive and negative attitudes towards school and education.* Slough: National Foundation for Educational Research.

Keys, W., Harris, S. and Fernandes, C. (1995) *Attitudes to School of Top Primary and First-Year Secondary Pupils.* Slough: National Foundation for Educational Research.

Keys, W., Harris, S. and Fernandes, C. (1997a) *Third International Mathematics and Science Study, First National Report. Part 2: Patterns of mathematics and science teaching in lower secondary schools in England and ten other countries.* Slough: National Foundation for Educational Research.

Keys, W., Harris, S. and Fernandes, C. (1997b) *Third International Mathematics and Science Study, Second National Report. Part 2: Patterns of mathematics and science teaching in upper primary schools in England and eight other countries.* Slough: National Foundation for Educational Research.

Keys, W., Mawson, C. and Maychell, K. (1999) *Out-of-Lesson-Time Learning Activities: Surveys of headteachers and pupils.* London: Department for Education and Employment.

Keys, W. and Wilkinson, D. (1999) *Study Support: A survey of local education authorities* (Research Brief 128). London: Department for Education and Employment.

Kibble, D. (1991) 'Parents' perceptions of GCSE homework'. *Pastoral Care in Education*, 9 (4), 5–8.

Kitsantas, A., Cheema, J. and Ware, H.W. (2011) 'Mathematics achievement: The role of homework and self-efficacy beliefs'. *Journal of Advanced Academics*, 22 (2), 310–39.

Knollmann, M. and Wild, E. (2007) 'Quality of parental support and students' emotions during homework: Moderating effects of students' motivational orientations'. *European Journal of Psychology of Education*, 22 (1), 63–76.

Knorr, C.L. (1981) 'A synthesis of homework research and related literature'. Paper presented to the Lehigh Chapter of Phi Delta Kappa, Bethlehem, Pennsylvania, 24 January 1981.

Kohn, A. (2006) *The Homework Myth: Why our kids get too much of a bad thing.* Cambridge, MA: Da Capo Press.

Kotsopoulou, A. (2001) 'A Cross Cultural Study of the Use and Perceived Effects of Background Music in Studying'. Unpublished PhD thesis, Institute of Education, University of London.

Kotsopoulou, A. and Hallam, S. (2010) 'The perceived impact of playing music while studying: Age and cultural differences', *Educational Studies*, 36 (4), 431–40.

Kremer, K.P., Maynard, B.R., Polanin, J.R., Vaughn, M.G. and Sarteschi, C.M. (2015) 'Effects of after-school programs with at-risk youth on attendance and externalizing behaviors: A systematic review and meta-analysis'. *Journal of Youth and Adolescence*, 44 (3), 616–36.

Kronberg, J. (2014) *Inquiry into the Approaches to Homework in Victorian Schools*. Melbourne: Parliament of Victoria Education and Training Committee.

Kryger, N. and Ravn, B. (2009) 'Homework in Denmark: What kind of links between family and school?'. In Deslandes, R. (ed.) *International Perspectives on Student Outcomes and Homework: Family–school–community partnerships*. London: Routledge, 7–24.

Kukliansky, I., Shosberger, I. and Eshach, H. (2016) 'Science teachers' voice on homework: Beliefs, attitudes, and behaviors'. *International Journal of Science and Mathematics Education*, 14 (Supplement 1), S229–50.

Kuyper, H. and Swint, F.E. (1996) *Microscopisch schoolloopbanenonderzoek*. Groningen: GION, Rijksuniversiteit Groningen.

LaConte, R.T. (1981) *Homework as a Learning Experience (What Research Says to the Teacher)*. Washington, DC: National Education Association.

Lage, M.J., Platt, G.J. and Treglia, M. (2000) 'Inverting the classroom: A gateway to creating an inclusive learning environment'. *Journal of Economic Education*, 31 (1), 30–43.

Laing, R.A. (1970) 'Relative Effects of Massed and Distributed Scheduling of Topics on Homework Assignments of Eighth Grade Mathematics Students'. Unpublished PhD thesis, Ohio State University.

Lam, J.W.-Y. (1996) 'The Employment Activity of Chinese-American High School Students and its Relationship to Academic Achievement'. Unpublished MA thesis, University of Texas at Arlington.

Lapointe, A.E., Mead, N.A. and Askew, J.M. (1992) *Learning Mathematics* (Report No. 22-CAEP-01). Princeton, NJ: Educational Testing Service.

Lareau, A. (2000) *Home Advantage: Social class and parental intervention in elementary education*. 2nd ed. Lanham, MD: Rowman and Littlefield.

Larue, R. (1995) 'Le travail personnel des élèves en dehors de la classe'. *Éducation et formation*, 44, décembre, 5–9.

Lash, S.W.E. (1971) 'A Comparison of Three Types of Homework Assistance for High School Geometry'. Unpublished EdD thesis, Temple University.

Lauer, P.A., Akiba, M., Wilkerson, S.B., Apthorp, H.S., Snow, D. and Martin-Glenn, M.L. (2006) 'Out-of-school-time programs: A meta-analysis of effects for at-risk students'. *Review of Educational Research*, 76 (2), 275–313.

Lee, F.-L. and Heyworth, R.M. (2000) 'Electronic homework'. *Journal of Educational Computing Research*, 22 (2), 171–86.

Lee, J.F. and Pruitt, K.W. (1979) 'Homework assignments: Classroom games or teaching tools?'. *The Clearing House*, 53 (1), 31–5.

Le Métais, J. (1985) *Homework Policy and Practice in Selected European Countries*. Brussels: Eurydice Central Unit.

Leung, J.J. (1993) 'Caucasian- and Chinese-American children's attitudes towards schoolwork and perception of parental behaviors that support schoolwork'. University of Wisconsin-Oshkosh.

Levin, I., Levy-Shiff, R., Appelbaum-Peled, T., Katz, I., Komar, M. and Meiran, N. (1997) 'Antecedents and consequences of maternal involvement in children's homework: A longitudinal analysis'. *Journal of Applied Developmental Psychology*, 18 (2), 207–27.

Liang, X. (2010) 'Assessment use, self-efficacy and mathematics achievement: Comparative analysis of PISA 2003 data of Finland, Canada and the USA'. *Evaluation and Research in Education*, 23 (3), 213–29.

Loitz, P.A. and Kratochwill, T.R. (1995) 'Parent consultation: Evaluation of a self-help manual for children's homework problems'. *School Psychology International*, 16 (4), 389–96.

London County Council (1937) *Homework Classes and Evening Library Classes*. London: County Hall.

Lorenz, F. and Wild, E. (2007) 'Parental involvement in schooling: Results concerning its structure and impact on students' motivation'. In Prenzel, M. (ed.) *Studies on the Educational Quality of Schools: The final report on the DFG Priority Programme*. Münster: Waxmann, 299–316.

Lubbers, M.J., van der Werf, M.P.C., Kuyper, H. and Hendriks, A.A.J. (2010) 'Does homework behavior mediate the relation between personality and academic performance?'. *Learning and Individual Differences*, 20 (3), 203–8.

Luo, W., Ng, P.T., Lee, K. and Aye, K.M. (2016) 'Self-efficacy, value, and achievement emotions as mediators between parenting practice and homework behavior: A control-value theory perspective'. *Learning and Individual Differences*, 50, 275–82.

Ma, X. (1996) 'The effects of cooperative homework on mathematics achievement of Chinese high school students'. *Educational Studies in Mathematics*, 31 (4), 379–87.

MacBeath, J. (1993) *Learning for Yourself: Supported study in Strathclyde Schools*. Glasgow: Strathclyde Regional Council.

MacBeath, J. (1996) 'The homework question'. *Managing Schools Today*, 5 (7), 20–4.

MacBeath, J. (2000) 'New coalitions for promoting school effectiveness'. In Wolfendale, S. and Bastiani, J. (eds) *The Contribution of Parents to School Effectiveness*. London: David Fulton, 37–51.

MacBeath, J., Kirwan, T., Myers, K., McCall, J., Smith, I., McKay, E., Sharp, C., Bhabra, S., Weindling, D. and Pocklington, K. (2001) *The Impact of Study Support: A report of a longitudinal study into the impact of participation in out-of-school-hours learning on the academic attainment, attitudes and school attendance of secondary school students* (Research Report 273). London: Department for Education and Skills.

MacBeath, J. and Turner, M. (1990) *Learning out of School: Homework, policy and practice: A research study commissioned by the Scottish Education Department*. Glasgow: Jordanhill College.

MacFarlane, E. (1987) 'Down with homework – bring back prep'. *Times Educational Supplement*, 20 November (3725), 25.

Maclachlan, K. (1996) 'Good mothers are women too: The gender implications of parental involvement in education'. In Bastiani, J. and Wolfendale, S. (eds) *Home–School Work in Britain: Review, reflection and development*. London: David Fulton, 28–38.

Madjar, N., Shklar, N. and Moshe, L. (2016) 'The role of parental attitudes in children's motivation toward homework assignments'. *Psychology in the Schools*, 53 (2), 173–88.

Maertens, N. and Johnston, J. (1972) 'Effects of arithmetic homework upon the attitudes and achievement of fourth, fifth and sixth grade pupils'. *School Science and Mathematics*, 72 (2), 117–26.

Maharaj-Sharma, R. and Sharma, A. (2016) 'What students say about homework: Views from a secondary school science classroom in Trinidad and Tobago'. *Australian Journal of Teacher Education*, 41 (7), Article 9, 146–57.

Mahoney, J.L., Harris, A.L. and Eccles, J.S. (2006) 'Organized activity participation, positive youth development, and the over-scheduling hypothesis'. *Social Policy Report*, 20 (4), 1–31.

Maltese, A.V., Tai, R.H. and Fan, X. (2012) 'When is homework worth the time? Evaluating the association between homework and achievement in high school science and math'. *High School Journal*, 96 (1), 52–72.

Markow, D., Kim, A. and Liebman, M. (2007) *The MetLife Survey of the American Teacher: The homework experience: A survey of students, teachers and parents*. New York: Metropolitan Life Insurance Company.

Marshall, P.M. (1983) 'Homework and Social Facilitation Theory in Teaching Elementary School Mathematics'. Unpublished PhD thesis, Stanford University.

Martin, M.O., Mullis, I.V.S., Beaton, A.E., Gonzalez, E.J., Smith, T.A. and Kelly, D.L. (1997) *Science Achievement in the Primary School Years: IEA's Third International Mathematics and Science Study (TIMSS)*. Chestnut Hill, MA: Center for the Study of Testing, Evaluation, and Educational Policy, Boston College.

Martinez, S. (2011) 'An examination of Latino students' homework routines'. *Journal of Latinos and Education*, 10 (4), 354–68.

Marzano, R.J. and Pickering, D.J. (2007) 'Special topic: The case for and against homework'. *Educational Leadership*, 64 (6), 74–9.

Marzano, R.J., Pickering, D.J. and Pollock, J.E. (2001) *Classroom Instruction that Works: Research-based strategies for increasing student achievement*. Alexandria, VA: Association for Supervision and Curriculum Development.

Mason, K., Bhabra, S., Mawson, C., Spear, M., Wray, M., Sharp, C. and Rees, F. (1999) *Out-of-School-Hours Learning Activities: An evaluation of fifty pilot schemes* (Research Report 178). London: Department for Education and Employment.

Massoni, E. (2011) 'Positive effects of extra curricular activities on students'. *ESSAI*, 9, Article 27, 84–7.

Mau, W.-C. and Lynn, R. (1999) 'Racial and ethnic differences in motivation for educational achievement in the United States'. *Personality and Individual Differences*, 27 (6), 1091–6.

Mayo, A. and Siraj, I. (2015) 'Parenting practices and children's academic success in low-SES families'. *Oxford Review of Education*, 41 (1), 47–63.

McCaslin, M. and Murdock, T.B. (1991) 'The emergent interaction of home and school in the development of students' adaptive learning'. In Maehr, M.L. and Pintrich, P.R. (eds) *Advances in Motivation and Achievement: A research annual* (vol. 7). Greenwich, CT: JAI Press, 213–59.

McComb, E.M. and Scott-Little, C. (2003) 'A review of research on participant outcomes in after-school programs: Implications for school counselors' (ERIC Digest ED482765). https://files.eric.ed.gov/fulltext/ED482765.pdf (accessed 11 April 2018).

McDermott, R.P., Goldman, S.V. and Varenne, H. (1984) 'When school goes home: Some problems in the organization of homework'. *Teachers College Record*, 85 (3), 391–409.

McGill, R.K., Hughes, D., Alicea, S. and Way, N. (2012) 'Academic adjustment across middle school: The role of public regard and parenting'. *Developmental Psychology*, 48 (4), 1003–18.

Mc Loughlin, L. (2012) 'A Study of the Effects of Participation in an After-School Homework Club'. Unpublished HDip (Psych) dissertation, DBS School of Arts, Dublin. Online. http://esource.dbs.ie/bitstream/handle/10788/443/dip_mcgloughlin_l_2012.pdf (accessed 28 April 2017).

McMullen, S. and Busscher, D. (2010) 'Homework and academic achievement in elementary school'. Working paper, Calvin College.

McNary, S.J., Glasgow, N.A. and Hicks, C.D. (2005) *What Successful Teachers Do in Inclusive Classrooms: 60 research-based teaching strategies that help special learners succeed*. Thousand Oaks, CA: Corwin Press.

McNaughton, S. (1995) *Patterns of Emergent Literacy: Processes of development and transition*. Melbourne: Oxford University Press.

Mendicino, M., Razzaq, L. and Heffernan, N.T. (2009) 'A comparison of traditional homework to computer-supported homework'. *Journal of Research on Technology in Education*, 41 (3), 331–59.

Merttens, R. and Newland, A. (1996) 'Home works: Shared maths and shared writing'. In Bastiani, J. and Wolfendale, S. (eds) *Home–School Work in Britain: Review, reflection and development*. London: David Fulton, 106–17.

Miller, B.M. (2003) 'Critical hours: Afterschool programs and educational success'. Commissioned by the Nellie Mae Education Foundation, Quincy, MA.

Miller, D.L. and Kelley, M.L. (1991) 'Interventions for improving homework performance: A critical review'. *School Psychology Quarterly*, 6 (3), 174–85.

Miller, D.L. and Kelley, M.L. (1994) 'The use of goal setting and contingency contracting for improving children's homework performance'. *Journal of Applied Behavior Analysis*, 27 (1), 73–84.

Miller, L.R. (1947) 'Some effects of radio-listening on the efficiency of reading-type study activities'. *Journal of Educational Psychology*, 38 (2), 105–18.

Mims, A., Harper, C., Armstrong, S.W. and Savage, S. (1991) 'Effective instruction in homework for students with disabilities'. *Teaching Exceptional Children*, 24 (1), 42–4.

Mirza, H.S. (1992) *Young, Female and Black*. London: Routledge.

Mitchell, A.H. (1949) 'The effect of radio programs on silent reading achievement of ninety-one sixth grade students'. *Journal of Educational Research*, 42 (6), 460–70.

MORI (Market and Opinion Research International) (2004) *Study Support Survey 2004* (Research Report 591). Nottingham: Department for Education and Skills.

Mori, I. and Baker, D. (2010) 'The origin of universal shadow education: What the supplemental education phenomenon tells us about the postmodern institution of education'. *Asia Pacific Education Review*, 11 (1), 36–48.

Mullis, I.V.S., Martin, M.O., Beaton, A.E., Gonzalez, E.J., Kelly, D.L. and Smith, T.A. (1997) *Mathematics Achievement in the Primary School Years: IEA's Third International Mathematics and Science Study (TIMSS)*. Chestnut Hill, MA: Center for the Study of Testing, Evaluation, and Educational Policy, Boston College.

Murillo, F.J. and Martínez-Garrido, C. (2013) 'Homework influence on academic performance: A study of Iberoamerican students of primary education'. *Revista de Psicodidáctica*, 18 (1), 157–78.

Murillo, F.J. and Martínez-Garrido, C. (2014) 'Homework and primary-school students' academic achievement in Latin America'. *International Review of Education*, 60 (5), 661–81.

Murphy, J. and Decker, K. (1989) 'Teachers' use of homework in high schools'. *Journal of Educational Research*, 82 (5), 261–9.

Murphy, P. and Elwood, J. (1998) 'Gendered experiences, choices and achievement: Exploring the links'. *International Journal of Inclusive Education*, 2 (2), 95–118.

Nadis, M.L. (1965) 'A Status Study of Homework Practices and Attitudes of Detroit Ninth Grade Social Studies Teachers and Ninth Grade Students including a Pilot Experimental Study of Two Ninth Grade Social Studies Classes'. Unpublished EdD thesis, Wayne State University.

National Commission on Excellence in Education (1983) *A Nation at Risk: The imperative for educational reform*. Washington, DC: National Commission on Excellence in Education.

Natriello, G. and McDill, E.L. (1986) 'Performance standards, student effort on homework, and academic achievement'. *Sociology of Education*, 59 (1), 18–31.

Nelson, J.S., Epstein, M.H., Bursuck, W.D., Jayanthi, M. and Sawyer, V. (1998) 'The preferences of middle school students for homework adaptations made by general education teachers'. *Learning Disabilities Research and Practice*, 13 (2), 109–17.

Newsom, J. (1963) *Half Our Future: A report of the Central Advisory Council for Education (England)*. London: HMSO.

New South Wales Department of Education and Communities (2012) *Homework Policy: Guidelines*. Sydney: Government of New South Wales.

Nicol, D.J. and Macfarlane-Dick, D. (2006) 'Formative assessment and self-regulated learning: A model and seven principles of good feedback practice'. *Studies in Higher Education*, 31 (2), 199–218.

Niggli, A., Trautwein, U., Schnyder, I., Lüdtke, O. and Neumann, M. (2007) 'Elterliche Unterstützung kann hilfreich sein, aber Einmischung schadet: Familiärer Hintergrund, elterliches Hausaufgabenengagement und Leistungsentwicklung [Parental homework support can be beneficial, but parental intrusion is detrimental: Family background, parental homework supervision and performance gains]'. *Psychologie in Erziehung und Unterricht*, 54 (1), 1–14.

Nolen-Hoeksema, S., Wolfson, A., Mumme, D. and Guskin, K. (1995) 'Helplessness in children of depressed and nondepressed mothers'. *Developmental Psychology*, 31 (3), 377–87.

North, S. and Pillay, H. (2002) 'Homework: Re-examining the routine'. *ELT Journal*, 56 (2), 137–45.

North Carolina Department of Public Instruction (1983) *Report on Student Homework and Achievement, Spring 1982 and Spring 1983* (Special Research Studies, 1983–1984). Raleigh, NC: Division of Research, North Carolina Department of Public Instruction.

Nova Scotia Department of Education and Early Childhood Development (2015a) *Provincial Homework Policy (Grades P–12)*. Halifax, NS: Department of Education and Early Childhood Development.

Nova Scotia Department of Education and Early Childhood Development (2015b) *The 3 Rs: Renew, refocus, rebuild – Nova Scotia's Action Plan for Education*. Halifax, NS: Department of Education and Early Childhood Development.

Núñez, J.C., Rosário, P., Vallejo, G. and González-Pienda, J.A. (2013) 'A longitudinal assessment of the effectiveness of a school-based mentoring program in middle school'. *Contemporary Educational Psychology*, 38 (1), 11–21.

Núñez, J.C., Suárez, N., Cerezo, R., González-Pienda, J., Rosário, P., Mourão, R. and Valle, A. (2015) 'Homework and academic achievement across Spanish compulsory education'. *Educational Psychology*, 35 (6), 726–46.

Núñez, J.C., Suárez, N., Rosário, P., Vallejo, G., Cerezo, R. and Valle, A. (2015) 'Teachers' feedback on homework, homework-related behaviors, and academic achievement'. *Journal of Educational Research*, 108 (3), 204–16.

Núñez, J.C., Suárez, N., Rosário, P., Vallejo, G., Valle, A. and Epstein, J.L. (2015) 'Relationships between perceived parental involvement in homework, student homework behaviors, and academic achievement: Differences among elementary, junior high, and high school students'. *Metacognition and Learning*, 10 (3), 375–406.

Núñez, J.C., Vallejo, G., Rosário, P., Tuero, E. and Valle, A. (2014) 'Student, teacher, and school context variables predicting academic achievement in biology: Analysis from a multilevel perspective'. *Revista de Psicodidáctica*, 19 (1), 145–71.

O'Connor, W.L. (1985) 'Two Methods of Grading Homework and Their Effect upon Student Achievement'. Unpublished MA thesis, University of Texas at Austin.

OCR and Shireland Collegiate Academy (n.d.) 'Flipped learning'. Online. www.ocr.org.uk/about/what-we-do/supporting-education/shireland-collegiate-academy/flipped-learning/ (accessed 28 August 2017).

OECD (Organisation for Economic Co-operation and Development) (2001) *Knowledge and Skills for Life: First results from the OECD Programme for International Student Assessment (PISA) 2000*. Paris: OECD Publishing.

OECD (Organisation for Economic Co-operation and Development) (2013) *PISA 2012 Results: Excellence through equity: Giving every student the chance to succeed (volume II)*. Paris: OECD Publishing.

OECD (Organisation for Economic Co-operation and Development) (2014) 'Does homework perpetuate inequities in education?'. *PISA in Focus*, 46, 1–4.

OECD (Organisation for Economic Co-operation and Development) (2015) *The ABC of Gender Equality in Education: Aptitude, behaviour, confidence*. Paris: OECD Publishing.

OECD (Organisation for Economic Co-operation and Development) (2016) 'Are there differences in how advantaged and disadvantaged students use the internet?'. *PISA in Focus*, 64, 1–4.

Offer, S. (2013) 'Family time activities and adolescents' emotional well-being'. *Journal of Marriage and Family*, 75 (1), 26–41.

Ofsted (Office for Standards in Education) (1994) *Taught Time: A report on the relationship between the length of the taught week and the quality and standards of pupils' work, including examination results*. London: Office for Standards in Education.

Ofsted (Office for Standards in Education) (1995) *Homework in Primary and Secondary Schools: A report from the Office of Her Majesty's Chief Inspector of Schools*. London: HMSO.

Ofsted (Office for Standards in Education) (2012) *Free Guide: The New Ofsted Framework: A guide to being outstanding*. London: HMSO.

Olympia, D.E., Sheridan, S.M., Jenson, W.R. and Andrews, D. (1994) 'Using student-managed interventions to increase homework completion and accuracy'. *Journal of Applied Behavior Analysis*, 27 (1), 85–99.

O'Melia, M.C. and Rosenberg, M.S. (1994) 'Effects of cooperative homework teams on the acquisition of mathematics skills by secondary students with mild disabilities'. *Exceptional Children*, 60 (6), 538–48.

Ontario Ministry of Education (2012) 'Homework Help'. Online. www.edu.gov.on.ca/elearning/homework.html (accessed 28 August 2017).

Osgood, J. and Keys, W. (1998) *Headteachers' Main Concerns* (Annual Survey of Trends in Education, Digest No. 5). Slough: National Foundation for Educational Research.

Otto, H.J. (1941) 'Elementary education'. In Monroe, W.S. (ed.) *Encyclopedia of Educational Research*. New York: Macmillan.

Otto, H.J. (1950) 'Elementary education'. In Monroe, W.S. (ed.) *Encyclopedia of Educational Research*. 2nd ed. New York: Macmillan.

Otto, W. (1985) 'Homework: A meta-analysis'. *Journal of Reading*, 28 (8), 764–6.

Oubrayrie-Roussel, N. and Safont-Mottay, C. (2011) 'Adolescent homework management strategies and perceptions of parental involvement'. *International Journal about Parents in Education*, 5 (2), 78–85.

Pabilonia, S.W. (2015) 'Children's media use and homework time' (IZA Discussion Paper 9126). Bonn: Institute for the Study of Labor.

Paschal, R.A., Weinstein, T. and Walberg, H.J. (1984) 'The effects of homework on learning: A quantitative synthesis'. *Journal of Educational Research*, 78 (2), 97–104.

Patall, E.A., Cooper, H. and Robinson, J.C. (2008) 'Parent involvement in homework: A research synthesis'. *Review of Educational Research*, 78 (4), 1039–1101.

Patall, E.A., Cooper, H. and Wynn, S.R. (2010) 'The effectiveness and relative importance of choice in the classroom'. *Journal of Educational Psychology*, 102 (4), 896–915.

Patton, J.E., Stinard, T.A. and Routh, D.K. (1983) 'Where do children study?'. *Journal of Educational Research*, 76 (5), 280–6.

Paul Hamlyn Foundation (2015) 'STAR Communities First'. Paul Hamlyn Foundation. London. Online. www.phf.org.uk/wp-content/uploads/2015/06/STAR-case-study.pdf (accessed 28 August 2017).

Pendergrass, R.A. (1985) 'Homework: Is it really a basic?'. *The Clearing House*, 58 (7), 310–14.

Peng, Y., Hong, E., Li, X., Wan, M. and Long, Y. (2010) 'Homework problems: Do students from rural and urban schools perceive differently?'. *International Journal of Learning*, 17 (3), 81–96.

Penn, J.H., Nedeff, V.M. and Gozdzik, G. (2000) 'Organic chemistry and the internet: A web-based approach to homework and testing using the WE_LEARN system'. *Journal of Chemical Education*, 77 (2), 227–31.

Penserio, N. and Green, F. (2017) 'Out-of-school-time study programmes: Do they work?' *Oxford Review of Education*, 43 (1), 127–47.

Perkins, P.G. and Milgram, R.M. (1996) 'Parent involvement in homework: A double-edged sword'. *International Journal of Adolescence and Youth*, 6 (3), 195–203.

Peterson, E.R. and Irving, S.E. (2008) 'Secondary school students' conceptions of assessment and feedback'. *Learning and Instruction*, 18 (3), 238–50.

Peterson, J.C. (1969) 'Effect of Exploratory Homework Exercises upon Achievement in Eighth Grade Mathematics'. Unpublished PhD thesis, Ohio State University.

Pocklington, K. (1996) 'The evaluator's view'. In Myers, K. (ed.) *School Improvement in Practice: Schools Make a Difference project*. London: Falmer Press, 126–60.

Polloway, E.A., Foley, R.M. and Epstein, M.H. (1992) 'A comparison of the homework problems of students with learning disabilities and nonhandicapped students'. *Learning Disabilities Research and Practice*, 7 (4), 203–9.

Pomerantz, E.M. and Eaton, M.M. (2001) 'Maternal intrusive support in the academic context: Transactional socialization processes'. *Developmental Psychology*, 37 (2), 174–86.

Pomerantz, E.M., Grolnick, W.S. and Price, C.E. (2005) 'The role of parents in how children approach achievement: A dynamic process perspective'. In Elliot, A.J. and Dweck, C.S. (eds) *Handbook of Competence and Motivation*. New York: Guilford Press, 259–78.

Pomerantz, E.M., Moorman, E.A. and Litwack, S.D. (2007) 'The how, whom, and why of parents' involvement in children's academic lives: More is not always better'. *Review of Educational Research*, 77 (3), 373–410.

Pomerantz, E.M., Ng, F.F.-Y. and Wang, Q. (2006) 'Mothers' mastery-oriented involvement in children's homework: Implications for the well-being of children with negative perceptions of competence'. *Journal of Educational Psychology*, 98 (1), 99–111.

Posner, J.K. and Vandell, D.L. (1994) 'Low-income children's after-school care: Are there beneficial effects of after-school programs?'. *Child Development*, 65 (2), 440–56.

Pratt, M.W., Green, D., MacVicar, J. and Bountrogianni, M. (1992) 'The mathematical parent: Parental scaffolding, parenting style, and learning outcomes in long-division mathematics homework'. *Journal of Applied Developmental Psychology*, 13 (1), 17–34.

Pressey, S.L. (1927) 'A machine for automatic teaching of drill material'. *School and Society*, 25, 549–52.

Pressman, R.M., Sugarman, D.B., Nemon, M.L., Desjarlais, J., Owens, J.A. and Schettini-Evans, A. (2015) 'Homework and family stress: With consideration of parents' self confidence, educational level, and cultural background'. *American Journal of Family Therapy*, 43 (4), 297–313.

Preston, C., Gohil, N. and Langan, F. (2014) 'About Show My Homework: Report summary'. MirandaNet, London. Online. http://39lu337z5lllzjr1i1ntpio4-wpengine.netdna-ssl.com/wp-content/uploads/2015/10/SMHW_research_paper.pdf (accessed 15 September 2017).

Project Tomorrow (2015) *Closing the Homework Gap with Mobile Devices and Wireless Connectivity.* Online. www.qualcomm.com/documents/closing-homework-gap-mobile-devices-wireless-connectivity (accessed 28 April 2017).

Puustinen, M., Lyyra, A.-L., Metsäpelto, R.-L. and Pulkkinen, L. (2008) 'Children's help seeking: The role of parenting'. *Learning and Instruction*, 18 (2), 160–71.

Ramdass, D. and Zimmerman, B.J. (2011) 'Developing self-regulation skills: The important role of homework'. *Journal of Advanced Academics*, 22 (2), 194–218.

Rankin, P.T. (1967) 'The relationship between parent behavior and achievement of inner city elementary school children'. Paper presented at the American Educational Research Association (AERA) Annual Meeting, New York, 18 February 1967.

Reach, K. and Cooper, H. (2010) 'Homework hotlines: Recommendations for successful practice'. *Theory into Practice*, 43 (3), 234–41.

Reay, D. (1998) *Class Work: Mothers' involvement in their children's primary schooling.* London: UCL Press.

Reetz, L.J. (1991) 'Parental perceptions of homework'. *Rural Educator*, 12 (2), 14–19.

Richards, L., Garratt, E., Heath, A.F., Anderson, L. and Altintaş, E. (2016) *The Childhood Origins of Social Mobility: Socio-economic inequalities and changing opportunities.* London: Social Mobility Commission.

Rickards, J.P. (1982) 'Homework'. In Mitzel, H.E. (ed.) *Encyclopedia of Educational Research* (vol. 2). 5th ed. New York: Free Press, 831–4.

Rideout, V. and Katz, V.S. (2016) *Opportunity for All? Technology and learning in lower-income families.* New York: Joan Ganz Cooney Center at Sesame Workshop.

Roderique, T.W., Polloway, E.A., Cumblad, C., Epstein, M.H. and Bursuck, W.D. (1994) Homework: A survey of policies in the United States. *Journal of Learning Disabilities*, 27 (8), 481–7.

Rogers, L. (2013a) 'Perceptions of studying during adolescence: Student typologies and the relationship with attainment'. *Educational Studies*, 39 (3), 298–314.

Rogers, L. (2013b) 'Underlying factors in perceptions of studying during adolescence'. *Research Papers in Education*, 28 (4), 443–58.

Rogers, L. and Hallam, S. (2006) 'Gender differences in approaches to studying for the GCSE among high-achieving pupils'. *Educational Studies*, 32 (1), 59–71.

Rogers, L. and Hallam, S. (2010) 'Gender differences in perceptions of studying for the GCSE'. *International Journal of Inclusive Education*, 14 (8), 795–811.

Ronen, M. and Eliahu, M. (1999) 'Simulation as a home learning environment: Students' views'. *Journal of Computer Assisted Learning*, 15 (4), 258–68.

Rønning, M. (2011) 'Who benefits from homework assignments?'. *Economics of Education Review*, 30 (1), 55–64.

Rosário, P., González-Pienda, J.A., Cerezo, R., Pinto, R., Ferreira, P., Abilio, L. and Paiva, O. (2010) 'Eficacia del programa "(Des)venturas de Testas" para la promoción de un enfoque profundo de studio [Efficacy of the programme "Testas's (mis)adventures" in promoting the deep approach to learning]'. *Psicothema*, 22 (4), 828–34.

Rosário, P., Mourão, R., Baldaque, M., Nunes, T., Núñez, J.C., Gonzalez-Pienda, J.A., Cerezo, R. and Valle, A. (2009) 'Homework, self-regulated learning and math achievement'. *Revista de Psicodidáctica*, 14 (2), 179–92.

Rosário, P., Núñez, J.C., Valle, A., González-Pienda, J. and Lourenço, A. (2013) 'Grade level, study time, and grade retention and their effects on motivation, self-regulated learning strategies, and mathematics achievement: A structural equation model'. *European Journal of Psychology of Education*, 28 (4), 1311–31.

Rosário, P., Núñez, J.C., Valle, A., Paiva, O. and Polydoro, S. (2013) 'Approaches to teaching in high school when considering contextual variables and teacher variables'. *Revista de Psicodidáctica*, 18 (1), 25–46.

Rosário, P., Núñez, J.C., Vallejo, G., Cunha, J., Azevedo, R., Pereira, R., Nunes, A.R., Fuentes, S. and Moreira, T. (2016) 'Promoting Gypsy children school engagement: A story-tool project to enhance self-regulated learning'. *Contemporary Educational Psychology*, 47, 84–94.

Rosário, P., Núñez, J.C., Vallejo, G., Cunha, J., Nunes, T., Suárez, N., Fuentes, S. and Moreira, T. (2015) 'The effects of teachers' homework follow-up practices on students' EFL performance: A randomized-group design'. *Frontiers in Psychology*, 6, Article 1528, 1–11.

Roschelle, J., Feng, M., Murphy, R.F. and Mason, C.A. (2016) 'Online mathematics homework increases student achievement'. *AERA Open*, 2 (4), 1–12.

Rosen, L.D., Carrier, L.M. and Cheever, N.A. (2013) 'Facebook and texting made me do it: Media-induced task-switching while studying'. *Computers in Human Behavior* 29 (3), 948–58.

Rosenberg, M.S. (1989) 'The effects of daily homework assignments on the acquisition of basic skills by students with learning disabilities'. *Journal of Learning Disabilities*, 22 (5), 314–23.

Rosenzweig, C. (2000) 'A Meta-analysis of Parenting and School Success: The role of parents in promoting students' academic performance'. Unpublished EdD thesis, Hofstra University.

Rutter, M., Maughan, B., Mortimore, P., Ouston, J. and Smith, A. (1979) *Fifteen Thousand Hours: Secondary schools and their effects on children*. Cambridge, MA: Harvard University Press.

Ryan, R.M. and Connell, J.P. (1989) 'Perceived locus of causality and internalization: Examining reasons for acting in two domains'. *Journal of Personality and Social Psychology*, 57 (5), 749–61.

Sadler, D.R. (2005) 'Interpretations of criteria-based assessment and grading in higher education'. *Assessment and Evaluation in Higher Education*, 30 (2), 175–94.

Safont-Mottay, C., Oubrayrie-Roussel, N. and Lescarret, O. (2009) 'Parent–child dyad's representations regarding homework and primary pupils' views of parental involvement in homework'. In Deslandes, R. (ed.) *International Perspectives on Student Outcomes and Homework: Family–school–community partnerships*. London: Routledge, 95–110.

Salend, S.J. and Schliff, J. (1989) 'An examination of the homework practices of teachers of students with learning disabilities'. *Journal of Learning Disabilities*, 22 (10), 621–3.

Sammons, P., Sylva, K., Melhuish, E., Siraj, I., Taggart, B., Toth, K. and Smees R. (2014) *Influences on Students' GCSE Attainment and Progress at Age 16: Effective Pre-School, Primary and Secondary Education Project (EPPSE)* (Research Report 352). London: Department for Education.

Savage, J.F. (1966) 'The Opinions of New England School Superintendents, Elementary Principals, Teachers, Parents, and Children Relative to the Value of Homework in the Middle Grades of the Elementary School'. Unpublished EdD thesis, Boston University.

Schunert, J. (1951) 'The association of mathematical achievement with certain factors resident in the teacher, in the teaching, in the pupil, and in the school'. *Journal of Experimental Education*, 19 (3), 219–38.

Sénéchal, M. and Young, L. (2008) 'The effect of family literacy interventions on children's acquisition of reading from kindergarten to grade 3: A meta-analytic review'. *Review of Educational Research*, 78 (4), 880–907.

Sharp, C., Keys, W., Benefield, P., Flanagan, N., Sukhnandan, L., Mason, K., Hawker, J., Kimber, J., Kendall, L. and Hutchison, D. (2001) *Recent Research on Homework: An annotated bibliography*. Slough: National Foundation for Educational Research.

Sheldon, S.B. and Epstein, J.L. (2002) 'Improving student behavior and school discipline with family and community involvement'. *Education and Urban Society*, 35 (1), 4–26.

Shute, V.J. (2008) 'Focus on formative feedback'. *Review of Educational Research*, 78 (1), 153–89.

Sidhu, G.K. and Fook, C.Y. (2010) 'Organisation of homework: Malaysian teachers' practices and perspectives'. *Research Journal of International Studies*, 13, 63–78.

Silinskas, G., Niemi, P., Lerkkanen, M.-K. and Nurmi, J.-E. (2013) 'Children's poor academic performance evokes parental homework assistance – but does it help?'. *International Journal of Behavioral Development*, 37 (1), 44–56.

Singh, J.M. (1969) 'An Investigation of the Effect of Individualized Enrichment Homework upon the Academic Achievement of Children in the Fourth, Fifth, and Sixth Grades'. Unpublished EdD thesis, Arizona State University.

Singh, R., Saleem, M., Pradhan, P., Heffernan, C., Heffernan, N., Razzaq, L., Dailey, M., O'Connor, C. and Mulcah, C. (2011) 'Feedback during web-based homework: The role of hints'. In Biswas, G., Bull, S., Kay, J. and Mitrovic, A. (eds) *Artificial Intelligence in Education: 15th International Conference (AIED 2011), Auckland, New Zealand, June 28–July 1, 2011* (Lecture Notes in Artificial Intelligence 6738). Heidelberg: Springer, 328–36.

Skaliotis, E. (2010) 'Changes in parental involvement in secondary education: An exploration study using the longitudinal study of young people in England'. *British Educational Research Journal*, 36 (6), 975–94.

Skinner, B.F. (1958) 'Teaching machines'. *Science*, 128 (3330), 969–77.

Small, D.E., Holtan, B.D. and Davis, E.J. (1967) 'A study of two methods of checking homework in a high school geometry class'. *Mathematics Teacher*, 60 (2), 149–52.

Smilansky, S. and Fisher, N. (1982) *Problems Raised by Mothers in Parent-Education Groups*. Jerusalem: Ministry of Education and Culture, Publication no. 606.

Smilansky, S., Fisher, N. and Shefatya, L. (1986) *The Family and the School: Towards a model of relationship*. Tel Aviv: Am Oved.

Snead, D. and Burris, K.G. (2016) 'Middle school teachers' perceptions regarding the motivation and effectiveness of homework'. *Journal of Inquiry and Action in Education*, 7 (2), 62–80.

Soderlund, J., Bursuck, B., Polloway, E.A. and Foley, R.A. (1995). 'A comparison of the homework problems of secondary school students with behavior disorders and nondisabled peers'. *Journal of Emotional and Behavioral Disorders*, 3 (3), 150–5.

Solomon, Y., Warin, J. and Lewis, C. (2002) 'Helping with homework? Homework as a site of tension for parents and teenagers'. *British Educational Research Journal*, 28 (4), 603–22.

Sparks, S.D. (2011) 'Schools "flip" for lesson model promoted by Khan Academy'. *Education Week*, 31 (5), 1–14.

Stainburn, S. (2014) 'High schools assign 3.5 hours of homework a night, survey estimates'. *Education Week* blog, 27 February. Online. http://blogs.edweek.org/edweek/time_and_learning/2014/02/high_schools_assign_3.5_hours.html (accessed 11 February 2018).

Stewart, L.G. and White, M.A. (1976) 'Teacher comments, letter grades, and student performance: What do we really know?'. *Journal of Educational Psychology*, 68 (4), 488–500.

Stoeger, H. and Ziegler, A. (2008) 'Evaluation of a classroom based training to improve self-regulation in time management tasks during homework activities with fourth graders'. *Metacognition and Learning*, 3 (3), 207–30.

Strand, S. (2011) 'The limits of social class in explaining ethnic gaps in educational attainment'. *British Educational Research Journal*, 37 (2), 197–229.

Strandberg, M. (2013) 'Homework – is there a connection with classroom assessment? A review from Sweden'. *Educational Research*, 55 (4), 325–46.

Strang, R.M. (1960) 'Homework and guided study'. In Harris, C.W. (ed.) *Encyclopedia of Educational Research*. 3rd ed. New York: Macmillan, 675–9.

Strang, R.M. (1968) *Guided Study and Homework* (What Research Says to the Teacher). Rev. ed. Washington, DC: National Education Association.

Straw, S., Quinlan, O., Harland, J. and Walker, M. (2015) *Flipped Learning: Research report*. London: Nesta.

Strukoff, P.M., McLaughlin, T.F. and Bialozor, R.C. (1987) 'The effects of a daily report card system in increasing homework completion and accuracy in a special education setting'. *Techniques*, 3 (1), 19–26.

Suárez, N., Regueiro, B., Epstein, J.L., Piñeiro, I., Díaz, S.M. and Valle, A. (2016) 'Homework involvement and academic achievement of native and immigrant students'. *Frontiers in Psychology*, 7, Article 1517, 1–8.

Suárez Riveiro, J.M., Gonzalez Cabanach, R. and Valle Arias, A. (2001) 'Multiple-goal pursuit and its relation to cognitive, self-regulatory, and motivational strategies'. *British Journal of Educational Psychology*, 71 (4), 561–72.

Sylva, K., Melhuish, E., Sammons, P., Siraj, I., Taggart, B., Smees, R., Toth, K., Welcomme, W. and Hollingworth, K. (2014) *Students' Educational and Developmental Outcomes at Age 16: Effective Pre-School, Primary and Secondary Education (EPPSE 3–16) Project* (Research Report 354). London: Department for Education.

Symeou, L. (2001) 'Family–school liaisons in Cyprus: An investigation of families' perspectives and needs'. In Smit, F., van der Wolf, K. and Sleegers, P. (eds) *A Bridge to the Future: Collaboration between parents, schools and communities*. Nijmegen: Institute for Applied Social Sciences, 33–43.

Symeou, L. (2002) 'Present and future home–school relations in Cyprus: An investigation of teachers' and parents' perspectives'. *School Community Journal*, 12 (2), 7–34.

Symeou, L. (2009) 'Mind the gap! Greek-Cypriot parents and their children's homework'. In Deslandes, R. (ed.) *International Perspectives on Student Outcomes and Homework*. London: Routledge, 92–110.

Tait, H. and Entwistle, N. (1996) 'Identifying students at risk through ineffective study strategies'. *Higher Education*, 31 (1), 97–116.

Tam, V.C. and Chan, R.M.C. (2016) 'What is homework for? Hong Kong primary school teachers' homework conceptions'. *School Community Journal*, 26 (1), 25–44.

Tas, Y., Vural, S.S. and Öztekin, C. (2014) 'A study of science teachers' homework practices'. *Research in Education*, 91 (1), 45–64.

Thin, D. (2008) 'Les familles populaires face aux devoirs'. *Cahiers pédagogiques*, 468, 23–4.

Thoennessen, M. and Harrison, M.J. (1996) 'Computer-assisted assignments in a large physics class'. *Computers and Education*, 27 (2), 141–7.

Thriving Places (2017) 'Family Meal and Homework Club'. Thriving Places blog, 18 May. Online. https://thrivingpdc.wordpress.com/2017/05/18/family-meal-homework-club/ (accessed 15 September 2017).

Timperley, H., McNaughton, S., Parr, J. and Robinson, V. (1992) *Community–School Collaboration: Beliefs and practices*. Auckland: Auckland UniServices.

Toomey, D. (1989) 'How home–school relations policies can increase educational inequality: A three-year follow-up'. *Australian Journal of Education*, 33 (3), 284–98.

Tower Hamlets Study Support Project (1997) *Closing the Gap: Tower Hamlets Study Support Project*. London: Tower Hamlets Study Support Project.

Train, B., Nankivell, C., Shoolbred, M. and Denham, D. (2000) *The Value and Impact of Homework Clubs in Public Libraries* (Library and Information Commission Research Report 32). London: Library and Information Commission.

Trammel, D.L., Schloss, P.J. and Alper, S. (1994) 'Using self-recording, evaluation, and graphing to increase completion of homework assignments'. *Journal of Learning Disabilities*, 27 (2), 75–81.

Trautwein, U. (2007) 'The homework–achievement relation reconsidered: Differentiating homework time, homework frequency, and homework effort'. *Learning and Instruction*, 17 (3), 372–88.

Trautwein, U., Köller, O., Schmitz, B. and Baumert, J. (2002) 'Do homework assignments enhance achievement? A multilevel analysis in 7th-grade mathematics'. *Contemporary Educational Psychology*, 27 (1), 26–50.

Trautwein, U. and Kropf, M. (2004) 'Students' homework motivation and behavior – and their parents' knowledge of it'. *Psychologie in Erziehung und Unterricht*, 51 (4), 285–95.

Trautwein, U. and Lüdtke, O. (2007) 'Students' self-reported effort and time on homework in six school subjects: Between-students differences and within-student variation'. *Journal of Educational Psychology*, 99 (2), 432–44.

Trautwein, U. and Lüdtke, O. (2009) 'Predicting homework motivation and homework effort in six school subjects: The role of person and family characteristics, classroom factors, and school track'. *Learning and Instruction*, 19 (3), 243–58.

Trautwein, U., Lüdtke, O., Kastens, C. and Köller, O. (2006a) 'Effort on homework in grades 5–9: Development, motivational antecedents, and the association with effort on classwork'. *Child Development*, 77 (4), 1094–111.

Trautwein, U., Lüdtke, O., Schnyder, I. and Niggli. A. (2006b) 'Predicting homework effort: Support for a domain-specific, multilevel homework model'. *Journal of Educational Psychology*, 98 (2), 438–56.

Trautwein, U., Niggli, A., Schnyder, I. and Lüdtke, O. (2009) 'Between-teacher differences in homework assignments and the development of students' homework effort, homework emotions, and achievement'. *Journal of Educational Psychology*, 101 (1), 176–89.

Trautwein, U., Schnyder, I., Niggli, A., Neumann, M. and Lüdtke, O. (2009) 'Chameleon effects in homework research: The homework–achievement association depends on the measures used and the level of analysis chosen'. *Contemporary Educational Psychology*, 34 (1), 77–88.

Tymms, P.B. and Fitz-Gibbon, C.T. (1992) 'The relationship of homework to A-level results'. *Educational Research*, 34 (1), 3–10.

UK Parliament (1886) *First Report of the Royal Commission Appointed to Inquire into the Working of the Elementary Education Acts (England and Wales)*. Parliamentary Papers 1886. London: HMSO.

Ulich, K. (1989) 'Eltern und Schüler: Die Schule als Problem in der Familienerziehung [Parents and students: The impact of the school on education in the family]'. *Zeitschrift für Sozialisationsforschung und Erziehungssoziologie*, 9, 179–94.

University of Phoenix College of Education (2014) 'Homework anxiety: Survey reveals how much homework K-12 students are assigned and why teachers deem it beneficial'. *UOPX News*, 25 February. Online. www.phoenix.edu/news/releases/2014/02/survey-reveals-how-much-homework-k-12-students-are-assigned-why-teachers-deem-it-beneficial.html (accessed 1 September 2017).

US Office of the Press Secretary (2015) 'FACT SHEET: ConnectHome: Coming Together to Ensure Digital Opportunity for All Americans', 15 July. Online. https://obamawhitehouse.archives.gov/sites/default/files/docs/wh_connect_home_fact_sheet.pdf (accessed 17 April 2018).

Valle, A., Núñez, J.C., Cabanach, R.G., Rodríguez, S., Rosário, P. and Inglés, C.J. (2015) 'Motivational profiles as a combination of academic goals in higher education'. *Educational Psychology*, 35 (5), 634–50.

Valle, A., Regueiro, B., Núñez, J.C., Rodríguez, S., Piñeiro, I. and Rosário, P. (2016) 'Academic goals, student homework engagement, and academic achievement in elementary school'. *Frontiers in Psychology*, 7, Article 463, 1–10.

Van Voorhis, F.L. (2001) 'Interactive science homework: An experiment in home and school connections'. *NASSP Bulletin*, 85 (627), 20–32.

Van Voorhis, F.L. (2003) 'Interactive homework in middle school: Effects on family involvement and science achievement'. *Journal of Educational Research*, 96 (6), 323–38.

Van Voorhis, F.L. (2011) 'Costs and benefits of family involvement in homework'. *Journal of Advanced Academics*, 22 (2), 220–49.

Vatterott, C. (2011) 'Making homework central to learning'. *Educational Leadership*, 69 (3), 60–4.

Villas-Boas, A. (1998) 'The effects of parental involvement in homework on student achievement in Portugal and Luxembourg'. *Childhood Education*, 74 (6), 367–71.

Vincent, C. (1996) *Parents and Teachers: Power and participation*. London: Falmer Press.

Wain, G.T. and Flower, S. (1992) 'Mathematics homework on a micro'. *Mathematics in School*, 21 (3), 8–11.

Walberg, H.J. (1991) 'Does homework help?'. *School Community Journal*, 1 (1), 13–15.

Walberg, H.J. and Paik, S.J. (2000) *Effective Educational Practices* (Educational Practices 3). Brussels: International Academy of Education.

Walberg, H.J., Paschal, R.A. and Weinstein, T. (1985) 'Homework's powerful effects on learning'. *Educational Leadership*, 42 (7), 76–9.

Walberg, H.J., Paschal, R. and Weinstein, T. (1986) 'Walberg and colleagues reply: Effective schools use homework effectively'. *Educational Leadership*, 43 (8), 58.

Wallinger, L.M. (2000) 'The role of homework in foreign language learning'. *Foreign Language Annals*, 33 (5), 483–96.

Walsh, L., Lemon, B., Black, R., Mangan, C. and Collin, P. (2011) *The Role of Technology in Engaging Disengaged Youth: Final report*. Canberra: Australian Flexible Learning Framework.

Ward, J.C. (1948) *Children out of School: An inquiry into the leisure interests and activities of children out of school hours carried out for the Central Advisory Council for Education (England) in November–December 1947*. London: Central Office of Information.

Warrington, M. and Younger, M. (1999) 'Perspectives on the gender gap in English secondary schools'. *Research Papers in Education*, 14 (1), 51–77.

Warrington, M., Younger, M. and Williams, J. (2000) 'Student attitudes, image and the gender gap'. *British Educational Research Journal*, 26 (3), 393–407.

Warton, P.M. (1997) 'Learning about responsibility: Lessons from homework'. *British Journal of Educational Psychology*, 67 (2), 213–21.

Warton, P.M. (2001) 'The forgotten voices in homework: Views of students'. *Educational Psychologist*, 36 (3), 155–65.

Weeden, P., Winter, J. and Broadfoot, P. (2000) 'The LEARN Project Phase 2: Guidance for schools on assessment for learning'. Qualifications & Curriculum Authority (QCA).

Weeden, P., Winter, J.C., Broadfoot, P.M., Hinett, K.V., McNess, E.M., Tidmarsh, C.R., Triggs, P.A. and Wilmut, J. (1999) 'The LEARN Project: Learners' expectations of assessment requirements nationally'. Qualifications and Curriculum Authority.

Weston, P. (1999) *Homework: Learning from practice*. London: Stationery Office.

Wiener, W. (1912) 'Home-study reform'. *School Review*, 20 (8), 526–31.

Wiesenthal, R., Cooper, B.S., Greenblatt, R. and Marcus, S. (1997) 'Relating school policies and staff attitudes to the homework behaviours of teachers: An empirical study'. *Journal of Educational Administration*, 35 (4), 348–70.

Wilder, S. (2014) 'Effects of parental involvement on academic achievement: A meta-synthesis'. *Educational Review*, 66 (3), 377–97.

Wilson, J. and Rhodes, J. (2010) 'Student perspectives on homework'. *Education*, 131 (2), 351–8.

Wober, J.M. (1990) 'Never mind the picture, sense the screen'. *Journal of Educational Television*, 16 (2), 87–93.

Wober, J.M. (1992) 'Text in a texture of television: Children's homework experience'. *Journal of Educational Television*, 18 (1), 23–34.

Wolf, R.M. (1979) 'Achievement in the United States'. In Walberg, H.J. (ed.) *Educational Environments and Effects: Evaluation, policy, and productivity*. Berkeley, CA: McCutchan Publishing Corporation, 313–30.

Wolters, C.A. (2011) 'Regulation of motivation: Contextual and social aspects'. *Teachers College Record*, 113 (2), 265–83.

Worrell, F.C., Gabelko, N.H., Roth, D.A. and Samuels, L.K. (1999) 'Parents' reports on homework amount and problems in academically talented elementary students'. *Gifted Child Quarterly*, 43 (2), 86–94.

Xu, J. (1994) 'Doing Homework: A study of possibilities'. Unpublished EdD thesis, Teachers College, Columbia University.

Xu, J. (2005) 'Purposes for doing homework reported by middle and high school students'. *Journal of Educational Research*, 99 (1), 46–55.

Xu, J. (2006) 'Gender and homework management reported by high school students'. *Educational Psychology*, 26 (1), 73–91.

Xu, J. (2007) 'Middle-school homework management: More than just gender and family involvement'. *Educational Psychology*, 27 (2), 173–89.

Xu, J. (2008) 'Models of secondary school students' interest in homework: A multilevel analysis'. *American Educational Research Journal*, 45 (4), 1180–1205.

Xu, J. (2009) 'School location, student achievement, and homework management reported by middle school students'. *School Community Journal*, 19 (2), 27–43.

Xu, J. (2010a) 'Gender and homework management reported by African American students'. *Educational Psychology*, 30 (7), 755–70.

Xu, J. (2010b) 'Predicting homework distraction at the secondary school level: A multilevel analysis'. *Teachers College Record*, 112 (7), 1937–69.

Xu, J. (2011) 'Homework completion at the secondary school level: A multilevel analysis'. *Journal of Educational Research*, 104 (3), 171–82.

Xu, J. (2012) 'Predicting students' homework environment management at the secondary school level'. *Educational Psychology*, 32 (2), 183–200.

Xu, J. (2013) 'Why do students have difficulties completing homework? The need for homework management'. *Journal of Education and Training Studies*, 1 (1), 98–105.

Xu, J. (2014) 'Regulation of motivation: Predicting students' homework motivation management at the secondary school level'. *Research Papers in Education*, 29 (4), 457–78.

Xu, J. (2015) 'Investigating factors that influence conventional distraction and tech-related distraction in math homework'. *Computers and Education*, 81, 304–14.

Xu, J. (2016) 'A study of the validity and reliability of the Teacher Homework Involvement Scale: A psychometric evaluation'. *Measurement*, 93, 102–7.

Xu, J. and Corno, L. (1998) 'Case studies of families doing third-grade homework'. *Teachers College Record*, 100 (2), 402–36.

Xu, J. and Corno, L. (2006) 'Gender, family help, and homework management reported by rural middle school students'. *Journal of Research in Rural Education*, 21 (2), 1–13.

Xu, J. and Wu, H. (2013) 'Self-regulation of homework behavior: Homework management at the secondary school level'. *Journal of Educational Research*, 106 (1), 1–13.

Xu, J. and Yuan, R. (2003) 'Doing homework: Listening to students', parents', and teachers' voices in one urban middle school community'. *School Community Journal*, 13 (2), 25–44.

Younger, M. and Warrington, M. (1996) 'Differential achievement of girls and boys at GCSE: Some observations from the perspective of one school'. *British Journal of Sociology of Education*, 17 (3), 299–313.

Zhao, N., Valcke, M., Desoete, A. and Verhaeghe, J.P. (2017) 'Can parents' homework assigned compensate for disadvantaged students' learning achievement in Mainland China?'. *International Journal of Research Studies in Education*, 6 (2), 3–18.

Zhu, Y. and Leung, F.K.S. (2012) 'Homework and mathematics achievement in Hong Kong: Evidence from the TIMSS 2003'. *International Journal of Science and Mathematics Education*, 10 (4), 907–25.

Zimmerman, B.J. and Kitsantas, A. (2005) 'Homework practices and academic achievement: The mediating role of self-efficacy and perceived responsibility beliefs'. *Contemporary Educational Psychology*, 30 (4), 397–417.

Zohar, A., Schwartzer, N. and Tamir, P. (1998) 'Assessing the cognitive demands required of students in class discourse, homework assignments and tests'. *International Journal of Science Education*, 20 (7), 769–82.

Index

Index